W9-ATK-761

OBJECTION!

NANCY GRACE

with DIANE CLEHANE

OBJE

CTION!

HOW HIGH-PRICED DEFENSE ATTORNEYS, CELEBRITY DEFENDANTS, AND A 24/7 MEDIA HAVE HIJACKED OUR CRIMINAL JUSTICE SYSTEM

NEW YORK

Copyright © 2005 Nancy Grace and Diane Clehane

All rights reserved. No part of this book may be used or reproduced in any manner whatsoever without the written permission of the Publisher. Printed in the United States of America. For information address Hyperion, 77 West 66th Street, New York, New York 10023-6298.

Library of Congress Cataloging-in-Publication Data

Grace, Nancy
  Objection! : how high-priced defense attorneys, celebrity defendants,
 and a 24/7 media have hijacked our criminal justice system / by Nancy
 Grace with Diane Clehane.—1st ed.
   p. cm.
  Includes bibliographical references.
  1. Trials—United States. 2. Defense (Criminal procedure)—United
 States—Popular works. 3. Lawyers—United States—Popular works.
 4. Celebrities—United States—Popular works. I. Clehane, Diane.
 II. Title.

 KF220.G73 2005
 345.73'05044—dc22

                 2004063230

Hyperion books are available for special promotions and premiums. For details contact Michael Rentas, Assistant Director, Inventory Operations, Hyperion, 77 West 66th Street, 12th floor, New York, New York 10023, or call 212-456-0133.

FIRST TRADE PAPERBACK EDITION

Trade Paperback ISBN: 1-4013-0848-1

10 9 8 7 6 5 4 3 2 1

To Keith

CONTENTS

OBJECTION!

INTRODUCTION

I REMEMBER AS IF IT WERE YESTERDAY, SITTING on the brick steps of my family's home in Georgia that August. It was so still and hot and soundless. Nothing moved. Not a breeze, not the song of a bird, not a single movement to be heard or felt. The heat was so intense it seemed as if I could actually hear it rising up off the dirt in visible waves. Not even a car drove by. The stillness and the heat that summer were oppressive and constant in my ears. I felt like I was being sucked into their vacuum.

A few weeks before, my fiancé had been murdered—"gunned down," as we say in the media. Keith was shot five times in his beautiful face and back. It was only a few months until our wedding, but the gunman couldn't wait. Violence doesn't acknowledge weddings and anniversaries, birthdays and celebrations.

Random violence entered my world.

The world I grew up in didn't know violence or hatred. The chimes in the Methodist church's steeple literally called everyone home at six o'clock with hymns like "God Will Take Care of You" and "His Eye Is on the Sparrow." My only encounters with violence and evil came through fleeting glimpses on the evening news at suppertime. All the horror seemed so far, far away. In my world, there was nothing as far as the eye could see but tall pine trees and soybean fields, peach orchards and rows and rows of corn and cotton, interspersed with pastureland.

I didn't know there was another world, one full of random violence bred from anger and desperation or, simply put, pure meanness. In my life at least, evil was a concept, not a reality. But that all changed in a single moment. Keith's funeral, the visits from our families and friends, the sympathy cards and the unnatural smell of hothouse flowers I received were all a blur. They still are. Sometimes I cried so much I couldn't open my eyes from the swelling. I was lost. Keith's world had ended, and mine had exploded.

I remember trying to go back to classes. I couldn't. The thought of sitting inside the four walls of a quiet college classroom studying Shakespearean literature, once my joy, was now like a heavy noose around my neck. I knew I could never go back to the world as I knew it. Wife, mother, and schoolteacher, it was not meant to be.

I escaped the vacuum the only way I could. I did eventually go back to school. To law school. I prayed that I would one day graduate from Mercer Law School and then start the fight. I prepared for years, studying and working late into the night with the lamp on beside my bed, reading. Sometimes I even carried a lawbook in church. I knew the law would be my sword and my shield. I had to be ready when the time came.

And it did. Seven years after Keith's murder, I tried my first jury trial. At that moment, in that Atlanta courtroom, I took to the fight like a fish to water. In trying to cure the injustice heaped on other victims of violent crime, I was cured. For the next ten years, I fought in the pit— in felony courtrooms in what was then the murder capital of the country, inner-city Atlanta. The drug trade made the city a targeted sweet spot for heroin, cocaine, and pot flooding in and out of Miami. The battle consumed me. I fell asleep at night with my files spread out on my bed. I jumped up even on nonjury days at 5:00 A.M., thinking somehow I was late to court. Every case was a cause I could take up, because every case represented a victim.

Guilty pleas caused me great personal turmoil. How was I to discern if today's shoplifter would become tomorrow's armed robber? I quickly gained a reputation for being unreasonable when negotiating pleas and vicious at trial. I didn't care. The battle was all that mattered. It is of those years that I am the proudest. I made next to nothing, but the reward to my heart and soul was priceless. I had the opportunity to be the voice of those who have no voice, most often women, children, and minorities, overlooked and never heard in our system. I learned what they don't teach you in law school, that the Constitution protects the accused, blanketing them and safeguarding their "rights." Victims have no voice, no face, and no recourse. The Founding Fathers, with all due respect, did not consider them, and today our courtrooms, our judges, our lawmakers follow suit.

My transition from a courtroom in Atlanta to a New York City television studio was by happenstance. While serving as a special prosecutor in Atlanta, I was called to sit on a panel of legal experts in the Hall of Justice in New York City while still prosecuting in Atlanta. I happened to be seated between two renowned defense attorneys—Johnnie Cochran, straight off the O. J. Simpson case, and Roy Black, straight off a victory in the William Kennedy Smith rape case. Naturally we got into a huge fight!

Several months later, the elected district attorney in Atlanta, my boss, decided to retire. I was devastated. Not only had Mr. Slaton given me the chance to become a trial lawyer at a time when very few women in the South were litigating in courtrooms, he was like a grandfather to me. I didn't know what I would do. I hadn't gone to law school to handle slip-and-falls, argue whiplash car accidents, or haggle over contracts. I wanted justice for crime victims. Nothing else was important to me.

I considered public service with the battered-women's center, but then, the founder of Courtroom Television Network, Steve Brill, flew to Atlanta and asked me face-to-face to join his new experiment, co-anchoring a legal talk show with Johnnie Cochran. I deeply disagreed with the Simpson defense, and with the option of high-priced defense work looming, I wanted to take Cochran on. I took off for New York shortly after Mr. Slaton served out his office. In 1997, I arrived in New York City with two boxes of clothes, a curling iron, and $200 in my savings account. Even now, all these years later, while sitting on a dark set staring into a camera lens, I wonder if I should go back to the courtroom to battle adversaries who trick Lady Justice, taking them on one by one.

But I accept that just as I was led to the airwaves, I know God will lead me to my next battle, making my path clear. I continue on, grateful.

This is what I know . . . there is a very real struggle going on in our world today—the age-old struggle between good and evil. Maybe it sounds simplistic, but it is true nevertheless. We must stand up and fight for what is right, even when we know we could very well lose. I find my sharpest sword to be the truth and I use it whenever I can. When the sorrow, the frustration, the moments with Keith forever lost surface, my response is to fight. Herein is the truth as I see it. I'm on the inside of the struggle for justice, calling out to all who will listen. This is what I see and what I know, regardless of whether it is politically incorrect or disturbing or tastes bitter going down. The battle of good against evil is real and palpable and is being waged in your local courthouse.

The struggle for justice in this country didn't end with the writing of the Constitution and the Bill of Rights. It's happening now. The fight has only started, and is raging in courtrooms all across this country. Please, take a listen, friend.

CHAPTER ONE

DEFENSE ATTORNEYS AND OTHER WILY CHARACTERS I HAVE KNOWN

THE FIRST THING WE DO, LET'S KILL ALL THE LAWYERS.

—*William Shakespeare*

"I WAS JUST DOING MY JOB." THAT'S THE TIRED excuse offered up by every defense attorney whenever they're asked how they do what they do—how they pull the wool over jurors' eyes to make sure the repeat offender they're defending walks free. I'll never know how they can look in the mirror when their client goes out and commits yet another crime, causing more suffering to innocent victims. I've heard, "I'm just doing my job—it's in the Constitution," too many times to count. Just doing their jobs. They make it sound like they're making doughnuts, drawing the yellow line down the street with a spray gun, or manning a toll booth on the freeway, nothing personal, just doing their jobs. In response, I agree with Dickens: "If that's the law, then the law is an ass."

That same tired excuse has been used to explain away wrongdoing throughout history. Everyone from the repo-guy to the utility worker who cuts off electricity to the needy to the parking-lot attendant who won't refund your quarters after you lose them in a broken meter to banks who foreclose on Christmas . . . they all work the same excuse. They're all just doing their jobs. When it comes to defense attorneys singing the same chorus, I don't buy it. Justice is not "just a job." The duty of a jury is to render a true verdict, a verdict that speaks the truth. How is that attainable when the "job" of defense attorneys is to use every means possible to get their clients acquitted—regardless of the truth?

The 2002 murder trial of David Westerfield, found guilty of kidnapping and murdering his seven-year-old neighbor, Danielle van Dam, is one of the most horrifying examples of the true business of being a defense attorney. The minute her disappearance was made public, there was an intense, massive, and frantic search involving hundreds of volunteers, all desperately working around the clock to find any trace of this beautiful girl. They combed the hillsides, the brush, the canyons, and the creeks near the van Dams' San Diego home. Danielle's parents, Damon and Brenda van Dam, were completely distraught.

Brenda appeared on television over and over, begging for her daughter's return. Her face was swollen from crying, her eyes were raw and red. While this was going on, Westerfield's defense lawyer, Steven Feldman, was trying his best to bargain with prosecutors—to cut a plea deal. Feldman knew Westerfield had only one bargaining chip, the location of Danielle's body. In exchange for life behind bars as opposed to death by lethal injection as dictated by California law, Westerfield would give up the location of the little girl's remains.

Knowing full well his client was a child killer, Feldman went into open court to launch a defense that consisted of dragging the seven-year-old victim's parents through the mud, ruining their reputations within the community, and revealing to the jury and the world that the couple had once been swingers. The defense boldly claimed the van Dams had unwittingly introduced a sexual predator into their own home. Knowing it wasn't true, Feldman argued someone else had killed Danielle—some predator linked to her parents. Nothing could be further from the truth. The predator was David Westerfield.

Feldman also chose to twist science itself to prove a series of lies to the jury. He produced a forensic entomologist to tell the jury that the larvae (maggots) on this beautiful child's body were of such an age as to preclude Westerfield from suspicion. He reasoned that the larvae were hatched on the body at a time when Westerfield was already under tight surveillance by police, and therefore he could not possibly be the killer who disposed of the child's body.

The argument was incredibly scientific and innovative—but hardly original. Turns out Feldman had used the exact same defense and the exact same "expert" in another murder trial and snagged an acquittal because of it. The second time around, it wasn't creative, innovative, or clever, just tired and rehearsed. Most important, the defense didn't fit the facts of the case or the truth.

I am sick at heart that an officer of the court concocted that defense while knowing the whole time his own client knew where Danielle was hidden. Feldman is a veteran trial lawyer and under the law is entitled to put on the best case he can on behalf of his client. Still, it's so disheartening that juries are hoodwinked every day by defense lawyers just "doing their jobs." Our adversarial system allows it—in fact, encourages it. They get paid tons of money to do it. Successful defense attorneys are idolized, treated like rock stars.

And hey, they're just doing their jobs.

"THE DARK SIDE"

Lewis R. Slaton was the elected district attorney of Fulton County in inner-city Atlanta, where I tried cases for ten years. He was like a grandfather to me, and when he announced he was retiring after thirty-seven years in office, I was shocked. I went to his office and begged him to serve another term. I said the public—and, most important, the city's crime victims—needed him. But he was well into his seventies and wanted to spend his remaining years with his wife and say good-bye to the courthouse. What could I say? I walked from his office with my head reeling, not knowing what I would do. I knew that the newly elected district attorney would likely fire all the top litigators left over from Slaton's administration, as is the custom, and I would be left with the alternative every veteran prosecutor faces at some point: being out of a job and considering the "dark side"—defense work.

I hadn't gone to law school to do slip-and-falls, write wills, or do real estate closings. After my fiancé's murder, I abandoned my plan to teach college literature and entered law school specifically to help other crime victims—to try to do right. All I knew, all I wanted, and all I loved, was criminal prosecution and victims' rights. In court, I was finally home.

When Slaton's announcement was made public, I discovered a myriad of job possibilities to consider—all for a lot of money to boot. Unsolicited offers from criminal-defense firms started pouring in. The salaries thrown my way were more than I had ever dreamed of. If I took a defense job, I could say good-bye to my second (and third) jobs, exchange my car with the smoking engine for one that actually ran every day, and stop shopping exclusively at Marshalls and Kmart. But from the get-go, it was wrong. All wrong.

I accepted that as soon as the newly elected district attorney fired me, I'd rather teach law school than be a defense lawyer. I sent out my résumé to local colleges and universities and hoped for the best. Then, out of the blue, came Court TV, which gave me a platform to speak out on behalf of victims' rights. After an entire career as a public servant, a trial lawyer, I packed up and headed to New York.

There was no way I could ever stand in front of a jury and use the knowledge and talents God gave me to "just do my job." No way. I knew that if I ever did, I'd look in the mirror every morning and see Keith's blue eyes looking back at me.

DEFENDING THE
INDEFENSIBLE

One night in July 2002, I did on-air battle on *Larry King Live* with John Pozza, the articulate and engaging defense attorney who got Alejandro Avila, the accused killer of five-year-old Samantha Runnion, off the hook on child-molestation charges at Avila's first jury trial in 2001. From my perspective, that one court case could have saved Samantha's life.

The Orange County, California, girl was abducted in broad daylight on July 15, 2002, as she played with her little friend in front of her house on a quiet residential street. Her grandmother was just steps away. The man who took her approached her by asking for help finding a lost puppy. Samantha's lifeless, nude body was found the following day, disposed of like trash alongside a rural highway and posed in a position suggesting sexual assault. Police suspected it was the work of a serial rapist who would strike again.

Based in part on tips from the public and a physical description given by Samantha's five-year-old playmate, twenty-seven-year-old Avila, a production line supervisor at a medical-supply plant, was arrested on July 19 and charged with kidnap, murder, and sex crimes. Orange County Sheriff Mike Carona indicated forensic evidence, DNA, proved that Samantha was sexually molested before her death. The death penalty can be sought in that jurisdiction if murder occurs during the commission of another felony such as rape or kidnapping. In this case, both occurred. If convicted, Avila could face death by lethal injection.

At his court appearance, Avila, dressed in an orange jumpsuit over a white T-shirt and sporting a goatee, stood demurely beside his court-appointed lawyer, paid for by us, the taxpayers. He gave only monosyllabic responses to the court's questions and was careful not to reveal any more than he had to in open court. He denied any involvement in Samantha's kidnapping. His mother, Adelina Avila, "alibied" him, saying he was at a local mall when Samantha went missing, although Avila's cell-phone records apparently indicate otherwise.

Samantha's horrific death could have been avoided. She could have lived and been spared the pain of kidnap, sex assault, and murder by asphyxiation. If she had lived, right now she'd be in grammar school like her other little friends. That dream died when John Pozza, Avila's defense attorney at his first trial, waged war against the two nine-year-old girls his client was accused of molesting.

I was sick when I learned Avila had been charged with the molestations of the first two victims. During that trial, Pozza argued the girls had been coached into making their claims of abuse, and, with a straight face, he claimed police had somehow planted pornography on Avila's computer. These claims hadn't a shred of truth, but the defense lawyer argued them anyway. In January 2001, Avila was acquitted on all counts, rode down in the elevator just like the jury did, and walked from the courthouse a free man.

"Quite frankly, I was surprised," Pozza later said of the acquittal he himself had engineered. "A lot of the evidence that the prosecution or the police had gathered would give one the impression that there was evidence of guilt there, and certainly it would be our job as his defense team to look very closely at that evidence," he said. Pozza reported he was "shocked" when he learned his former client was charged with molesting and murdering five-year-old Samantha. Shortly after Avila's arrest, he told CNN, "It has thrown my entire world off course." I can't imagine why. Criminal-defense lawyers and prosecutors alike know full well that molesters, especially, will strike again. They can't help themselves. They may not get caught, but they *will* strike again. So why was he surprised?

He was likely concerned, however, that the public had found out that his mission in court—to attack the truth and hide evidence from the jury—had had disastrous results and that people would begin to question his role, not just his client's. The word was out. The world had actually learned that defense attorneys obscure the truth from the jury and that this time, as a result, a little girl had endured a brutal sex attack before being murdered. Pozza has stated that he was rethinking his career since Samantha's death, but to one little girl's loved ones that epiphany came too late.

Disagree with me if you want, but that's how I see it. But for the fact that Pozza argued that cops planted porn on Avila's computer, that two unsuspecting little girls had fabricated a story of sex abuse—while Pozza knew full well that Avila flunked his polygraph—Avila would have been behind bars that sunny afternoon when Samantha's grandmother let her go outside and play. The afternoon Samantha thought she was helping a man find his puppy. The afternoon she was assaulted and murdered. Pozza can't hide behind his "duty" as a defense attorney. He can't wash his hands of Samantha's death.

Here's what he said the night Larry King asked him about his role in Avila's first trial:

KING: *Did you believe your client didn't do it at the time?*

POZZA: *You know—at the time, Larry, I cannot say whether or not I believed his guilt or innocence. And really, I am not the finder of facts. So I try to remove myself from that and, basically, present the best defense I can for my client. That's what I do for every client.*

I was shocked to hear a defense attorney admit he tries to remove himself from the actual truth of his client's charges, especially when child victims are involved. I have no doubt in my mind his brand of practice is in part responsible for Samantha's death. Samantha's mother rightly widens the circle of blame in her daughter's death to include a jury who refused to believe two little girls, choosing instead to accept that the girls would lie and cops would plant pornography on Avila's computer.

A few nights earlier, Samantha's mom, Erin Runnion, told Larry, "I blame every juror who let him go. Every juror who sat on that trial and believed this man over those little girls. I will never understand. And that is why he was out. And that is why his sickness was allowed to do this."

That night, the *Larry King Live* staff had been very concerned for Runnion and worried about whether she could hold up for an entire hour's interview. I was sitting in the darkened control room with the CNN crew as backup in case Erin Runnion broke down and couldn't go on. I listened to her and my heart broke. I was overwhelmed with sorrow for this grieving mother. She was so brave. The next morning, that one single and very powerful quote regarding the jury's part in Samantha's death was picked up by hundreds of news outlets covering the story and instantly transmitted around the world.

As far as I'm concerned, the pedophile who killed Samantha is not the only one who's sick. When Pozza and I sparred on *Larry King Live*, producers kept telling me, in my earpiece, to go easy on the defense lawyer, but I couldn't. I was so distraught at what he had done. It turned into a knock-down, drag-out fight on air, with Larry breaking us up over and over. Another guest on the panel, defense-attorney-to-the-infamous Mark Geragos, also joined in the fray, taking Pozza's side. I cried the whole way home, torn up by the heartbreak that had shattered the Runnions' lives.

When I thought of what Samantha's mother had said about the little girl's having a huge poster from the Disney movie *Hercules* over her bed, I broke down once again. When Mrs. Runnion tried to warn her daughter about "bad people" whom she should be careful of, Samantha's response was so incredibly innocent. She said she'd "be like Hercules, Mom, I'll just run."

Samantha wasn't fast enough to outrun Avila, who had allegedly been trolling the neighborhood for little girls to molest. The justice system wasn't clever enough for the likes of his first trial lawyer, who, in spite of the truth, managed to get his client acquitted. Samantha is dead, and he wonders why?

Here's why: Because defense attorneys truly believe it's all a big game. A game they can win. Who can outsmart whom, who bests whom in court, who is clever enough to trick a jury into hating cops or disbelieving children who take the stand and swear to tell the truth. If I had to wake up every morning knowing my job was to get repeat offenders off the hook to roam the streets yet again, I swear I couldn't practice law at all. But it's all okay in their minds. They adhere to the rules of evidence and to their unique take on ethics. They are simply doing their jobs—according to them anyway. Not according to me.

The game Avila and his new defense attorney, public defender Denise Gragg, are playing with the system continues today. As of this writing, Avila's trial has been postponed numerous times. Delay is a defense lawyer's best friend for a multitude of reasons: lost witnesses, fading memories, overcrowded jails and courtrooms. Any number of things can happen the longer a jury is prevented from hearing the case. The underlying reason the defense so often tries to delay a trial is simple: Every day of delay is another day the defendant is not guilty under the law. It's another day of innocence!

Delays always happen; they happened in practically every jury trial I ever prosecuted. Often judges would even make defense lawyers and defendants bring actual doctor's notes to court to prove they were sick and couldn't perform at a trial. I believe there should be firm statutes on delay. Avila's trial is just one example of what can happen when there has been excessive delay. Another is the long-delayed trial of the actor Robert Blake, who was arrested in connection with the murder of his wife, Bonny Lee Bakley.* Blake fired one high-profile defense team after another, each time getting another continuance or delay, à la Michael Jackson. This makes the proceedings even more agonizing for the victims' families; their healing process can't even start until the trial is over and done, regardless of the outcome.

Right now, it's largely within the discretion of the trial judge as to whether the defense's feet are held to the fire and the accused goes to trial in a timely manner. Justice is rarely swift. Under the constitutional

---

*As this book went to press, on March 16, 2005, Robert Blake was acquitted of the murder of his wife, Bonny Lee Bakley. Blake was also found not guilty of solicitation of murder. The jury was deadlocked on the second solicitation charge, which was subsequently dismissed.

interpretations by defense attorneys, judges are faced with granting delays or, on appeal, postconviction, facing reversal because the defense claims it "wasn't ready." Clearly a remedy is needed. One possible remedy would allow a strict statutory number of continuances for either side. This would likely be contested, though, perceived as draconian. Another solution would be for the defense attorney to agree to a trial date at the end of the first trial calendar and then be held to it. That way, the trial date would be an agreement with the court up front and more likely to stick. Knowing the system, I suspect that, regarding trial delays, the defense bar has Lady Justice over a barrel.

Speaking as one who has watched justice unfold not only as a prosecutor but as a victim of violent crime, I assure you this is no game. Trials are the culmination of months, sometimes years, of pain and anguish. The unfinished business of justice looms, and finally the trial begins. To have the truth-seeking process boiled down to a game of wits between two sets of lawyers is almost more than crime victims and their families can bear. Ask Samantha Runnion. I'm sure she'll agree. But you'll have to wait a while. You can meet her only in Heaven.

A MATTER OF ETHICS

My deep-seated ethical problem with defense attorneys likely traces back to my being a witness in Keith's murder trial. The whole thing has always been a big blur to me, but I do distinctly remember going to the courthouse as a witness. The cavernous courtroom reminded me of the one in *To Kill a Mockingbird*. The witness stand was several feet high. I had to climb two sets of stairs with a landing in the middle to get to it, so I was up off the ground by a good six feet.

Directly below and in front of me sat the defendant and his lawyer. I don't really remember the lawyer, but I do remember looking down and seeing Keith's bloody clothes that had been laid out for the jury. The reality of what Keith had gone through was too much to take in.

I looked at the clothes and somehow wouldn't let myself connect them to the person I loved so deeply.

The other thing that I recall to this moment was that the defendant never looked at me in the face. He never could bring his eyes up to meet mine. I didn't know it at the time, but that must have been when I began to formulate my theory on the importance of what I call "behavioral evidence"—behavior that is so odd or disturbing, so abnormal or curious, it logically points to either guilt or pangs of conscience. If I had been on trial for the murder of another's loved one, I would scream out, "I didn't do it! I didn't do it! Please believe me! I would never hurt you!" But the defendant did nothing remotely like that. He just looked away, avoiding my eyes, because he knew he had murdered someone, and looking at me and at the rest of Keith's family, he had to realize the incredible pain he had caused—all over a wallet with thirty-five dollars in it.

There was no cross-examination that I recall. It was over. I just slowly stood up and made my way down the steps and out of the courtroom. No one said a word, and as I passed the defense table, I slowed down and looked at him. He never looked up.

Even the defense attorney looked away from me.

That trial became the foundation of my opinions on defense attorneys and defense strategies. They didn't crystallize until years after I graduated from law school and was working in the pit of a courtroom ten hours a day against defense lawyers. That's when it all came together for me. The truth really doesn't matter to the defense. Under our adversarial system as outlined in the Constitution, it's all okay because it's "ethical." Defense attorneys have a right to cross-examination, and the rules of evidence allow them to attack the state's case, including crime victims and witnesses who are telling nothing but the truth.

The rules allow defense attorneys to poke holes in a prosecutor's argument and kick the wheels of evidence. The good news is, prosecutors have the right to do the same thing to them and all of their witnesses. That's what our justice system is about. It's set up for the state to seek the truth behind the crime and for the defense to protect its client. Under the law, that's all well and good. To me, it is a distortion of the truth. There are systems of justice on this planet where both sides seek the truth, but that's not the case in this country.

Given those confines, I could never live with myself if I helped a violent felon by prostituting my law degree, my energy, and my experience to free someone that I know is guilty. I could never be responsible for the release of a violent criminal who would walk free, a predator among the innocent. Think I'm wrong? Talk to someone who's been victimized by a repeat offender—or to a bereaved family member, since so many victims are no longer among the living to speak for themselves. Because of unspeakable acts by repeat offenders, too many innocent voices have been silenced forever.

LEARNING FROM THE MASTER

One of the most high-profile, flamboyant, and effective defense attorneys of all time is Johnnie Cochran. He was my first on-air partner when I joined Court TV, and we were paired as the cohosts of *Cochran and Grace* in 1997. It took me a solid year to accept that Cochran was not the one responsible for the double murders of Nicole Brown and Ron Goldman. I constantly glared at him during shows, and frankly, I don't know how he stood it. I was so angry after the Simpson verdict, I'm surprised he didn't just walk off the set. I'd go after him about something as benign as a California proposition regarding marijuana use for glaucoma. He argued his points graciously and never lost his cool. I, on the other hand, was vicious no matter the issue, still harboring intense disillusionment over the Simpson verdict and Simpson himself.

Working with Cochran gave me the chance to study the king of criminal defense for the next couple of years, and I found it incredibly enlightening. I began to see something I'd never been able to see before: to understand what exactly it was that juries sometimes saw in defense lawyers.

I had always viewed them as quick and wily, like a beautiful snake that you keep in a cage but wouldn't dare touch. I still feel that way, but now I understand why juries can be captivated by lawyers like Johnnie Cochran. I studied him carefully. I watched the way he talked. I listened to the words he chose to use, his mannerisms, even the way he walked into a room. I learned that juries can be struck by someone who is charming, attractive, and affable. Cochran could give an opening and closing argument that could charm a bird out of a tree. I had always been so focused on the truth and the facts of a particular case, so hellbent on justice that I was almost immune to a defense attorney's charms. I learned through watching him why juries are sometimes bowled over by someone like Cochran.

In addition to being a master orator, Cochran puts together a practically unstoppable defense team. I recall when Sean "P. Diddy" Combs, the head of Bad Boy Entertainment, was charged with firing a weapon during a 1999 dispute at a Times Square club in which three bystanders were wounded. It was also alleged that Combs later promised his chauffeur $50,000 and a platinum ring to take the rap. Cochran was immediately called in and promptly tapped one of the toughest street-fighting lawyers I've ever seen, Benjamin Brafman, as co-counsel.

Cochran knows strategy. As everyone knows, the squad of lawyers and experts he assembled to defend O. J. Simpson (Barry Scheck, F. Lee Bailey, Robert Shapiro, and Dr. Henry Lee) were—and are—all specialists in their respective fields. Their reputations and work on the case earned them the title of the "Dream Team." Watching Cochran in action during the Simpson case made me realize how much more dangerous defense attorneys are than I had previously thought. Not only do they have a host of trial tactics at their disposal that I would never even consider, they can be charming and likable to a jury. Therein lies the danger. The Constitution didn't set up a jury trial to be a popularity test, but with a charismatic defense lawyer like Cochran, it can turn into the homecoming parade, not a search for the truth.

Although Cochran and I vehemently disagreed on many, many things—most notably the issue of Simpson's guilt—I consider myself to be a friend of Johnnie's. We agreed to disagree, but when it comes to Cochran, I know I am battling one of the best there is. Do I agree with him? Never. Do I acknowledge his abilities? I'd be a fool not to.

THE BUSIEST DEFENSE ATTORNEY OF 2004

The one thing that Mark Geragos and Johnnie Cochran have in common is that they are both incredibly charming. They're both attractive, likable, and unfailingly smooth. The major difference, as of this writing at least, is that Cochran has won all of his major high-profile cases. I in no way suggest that "winning" a felony case puts the defense in the right or is some litmus test of right or wrong, moral or immoral. To do so would be like putting perfume on a pig . . . it still stinks.

As for Mark Geragos, in the space of a single year, he has become one of this country's most famous lawyers for simultaneously taking on two of the most infamous defendants of the decade: Scott Peterson and Michael Jackson.

At the onset of the Peterson trial,* no one knew what to expect from Geragos, especially in light of his own words about his client before he signed on to defend him. Two days before Peterson's arrest, Geragos stated on air, "You'd be hard-pressed to find a prosecutor who couldn't put together an indictment, let alone a conviction. There are a lot of guys sitting in state prison on a lot less evidence. There is just an over-

---

*As this book went to press, on March 16, 2005, Scott Peterson was sentenced to death by lethal injection or, in the alternative, the California gas chamber, for the murders of his wife and their unborn child.

whelming amount of circumstantial evidence. His defense at this point is, 'Oh, my God, somebody else must have done it and was trying to set me up.' I don't think it's ever going to wash."

It's hard to ignore Geragos's own analysis of the case, offered up on *Larry King Live* on April 18, 2003, the day of Peterson's arrest. At the time, he said, "The most damning piece of circumstantial evidence [a marina receipt] comes out of his own mouth and his own hands. That is just a devastating thing. It's a damning, circumstantial case. The man is a sociopath if he did this crime. This is a guy who has, from day one, not helped himself in any way." Ten days later, during another television interview, Geragos was asked why Peterson lied to Amber Frey about being single. His response? "Because he's a cad. When guys commit adultery, guys lie to a single woman in order to get them into bed."

In the hours that followed, on April 29, Geragos met with Peterson in jail, and the next day he revealed he was considering signing on as Peterson's lead counsel. On May 2 he announced he had taken the case. Once he was retained, he suddenly saw the light. He clearly had an epiphany: Scott Peterson was innocent. My head was spinning. Hadn't Geragos practically finished the state's closing argument for them on air? In retrospect, why was I surprised?

I called him on it publicly just before he announced Peterson had hired him as his lead defense attorney. That evening, I noticed a sudden reversal in his previous opinion that Peterson would be convicted. I asked him on air, "What happened, Mark? What changed?" Geragos dodged the question—evasive as ever.

Geragos employed many disturbing strategies in handling the Peterson case. Nothing was more offensive to me than the treatment Sharon Rocha and her family received at the hands of the defense in the early stages of the case. After Laci Peterson's remains had washed up on the rocks in April 2003, her family was banned from Scott and Laci's house. Although the defense team and its investigators had been swarming the couple's Modesto, California, home for weeks and Peterson's family had been there during visits to their son, the defense still claimed with a straight face that it was a crime scene and couldn't be tampered with or contaminated by Laci's own family.

By having people come and go as they pleased, the house had long lost its value as an untampered-with crime scene. That fact didn't stop the defense from using it as a premise to prevent Laci's family from getting into the house and retrieving some of her personal belongings as mementos. A long tug of war ensued between Scott's camp and Laci's camp. Finally, Laci's family went over to the couple's house and collected a few items, including her wedding dress, some of her plants, some watering cans and diplomas. Sharon Rocha went into Laci's room simply to sit in Laci's rocking chair, trying to feel her daughter's presence.

And you know what happened that afternoon?

The Peterson defense team raced to the house and demanded police file a burglary report. As if the murder of their daughter weren't enough. Is it legal? Yes. Is it moral? Absolutely not. After realizing they had created a public-relations disaster, the defense backed off their strident calls to have Laci's mother arrested, and nothing more was said of it. For the defense, it was as if nothing had ever happened. For Laci's mother, it was another wound that will never heal.

With Geragos at the helm, Scott Peterson was transformed from an orange-jumpsuit-clad "Monster in Chains," as described by the *New York Post*, into a well-groomed, upper-middle-class, college-educated young man in tastefully subdued suits. The defendant's ill-advised dye job and facial hair were replaced with a close-cropped haircut, a clean-shaven face, and a thoughtful yet pensive look in court.

But Geragos couldn't whitewash Peterson's image as a cheating cad, and he had his work cut out for him in order to erase the idea his client was a man on the run. When Peterson was arrested in San Diego, police searched the 1984 Mercedes-Benz 500SEC he was driving. He wasn't traveling light. Among the items found in the car: $15,000 in cash, twelve Viagra tablets, several credit cards belonging to various members of the Peterson family, a water purifier, a knife, a fire starter, and tons of survival gear. The few superficial changes Geragos insti-gated had somehow managed, virtually overnight, to erase the damag-ing image of Peterson as a fugitive.

Unfortunately, the defense attorney couldn't control Peterson com-pletely. During one of the earliest days of the trial, the defendant went a little too far to win the title of Mr. Congeniality. Entering the courtroom, he lit up a thousand-watt, Hollywood-love-me smile for a huge jury pool. One potential juror summed it up beautifully as she was leaving the courtroom: "It was creepy." After that misstep, Geragos likely advised Peterson to hold back all that charm and just look down and take notes.

Geragos tried out a series of theories on the public via statements and court papers to see if any would stick. At the beginning of the trial, we heard a host of stories about people and events that might be tied to Laci's disappearance and murder. First came the story about a brown van and a missing shoe that would explain everything; then came a mysterious woman with important information. Those were followed by various and sundry tales, including "Donnie" the dope dealer, the evil burglars, the homeless killers, a besotted neighbor in love with Scott Peterson, a possible jewel heist, a deranged sex offender, a Hawaiian gang, and, of course, a satanic cult. A court-imposed gag order only added fuel to the flames of speculation.

An important word about leaks: Courthouse leaks can come from many sources, from calendar clerks to assistants who file documents to messenger services to the person responsible for collecting faxes off the courthouse machine. A leak could also come from a secretary at the de-fense lawyers' firm, a courier, or a law clerk. Identifying the source of leaks is always difficult, and that is why leaking is rarely punished—because so many people have the ability to get their mitts on court docu-ments. The bottom line is, most leaks are highly favorable to the defense, just as we saw in the Kobe Bryant case, where things got so bad that the judge had to issue a written apology to the alleged rape victim. In most cases, logic clearly suggests that the leaks are in fact orchestrated by the defense. Although it's pretty much impossible to stop leaks, I believe that if they were investigated as actual crimes against the court and then prosecuted, they would dry up pronto. This could easily be achieved through a contempt of court–like statute and proceedings.

Surprisingly, Peterson's trial quickly became a made-for-television spectacle. Geragos first asked for a closed preliminary hearing, which included the barring of reporters from even sitting in the courtroom, much less a camera watching Peterson's every move. When the idea of a closed courtroom was rejected, Geragos switched positions and argued the reverse—to allow television cameras to cover the entire proceeding live, a motion the judge also denied. Geragos is extremely savvy when it comes to working the media. We might never know why the telegenic defense attorney waffled on this issue, but, believe me, he had his reasons for switching gears, both in his representation of Peterson after pointing out his likely guilt on air and in his request not to allow cameras in court.

Although truth won out in the end, in Geragos's first major battle, he scored a victory when the court agreed to a change of venue out of Laci's hometown. After gauging the pulse of the Redwood City jurors, he asked for another venue change. That was denied, so Geragos dug in and the trial commenced. Shrewdly, however, whenever he got a chance, he renewed his dissatisfaction with the venue, announcing often that his client could not get a fair trial.

True to form, Geragos was charming and cordial in the courtroom. As demonstrated throughout jury selection and trial, only occasionally did he let the jury see another side of him, when he bullied witnesses and other lawyers. Another less-than-winning quality of the usually smooth defense lawyer is his penchant for sarcasm. In late July 2004, Detective Dodge Hendee was on the stand testifying about what he found while searching Scott Peterson's warehouse. During cross-examination, he told Geragos he found what appeared to be cement residue in what looked like five rings, which indicated that Peterson had made five anchors—but only one was found. Geragos, trying to punch holes in Hendee's theory, showed the pictures of the so-called rings and commented that they looked more like light right angles than rings. He mocked Hendee, saying, "Is this a ring? And is this a ring? Is this a circle?" His attempt at witty sarcasm fell flat. Although there were a few chuckles in the courtroom, some of the jurors looked disgusted by the treatment the detective received. He was a credible witness who deserved to be treated with respect. Evidently Geragos thought otherwise.

When Geragos's long-anticipated cross-exam of Peterson's former lover, Amber Frey, was set to commence, he deadpanned in open court, "No questions." He then paused for effect before adding, "Just kidding." While there were a few people who thought this was hilarious, certain members of the jury looked on stoically and never even cracked a smile, as if to relay the message, "What's funny about murder?"

There's no doubt Mark Geragos is a talented lawyer. How far can sheer talent take a defense when pitted against the truth? In *State v. Scott Peterson*, the truth won out.

A MATTER OF MONEY

One thing for sure about Geragos is that this million-dollar defense attorney not only knows the ropes, he knows how to tie them into a lasso for the prosecution. The *Modesto Bee* reported that two judges decided last July that taxpayer money would go to help Geragos defend Peterson. Stanislaus County Superior Court judges Roger M. Beauchesne and Linda McFadden met with Geragos behind closed doors in July 2003 and sent him their decision a few days later. At the time we couldn't know the facts supporting their decision, since the law requires that the ruling remain confidential. When asked about the motion, Geragos told reporters, "Look, if I did file, I couldn't tell you. If I didn't file, I still couldn't tell you."

The last time I checked, public funds are generally used with the public's knowledge, with the exception of secret FBI and CIA operations. There is *no* justification for keeping this information secret. While Geragos shouldn't be made to reveal trial strategy, taxpayers have a right to know how much money judges are forking over to the defense. As for his asking for any money at all, I firmly believe that he and other high-priced lawyers like him should be paid the same rates as court-appointed attorneys, prosecutors, and state experts.

Much of the public's money designated for defendants' attorneys goes to pay for court-appointed attorneys, not high rollers from silk-stocking law firms. It's the exception, not the rule, for defendants to hire expensive private attorneys, run out of money, and end up with their hands in our pockets.

Erik and Lyle Menendez, who gunned down their parents in Beverly Hills in 1989, and Danielle van Dam's killer, David Westerfield, received public money. If Geragos ever does reveal just who paid the bill, I suspect we won't hear the real story for quite a while.

A BRIEF VISIT TO NEVERLAND

When Geragos was in charge of Michael Jackson's defense in its early stages, virtually everything the defendant did was a horrendous mockery of the justice system. With a client like Michael Jackson and a lawyer like Mark Geragos, division of fault is pretty tricky. I do not necessarily believe that Geragos knew what was to come, but I have to wonder, did he have an inkling?

In January 2004, when Michael Jackson pled not guilty in his first hearing on child-molestation charges, the judge planned to keep a tight rein on the singer and the attorneys in the case. Judge Rodney Melville immediately set a strict tone and kicked off the day's proceedings by scolding Jackson for being twenty-one minutes late to court—laying down rules he expected attorneys on both sides to follow. The judge told the singer, "Mr. Jackson, you have started out on the wrong foot here. . . . I want to advise you that I will not put up with that. It's an insult to the court."

That was just the beginning. As if his court appearance were some sort of entertainment event, Jackson's website promised free transportation for fans wishing to travel to the courthouse as part of a "Caravan of Love." Well-wishers in tow, Jackson arrived late, although his route was planned well ahead of time and extra security—paid for by the taxpayers—was employed to ensure Jackson's arrival. Police Chief Danny Macagni told the Associated Press that 42 of the 107 officers in the Santa Maria Police Department were assigned to the courthouse that day, along with 50 sheriff's deputies. Already late, Jackson was further delayed after taking time to greet cheering fans, leaving Judge Melville inside the courtroom to cool his heels. The incident widened the gap between Jackson supporters and those who believe that he will be treated differently, more leniently—with kid gloves—because of his celebrity status. This one incident sowed the seeds of resentment among many court watchers.

Outside the courthouse, it got worse. The self-titled King of Pop broke into dance on top of an SUV and invited a throng of his fans to join him at a party at his Neverland Ranch. Meanwhile, some three thousand people, including fans and news media from as far away as Japan and Norway, clamored around the courthouse itself, making the event more like an awards show than a criminal proceeding. Even though there was no red carpet, Geragos had to have anticipated the throngs of reporters and fans. He had to see that Jackson was dressed as if he were in the front row of a fashion show or in an MTV video—complete with huge sunglasses, a black ensemble with a white armband, a military medallion, and glitter shoes—instead of a defendant facing child-molestation charges.

As Jackson drove away from the courthouse, fans mobbed his SUV. The singer only encouraged them by reaching out his window and waving. Fans were egged on by Jackson's camp, headed by Geragos, to travel from Southern California and Las Vegas in chartered buses and cars. About a thousand people came to Jackson's "after-party," a postarraignment affair at Neverland. Hundreds of cars were backed up on the two-lane country road that led to the estate. Rides were in full operation, and ice cream, popcorn, and soft drinks were provided.

What exactly were they celebrating? Jackson being indicted for child molestation? The anguish of a family who, along with their cancer-stricken son, must now endure a long, drawn-out trial? The entire episode was a bizarre mockery of the justice system. Regardless of whether Geragos orchestrated the whole performance, he let it happen.

At the onset of the case, I believed Geragos's strategy was to discredit the victim or the victim's family. The problem with that approach is that there could be many alleged molestation victims. But is everybody a liar? Everybody but Jackson? I don't think so.

Already, one young boy settled his case against Jackson in 1994 for $20 million under the direction of Johnnie Cochran. One thing that Cochran did do for Jackson that Geragos wasn't able to do was save him from an indictment.

In the end, Geragos himself fell victim to Jackson's erraticism. Following his formal indictment, Jackson booted his lawyers, including not only Geragos but also co-counsel Ben Brafman and two security teams in quick succession. Jackson then retained another high-profile lawyer who put up with actor Robert Blake for a period of time acting as his defense attorney, Tom Mesereau. My advice to Mesereau, since he didn't ask, is this: If Jackson can fire two veteran trial lawyers like Geragos and Brafman on a whim, don't work nights on your closing statement. No matter how good you are, you may not be around by then.

As for Geragos, even losing the Peterson trial vaulted him to stardom, to rock star status. The guilty verdict in the Winona Ryder case didn't faze him and neither did getting the boot from Michael Jackson. The outcome in Peterson's case is pretty much secondary to Geragos's own stardom. I predict he will end up commenting on air about legal cases as an expert. With his made-for-television manner, he'll likely land his own show. He's smooth, he's tanned, he's rested, and he's ready. It's just a matter of time.

HIDING BEHIND
THE CONSTITUTION

The Founding Fathers set up our Constitution in a way that allows defense attorneys and defendants to literally get away with murder. These are the rules lawyers have to play by—and they aren't going to change. They may fluctuate a tiny bit based on Supreme Court rulings, but, generally speaking, those are the rules. As a prosecutor, you fight to the finish. That's the way a trial is. You play by the rules of evidence, which are set up to protect the defendant. Nowhere in the Constitution is the victim of a crime ever mentioned. It plays out all across the country because of state and federal statutes that determine what's admissible and inadmissible in court. Nothing protects the victim.

In the Kobe Bryant case, we saw flagrant violations of the rape-shield law (which I will analyze in greater detail in a later chapter). In that case, the rules weren't just bent, they were broken—to accommodate a celebrity (also the subject of another chapter). Of course, there are legions of defense attorneys who argue the rules were not violated in the Bryant case, but I couldn't disagree more. The final insult is that not only is the truth being obscured by defense attorneys, it's being obscured by using something I deeply treasure—the Constitution. The reality is, there's no use in railing against it. These are the rules, and prosecutors must follow them.

There is nothing right about going before a jury of twelve unsuspecting souls and obscuring the truth by using defense tactics of all sorts, including smoke and mirrors. In the majority of cases, the defendant does not take the stand. I believe that's because there aren't very many defendants who could withstand a cross-examination. I think the truth would come out, and their true nature would be exposed. Defense attorneys very wisely dress clients in their Sunday best and have them sit there and look serious and thoughtful for the duration of the trial.

That might be the most obvious manipulation they employ, but it sure isn't the only trick they have up their sleeves.

NOT A LAUGHING MATTER

Once during a publicity photo shoot, someone took it upon himself to recite a series of lawyer jokes to me, starting with "What's the difference between a catfish and a lawyer?" The punchline was "One is a bottom-feeding, scum-sucking, cold-blooded parasite . . . and the other's a catfish." He looked at me, waiting for a response. I responded, all right. In no uncertain terms, I told him to call a catfish the next time he was in trouble.

But no doubt, there's a reason lawyers have become one of the most reviled groups in our culture. It's because it's perceived that lawyers will do practically anything for money—that they're nothing more than prostitutes of the court. Attorneys are so notorious for stealing money that there are calls for a federal referendum for tort reform so that they can't take more than a certain amount. As things stand now, it's in the hands of Congress.

This proposed legislation is very damaging to the client. Linda Mc-Dougal, forty-six, was diagnosed with an aggressive form of breast cancer in May 2002, based on a biopsy performed after a suspicious spot appeared on her mammogram. McDougal said she was told the cancer was so aggressive that her only chance to survive was a double mastectomy, chemotherapy, and radiation. Days after the surgery, the doctor revealed that McDougal's test results had been switched with another woman's. McDougal, it turns out, never had cancer. Both her breasts are gone, but proposed new federal legislation caps damages for cases just like Linda McDougal's at $250,000. The same would go for punitive damages.

Because lawyers have gotten such a horrible reputation after years of flimflamming, there is actually a proposed law to cap their take. The insurance industry is closing in for the kill and capitalizing on the public's perception of trial attorneys, proposing a one-size-fits-all limit on the compensation Linda McDougal and other victims of malpractice can receive for life-altering injuries. Greedy lawyers have had their hands in the cookie jar for so long that Congress may actually enact a law to stop them.

A LESSON IN BAD JUDGMENT

The lines are clearly drawn in court when the lawyers do battle: The state seeks the truth and the defense zealously defends its client. But what happens when the judge—the supposed impartial referee—thwarts justice? Here's my opening argument.

JUDGE LANCE ITO: READY FOR HIS CLOSE-UP

Presiding over the debacle later named the "trial of the century," State v. O. J. Simpson, was a then-little-known trial judge, Lance Ito. Somewhere during the Simpson trial, he went from trial judge to media sponge. The main reason Ito may have favored cameras is that he fell in love with the spotlight the moment the trial began and actually came to believe he was a media star. His nickname around the courthouse was "Judge Ego." Occasionally, in the middle of testimony—and remember, this was a double-murder trial—with the jury seated and the two teams of lawyers hunkered down at their respective tables, Ito suddenly, inexplicably, and without request by either side, would announce a break in the proceedings. It was later revealed that these were "star breaks." When a celebrity, of which there were many, would enter the courtroom to watch or cover the proceedings, Ito would halt the trial and have his bailiff summon the star to his chambers for a meet-and-greet. I wouldn't be surprised if he kept an instant camera at the ready for all those priceless Kodak moments.

After the trial, defense attorney Peter Neufeld told *Time* magazine, "I was very disappointed with Judge Ito, . . . the fact that he was so concerned about his status as a celebrity, his willingness to entertain personalities in chambers, to show the lawyers little videotapes of skits on television." Neufeld went on with his critique, describing an episode when Ito summoned the lawyers to chambers and played back a clip of the "Dancing Itos" from the *Tonight* show. When you are summoned to the judge's chambers to see a video, you expect, as a trial lawyer, to see a confession, a surveillance tape, or some other type of video or documentary evidence. Not this time. The joke was on Lady Justice.

The Simpson judge was quite the jokester. Don't get me wrong—it's not that serious cases can't use a touch of levity at times; but not at the expense of the victims. His inappropriate and tasteless remarks were no laughing matter. In his book *Outrage: The Five Reasons Why O. J. Simpson Got Away with Murder,* Charles Manson prosecutor Vincent Bugliosi writes that at the start of the case, Ito told Johnnie Cochran he had good news and bad news. The bad news was that police had found Simpson's blood outside Nicole Brown's home, the scene of the double murders. The good news, according to Ito, was that Simpson's cholesterol was low. I bet the victim's families thought that was really funny.

From day one, Ito was starstruck as well as overwhelmed by the Dream Team. This extended to the defense experts. It's true that Dr. Henry Lee is incredibly well respected, but judges are required by law to refrain from commenting on the evidence or on witnesses in the case they are hearing. During the Simpson trial, after Lee testified for the defense, just as cross-exam was to commence, Ito looked down at the assistant district attorney and said, "Frankly, if I were in your shoes I would cross-examine Dr. Lee for no more than half an hour. Accentuate the positive in a friendly and professional manner, given his reputation, and then get out." What the hay? Since when did the defense need a cheering section on the bench? Actually, in the future, we should just add the judge to the Dream Team—he'd make a perfect mascot.

Then there's the issue of an alleged confession made by Simpson to his friend Rosey Grier that Ito suppressed illegally. On November 13, 1994, the former NFL star Rosey Grier, also an ordained minister, visited Simpson in jail. A sheriff, Jeff Stuart, stood about ten feet away from the two as they spoke. According to a story in the *Globe* published on January 9, 1996, Simpson raised his voice and blurted out, "I didn't mean to do it! I'm sorry!"

Ito ruled the clergyman-penitent privilege waived because Simpson voluntarily spoke so loudly that he was overheard. But, amazingly, he then went on to exclude Simpson's admission on other grounds. Ito reasoned that Simpson had assumed privacy—with a sheriff ten feet away. This was a turning point in the case, in my mind.

Moreover, the way Ito treated prosecutor Marcia Clark throughout the trial was horrific. He often talked down to her as if she were on trial. Call me a women's libber if you want, but I watched the entire trial myself, and this tone was never used with the male attorneys. Bugliosi makes the same observation in his book. On July 20, 1995, Clark was only a few moments late for a very early court hearing. The jury was not there, so they were not inconvenienced in any way. Clark promptly apologized to the court and the other attorneys. Ito, all bravado, fined her office $250. When Clark pointed out, "Your Honor, may I remind the court that Mr. Shapiro kept the court waiting for twenty minutes— showing up at twenty minutes after nine when it was his witness on the stand—and suffered no sanctions?" Ito threw back, "Thank you. The fine will be one thousand dollars." He undermined Clark throughout the trial. I saw it with my own eyes.

And then the icing on the cake. At the end of this appalling miscarriage of justice, Ito not only thanked the jury for their time, he went totally overboard. The ringmaster of the three-ring circus that had shocked the world stated that society owed the jurors a "debt of gratitude." Nicole Brown and Ron Goldman, somewhere, had to be crying.

JUDGE HILLER ZOBEL:
HIJACKER OF JUSTICE

On November 10, 1997, Judge Hiller Zobel hijacked the justice system by reversing the will of the people in *Commonwealth of Massachusetts v. Louise Woodward*. On October 30, at the culmination of the trial that had riveted the country and horrified parents everywhere, the jury found the nineteen-year-old British au pair guilty of second-degree murder in the death of eight-month-old Matthew Eappen. But less than two weeks later, on that infamous fall day, Zobel took it upon himself to reduce the jury's verdict to manslaughter and slashed Woodward's sentence of life behind bars with parole possible in fifteen years, to time served. She walked out of jail.

Even before Zobel's outrageous actions, Woodward's murder trial ignited a firestorm of controversy for a number of reasons. It brought attention to working mothers' fears about whether the people hired to help care for the children they leave behind each day as they're out making a living are qualified for the job. It also brought to light a largely unregulated business, in-home nanny services. The "Nanny Trial," as it was dubbed, revolved around the death of a beautiful baby boy, Matty Eappen. Matty's parents, Deborah and Sunil Eappen, were both well-respected physicians, who left baby Matty in the care of Woodward, whom the couple hired in 1996. On February 4, 1997, Woodward called police and said that the baby was having difficulty breathing. When paramedics arrived at the Eappens' home, they discovered that Matty had a two-and-a-half-inch skull fracture. The Eappens kept vigil over their son while he spent four days on life support before he died on February 9. An autopsy revealed that Matty did indeed have a fractured skull and a month-old wrist fracture.

The defense team, headed by the brilliant but clearly misguided defense attorney Barry Scheck, attempted to place blame on the baby's own parents for Matty's skull fracture and intense brain damage associated with shaken-baby syndrome. Both sides agreed that Matthew Eappen died from massive bleeding inside his skull. The prosecution claimed the bleeding was caused by "a combination of extraordinarily violent shaking and overpowering contact with a hard flat surface, all occurring some time on February 4, 1997." The far-fetched defense theory was that the subdural bleeding had been a result of prior head injuries and that someone else had caused the trauma weeks before and it had gone undetected—obviously alluding to the parents.

Scheck also argued that a preexisting medical condition must have killed baby Matty. The attorneys also hinted that the Eappens' other child, two-year-old Brendan, may have had something to do with his brother's injuries—an outrageous claim that prosecutors were quick to discredit, saying no toddler could have inflicted that much trauma on a baby. Disgusting. Prosecutors argued that Woodward even admitted to shaking the baby, dropping him on floor, and tossing him on the bed. Medical examiners said Matty hit the floor with force equal to that of a fall from a second-story window.

In a major all-or-nothing gamble, and after both sides had rested, the defense fought like mad to preclude the jury from considering any count other than first- or second-degree murder—no manslaughter, no involuntary manslaughter. Punishment for first-degree murder is a mandatory life sentence; second-degree murder carries the same sentence with the possibility of parole after fifteen years. In order to convict Woodward of first-degree murder, prosecutors had to prove she knowingly acted with premeditated malice and extreme cruelty.

The state argued for the lesser included counts of voluntary and involuntary manslaughter in addition to murder in order to give the jury all possible alternative verdicts founded in the facts presented at trial. The Massachusetts Supreme Court agreed with prosecutors on this issue, stating, "As far as we are aware, no jurisdiction that has considered the issue has allowed a defendant to veto a lesser included offense instruction properly requested by the prosecution." The defense blocked their request, and the judge, contrary to the law, backed them up. It was all or nothing.

The jury surprised many court watchers, but not me. After watching Woodward's performance on the stand, I was more convinced than ever that she was guilty as sin. Her demeanor, combined with the incredible physical injuries this baby boy suffered after his parents left for work, was enough to convince me. The jury agreed. Louise Woodward was convicted of second-degree murder on October 30. The jury had deliberated for nearly thirty hours over the course of three days. The next morning at the sentencing, Woodward was sentenced to life with the possibility of parole in fifteen years.

But that wasn't the end of it. Days later, the defense filed a three-part motion to set aside the verdict and dismiss the case, or to set aside the verdict and get a new trial, and, finally, to reduce the charge to manslaughter. In a shocking turn of events, Judge Zobel took it upon himself to reverse the jury's verdict and reduce their finding to manslaughter. He also allowed Woodward to leave jail immediately, sentencing her to "time served." Under the law, the judge is allowed to correct erroneous jury verdicts. In my view, this verdict was not erroneous. Then the state supreme court, in a split decision, let Zobel off the hook by affirming his jury reversal. At least a few of the appellate judges had the guts to complain.

The former au pair is now free and clear, living back home in Great Britain. Her family managed to raise quite a bit of money for her "defense" (reports said Woodward's coffers once reached half a million dollars), although later her parents were accused of squandering portions of it. Woodward defaulted in the wrongful-death civil suit filed by the Eappens. Her attorneys said, "She is not in a financial position to defend the action in America. It is not an admission of guilt. She maintains her innocence." In the suit, the Eappens sought to prevent Woodward from profiting from the case. Woodward says she wants to be a mother. God help any little baby in her care.

Last year, Woodward got a two-year contract and started working as a lawyer in England. A partner in the firm told reporters that the former nanny, who served just 279 days for the death of baby Matty, wants to specialize in commercial law. Thank God she's given up the child-care business.

Aside from Woodward, Zobel is also a disturbing figure in this scenario. In reversing the jury's verdict, Zobel started off with a quote from John Adams. Adams must be spinning in his grave. Zobel wrote:

> The law, John Adams told a Massachusetts jury while
> defending British citizens on trial for murder, is inflexible,
> inexorable, and deaf: inexorable to the cries of the defendant; "deaf
> as an adder to the clamours of the populace." . . . A judge, in short,
> is a public servant who must follow his conscience, whether or not
> he counters the manifest wishes of those he serves. . . .

First Zobel bent over backward to encourage the defense's strategy and, in the end, reduced a hard-won murder conviction, giving Woodward a free pass to get out of jail. He devoted nearly half of his order to justifying his decision to downgrade the conviction. Ignoring the evidence so carefully presented by the state and relied upon by the jury, Zobel wrote that "although as a father and grandfather I particularly recognize and acknowledge the indescribable pain Matthew Eappen's death has caused his parents and grandparents, as a judge I am duty-bound to ignore it. I must look only at the evidence and the defendant." Zobel ruled that "the circumstances in which Defendant acted were characterized by confusion, inexperience, frustration, immaturity and some anger, but not malice (in the legal sense) supporting a conviction for second-degree murder."

Since when is brutalizing a helpless infant unable to defend himself not malice? He went on: "Frustrated by her inability to quiet the crying child, she was 'a little rough with him' under circumstances where another, perhaps wiser, person would have sought to restrain the physical impulse." *A little rough with him?* The baby died. Zobel actually wrote those words in his decision. The Eappens must have been sick at heart, not only over losing their precious baby son in such a brutal way but also because they saw justice, in the form of Judge Hiller Zobel, fail their beloved son as well.

I met and spoke with Zobel in Atlanta one afternoon. My eyes were obviously playing tricks on me, because in another setting, without the power of the bench or the temptation to abuse that power, he seemed almost grandfatherly. But looks can be deceiving. I will never forget the day Zobel, for all intents and purposes, rewrote the Constitution and not only robbed the Eappens of a jury's verdict but assaulted Lady Justice herself.

After the judge's stunning verdict reversal, Woodward had the gall to say she was disappointed in the decision because she was not totally exonerated. She wanted a full acquittal from Zobel. Woodward and her defense team—much like O. J. Simpson, who pledged to find Nicole and Ron's "real killer"—swore they would convene an independent review team of scientists to reexamine key medical and forensic evidence in the case to prove the true cause of death. Surprise! They haven't lifted a finger to do it. Not that they needed to. We know who caused Matty's death. Louise Woodward. And Judge Hiller Zobel let her get away with murder.

JUDGE TERRY RUCKRIEGLE – WHAT A FAN!

In the summer of 2004 in a courtroom in Colorado, Lady Justice was spinning like a top thanks to the ringmaster of the Kobe Bryant case—Judge Terry Ruckriegle. After allowing hours of closed-door questioning of the alleged rape victim on sexual behavior dating back a year before she met Kobe Bryant, he ruled that portions of the young woman's prior sex life would be brought before the jury. In addition, he then mistakenly released the closed-door transcripts on the Internet. When the young woman wanted a continuance following that disaster, Judge Ruckriegle refused.

The last "mistaken" release of information was one of many

episodes that can be traced back to the very beginning of the trial. The woman's name, as well as other case-sensitive information—always damning to the alleged victim—was repeatedly leaked. In comparison, nothing remotely disparaging to the defense was ever leaked. While the case was still in county court, Eagle County Judge Frederick Gannett took zero action (besides offering useless lip service) when Bryant's defense lawyer, Pamela Mackey, stated the young woman's name in open court multiple times.

That moment set the tone for the trial. Chief Judge Ruckriegle presided over the circuslike atmosphere that dominated the remainder of the proceedings, which ultimately led to the victim deciding to pack her bags and abandon the case. With no one protecting her rights, who can blame her? Whether or not Bryant was guilty of rape, Ruckriegle sent a clear message to rape victims all over the country: The court won't protect you. You will be mistreated in court and out because of the person wearing the robe. It's no wonder rape remains one of the single most underreported crimes on the books.

CHAPTER TWO
WE THE JURY

ON ELEVATORS AND IN RESTAURANTS, AT BUS
stops and airports, I am constantly asked, "What's the secret to winning
cases?" My response is always the same: You win or lose in jury selection. Once the jury's struck—twelve jurors who hear the case selected
from a pool of people—it's all over. Jury selection is the single most important part of a trial. As a prosecutor, I can say without question, if you
fumble your strikes by selecting a jury that's in a hurry, that doesn't
want to be bothered, that is inherently suspicious of police or is simply
cantankerous and not prone to compromise, you've got big problems.
The result can be a hung jury, or worse—a not-guilty verdict.

By the time a lawyer stands at the jury rail for opening statement,
they must firmly believe what they're saying is true. Before approach-
ing the rail, I always investigated my cases backward and forward myself, in addition to the police investigation. I interviewed witnesses,
carefully wrote out by hand their direct-exam, question by question, including notes on the appropriate juncture at which to introduce key
physical evidence. I always devised a strategy and prepared the ex-
hibits before the trial began. All of those things can be controlled or at
least laid out in advance. The unknown variable in every trial is the secret minds of the jurors: their belief systems, their values, and their

mind-sets. These things can't be controlled, but they can be dealt with through proper preparation.

This country's jury system is under attack as never before, largely because the juror mind-set has been left mostly unexplored and unchallenged. Many recent cases have resulted in downright shocking verdicts that have left veteran trial watchers and legal analysts shaking their heads in disbelief. But it was events surrounding jurors in three high-profile trials in 2004 that showed, without question, that the jury-selection process and the juror oath as it stands today are simply not working. Chappell Hartridge—the media-obsessed juror in the Martha Stewart trial—the allegedly disagreeable "Juror Number 4" in the Tyco mistrial, and the so-called stealth jurors attempting to fake their way into the jury box in the Scott Peterson case all caused varying degrees of chaos in the courtroom because of their confounding behavior and their unexplored mind-sets.

JURORS WHO LOATHE THE OATH

Hear out my argument and consider the following three examples of a jury system in peril:

EXHIBIT A: IT'S ALL ABOUT ME!

In the Martha Stewart case, everybody pointed the finger but nobody knew exactly whom rightfully to blame for the fact that Chappell Hartridge, Juror Number 8, had gotten on the jury in the first place. From what I can tell based on court filings, he withheld information during jury selection. The defense claimed that Hartridge lied about his arrest record on a questionnaire when he said he had never been in court other than for a minor traffic violation. Did he forget he'd been arrested for assaulting a woman he lived with? This could have been remedied during voir dire, which coincidentally means "to speak the truth," but Hartridge never murmured a word. Defense lawyer Robert Morvillo said Hartridge "dishonestly suppressed information concerning a gender-related incident . . . to be able to sit in judgment of a well-known and highly successful woman in a case alleging false statements."

Hartridge also allegedly failed to disclose on his jury questionnaire that he had been sued three times. The defense filing stated that civil judgments had been entered against him in each case. Hartridge's alleged juror misconduct alone wasn't enough for the trial judge to grant Stewart's request for a new trial. The reality is that, ironically, if the defense had known that Hartridge had been charged with a crime, they probably would have insisted he stay on the jury ("Here's a guy who's been accused of wrongdoing before—he'll side with Martha! We love him!"). The whole thing backfired. If anyone had wanted him off the jury, most likely it would have been the state.

In addition to lying during the jury oath, evidence suggests that Hartridge may have been guilty of juror greed as well. On the day of Martha Stewart's guilty verdict, he was all about justice, publicly declaring he believed the decision was "a victory for the little guys." Producers from every network scrambled to get him for their nightly news programs, eager to hear whatever insights he might have to offer about the deliberations. Not surprisingly, he disappeared from his impromptu press conference on the courthouse steps and reemerged soon afterward on NBC's myriad news outlets. He showed up at all hours of the day and night in the aftermath of the verdict on *Dateline NBC*, the *Today* show, and on MSNBC. But Hartridge's own greed preempted his multimedia moment. Dominick Dunne reported in *Vanity Fair* that at least one other show on another network dropped him from their lineup when he demanded money and a limousine for his appearance. Court documents filed by Morvillo seeking a new trial also accused Hartridge of seeking money for posttrial interviews. Incidentally, the same papers also alleged that Hartridge embezzled money from a local Little League team. The local Little League? Embezzlement?

No one knows for sure what Hartridge's motives were, but evidence suggests he had an issue with Martha Stewart and her millionaire lifestyle. It's not clear if his agenda involved getting Stewart convicted out of his own pecuniary interest or if he had some other, more personal reason, like exacting revenge against the rich, that was fulfilled by sitting on this jury. While there was no reversal and retrial in the Martha Stewart case because of Hartridge's lies, the fact that his past didn't prevent him from sitting on the jury is very troubling. Most people lie to get out of jury duty. It's very disturbing and completely bizarre to me that today there are people who see their jury summons as a temporary ticket to C-list stardom.

EXHIBIT B:
CAN'T WE ALL JUST GET ALONG?

When taking the jury oath, jurors assume the duty to deliberate with each other in a wholehearted attempt to render a verdict that speaks the truth. During the same head-spinning month that Chappell Hartridge monopolized the small screen, another courtroom meltdown was occurring in the Tyco case. The trial was thrown into chaos when Juror Number 4 was reported to have given the "AOK" sign to the defense team of CEO Dennis Kozlowski and codefendant Mark Swartz while leaving the courtroom. Claims flew that Juror Number 4 was neither impartial, as required by law, nor willing to deliberate—or, for that matter, even able get along with her fellow jurors.

In an astonishing breach of journalistic ethics, the *New York Post* and the *Wall Street Journal* revealed the juror's name. Robbed of her anonymity, seventy-nine-year-old Ruth Jordan went public with her story on *60 Minutes II* and denied she made such a gesture. But the genie was out of the bottle. She fell under siege by the media and told the judge she had received a threatening letter as a result of being identified. The judge in the case rightly declared a mistrial. The truth is, even if the jury had come back with a verdict in a timely fashion, there would have been a reversal on appeal because of an alleged threat to the juror. Whether the letter Jordan received was truly threatening is beside the point. The fact that Juror Number 4 perceived it to be so was all that mattered. A coerced jury verdict will not stand.

What disturbs me about this is that it's unearthed yet another way for defense attorneys to get a mistrial or a reversal. In the Tyco trial, the decision to declare a mistrial was a sound one, though we're left with some tough questions. How are defense attorneys now going to try to twist and turn the evidence of what a juror said or did in order to get a new trial? Every twitch of a nose, every wink or nod, will open up allegations of juror impartiality. How long will the appeals process be now that there's a whole new universe—inhabited by the sneaky juror—for the defense to explore? I refer to the defense as the instigator in these situations simply because, in order for there to be an appeal, there must first be a conviction. If the state loses a case, it rarely has grounds for appeal, making this an avenue almost exclusively tailored for the defense. Taxpayers, brace yourselves for a new round of appeals based on grounds like the Juror Number 4 allegations that will make it all the way up to the U.S. Supreme Court. Here's another news flash: You'll be paying for the ticket, first class.

EXHIBIT C:
THE STEALTH JUROR

People who lie in order to make it onto the jury in a high-profile trial have come to be known in the legal community as "stealth jurors." They have an agenda—which usually involves delivering their own brand of vigilante justice or profiting from their time in the jury box. If jurors are actually guilty as charged of having these ulterior motives, they become dangerous spoilers for a true verdict.

Scott Peterson's defense team claimed they spotted such a juror in a retired secretary and take credit for saving the jury. Juror Number 29308 was polite during questioning by the state, insisting she could definitely be fair and impartial. But then, defense attorney Mark Geragos abandoned his usually charming demeanor and went on the attack, grilling her over a senior-citizen bus trip she took to Reno, Nevada. "Did you tell people on that trip that you passed the test to get on the jury and Scott Peterson is 'going to get what is due to him'?" Geragos asked. The juror, a volunteer at a senior-citizen center, acknowledged the bus trip but denied talking about the Peterson case. Trial judge Al Delucchi ultimately booted her off the jury.

A short time afterward, Geragos told the judge he'd received a tip that another female juror, a thirty-three-year-old student, had boasted during an online session in a "spirituality" chatroom that she had lied on the questionnaire to get on the jury. When confronted by Geragos about these allegations, she denied them, but she, too, got the judicial boot.

These developments have incredibly far-reaching implications. The more Geragos could trump up the motives of allegedly dishonest jurors, the more likely his accusations become the basis for a venue change or an appeal. A new trial could conservatively cost the state millions, as it took months to get through the sixteen hundred jurors vetted for the trial. The bottom line is that these particular "stealth jurors" may be gone, but the damage has been done, and the system pays for it.

In general, the defense seems to believe the only acceptable juror is an uninformed juror, a juror who never reads the paper, listens to the radio, or watches television. Practically no one escapes hearing the facts reported on high-profile cases. I think people can and must have an opinion—we're human beings, not turnips. When I prosecuted cases, I wanted jurors who could listen to the evidence and, based on what they heard in the courtroom, reach a fair and impartial decision. The truth, as I see it, is that they are not hard to find.

Most prospective jurors might have commented on what they've heard to friends or family. That's not unusual. What would be unusual is for someone to live in our news-saturated society and *not* hear about cases. But now, as a result of the developments in these three cases, innocent comments can be held against a juror. In the past, jurors have been "rehabilitated" by attorneys' getting them to admit in court that, yes, they have heard about the case but will keep an open mind and listen to both sides before rendering a verdict. Up until now, jurors have been taken at their word on their solemn oath. People like Hartridge have given us pause to think about whether that's actually happening. The doubts they engender undermine the integrity of the jury and the system.

In court, I was always concerned about what the jurors thought. I had the habit of watching them like a hawk throughout the trial, for any clues in their faces. Now I find I'm even more worried about who exactly the jurors are—just who is sitting in the jury box? What effect will their foibles have on a true verdict? The events in the Stewart, Tyco, and Peterson trials are just the tip of the iceberg. It's impossible to know how far this will go. If a juror says at the end of a trial, "We knew he did it, and we weren't gonna let him get away with it," would that be grounds for a new trial? For throwing out a case?

I use that example because I distinctly remember a middle-aged male juror coming up to me after one especially hard-fought trial. I was standing at the curb waiting for the light to change when I felt a hand on my shoulder. When I turned around, I immediately recognized the man in a windbreaker standing before me from the jury box. He spoke these words: "Miss D.A., we knew he did it, and we weren't going to let him get away with it." My heart warmed, and I thanked him for rendering a true verdict and shook his hand. When the light turned green, we parted there and I never saw him again. In retrospect, I would have been struck to the core with fear if somehow the defense would claim "stealth juror!" Thankfully, that didn't happen, and justice was served.

It's largely because of the strange events in these three headline-grabbing cases that I believe we will see an increasing number of defense attorneys attacking the individuals on the jury—legitimately or not—for statements they may have made. In the Peterson trial example, ultimately the word of a tipster was taken over that of a juror. I still believe that most jurors are like most of us, people who sing in the choir or work around the corner at the local bank or deli—just ordinary people with no hidden agenda. Most of them don't even want to be there but attend out of a sense of duty to our justice system. Very rarely are you going to find somebody dying to get on jury service, anxious to be away from home or work. That's why Hartridge and others like him are so upsetting, because they give the system a bad name, leaving in their wake the impression that juror misconduct happens all the time.

"JUROR NUMBER 5"

Unless you've lived under a rock for the last year, you know exactly who Juror Number 5 is and what he meant to the case of *State v. Scott Peterson*. On June 23, 2004, the now-infamous Juror Number 5 was booted from the Scott Peterson jury and the world got a rare peek into one of the twelve minds in the Peterson jury box. When the press revealed Justin Falconer to be Juror Number 5, he became an overnight sensation. He was everywhere—on all the network morning shows, *Larry King Live*, Court TV, and on syndicated radio. Falconer told the world he believed that Peterson, on trial for the murders of his wife and unborn son, was innocent and that the state had failed to prove its case just weeks into the trial.

I unwittingly became part of the story. Falconer got the boot after video in the courthouse lobby showed him speaking directly to a witness in the case, Laci Peterson's brother, Brent Rocha. The judge, a seasoned trial veteran with plenty of death-penalty trials under his belt, summoned Falconer to his chambers to make sure no inappropriate discussions had taken place regarding the facts of the case. Prior to the exchange with Rocha, though, Falconer had become a point of interest to journalists and legal pundits alike for his seeming familiarity in court with Scott Peterson and his attorney, Mark Geragos. Allegedly, upon entering the courtroom each morning and when returning from breaks, Falconer would give encouraging smiles to the defense table as he walked by. Talk about nonverbal communication! If I had been the prosecutor, I would have been beside myself!

In any event, during the conversation with Judge Delucchi, it turns out that Falconer gave him an earful—including the fact that his (Falconer's) girlfriend was a frequent Court TV watcher and was so furious with the "Court TV lady" (me) that she wanted to "kick the crap" out of me. That apparently caused Delucchi to perk up his ears and put two and two together. However innocently, Falconer's girlfriend had been relaying tidbits of coverage about the Peterson trial to her boyfriend—a Peterson juror.

In the days leading up to the Falconer revelation, I had complained bitterly on air about the familiarity shown between Falconer and the defense camp and I made no secret of it. Of course, Geragos was furious after Falconer's dismissal and suggested that the media had somehow arranged the entire incident in order to pressure the judge to dismiss a pro-defense juror. Geragos even filed a motion for mistrial over the whole thing and called it an "outrage." What is an outrage is that Laci and Conner were murdered and dumped in the bay—but that's a whole other story.

I didn't like much of what Falconer had to say about the state's case or his take on it, including his insistence at the early stages of trial that the state had failed. In my mind, the evidence against Peterson was overwhelming. But here's the reality: I don't have to like it. Whether or not you agree with Falconer's assessment of the case, in his mind the state had failed. As a prosecutor, you never get a second chance in court, but Falconer gave the state that chance. Even though his medicine tasted bad going down, he opened their eyes to the perceived holes in their case. The state's duty is to convince the jury beyond a reasonable doubt, and whether Falconer was right or wrong, the state's duty was to convince him as well. I was shocked by his revelations, but I know I learned a lot about a juror's thinking, seeing the case through his eyes.

In the end, Delucchi denied the motion, and the case went on. The reality is that Falconer did wind up being incredibly pro-defense, even stating point-blank, "There's no way you could possibly convict him." I know that because I interviewed him on air myself. Since that time, he has visited me at the Court TV truck when I was in Redwood City covering the case. One time he even brought his girlfriend—and guess what? She didn't kick the crap out of me.

STARGAZING

Jurors throughout history have been swayed by their own prejudices, their likes and dislikes, their instinctive perceptions of a defendant, of the prosecutor, or even of a particular witness. People might not have had a voracious news media to deal with over two hundred years ago when the jury system was first created, but many of the same societal problems existed then as exist now. They have simply grown to twenty-first-century proportions.

In today's high-profile trials, the "public" now encompasses not only the whole country but the entire world. Information is communicated instantly around the globe via satellite. Our global village has a huge appetite for and an endless curiosity about celebrities, an appetite that can be satisfied any time, day or night, simply by clicking on the television. Every aspect of these revered stars' lives is available to us 24/7, including where they have their hair highlighted, what car they drive, where they shop, even where and with whom they had dinner the night before.

The "starstruck juror" is nothing new, and celebrity trials certainly aren't a new phenomenon either. As long as there has been a jury system, every village and city has always had its own "celebrities"—the wealthiest person in town, the mayor's wife, the high-school quarterback, the homecoming queen. There have always been those people, who for whatever reason (largely because we think these individuals have "perfect" lives) fascinate other people. Prosecutors have always had the additional hurdle in the burden of proof of overcoming celebrity status. It is extremely difficult for a prosecutor to get a celebrity convicted, be it an A-list athlete (O. J. Simpson), a politician's relative (William Kennedy Smith), or a Hollywood star (Sean "P. Diddy" Combs). The glaring spotlight of celebrity is often blinding. Die-hard fans continued to give Kobe Bryant and Michael Jackson their devotion regardless of the charges lodged against the two stars. But star defendants need not be A-listers like Jackson or Bryant to have the same effect on starstruck jurors. In July 2003, after a Houston jury acquitted then–Astros shortstop Julio Lugo of assaulting his wife, they pressed the infielder to sign autographs in the jury room.

Although the accused might not be a household name, juries seem equally dazzled by wealthy defendants. In 1982, John DeLorean, the creator of the futuristic eighties sports car, the DeLorean, was charged with conspiring to smuggle $24 million of cocaine into the United States. At his 1984 trial for drug trafficking, the prosecution showed videotape of DeLorean discussing the drug deal with undercover FBI agents. The defense maintained that the government had entrapped him and that DeLorean was a man driven to desperate acts because his company was on the brink of financial ruin. A jury found him not guilty.

History seems to be repeating itself. Before Judge Michael Obus declared a mistrial because of the perceived threats received by juror Jordan in the Tyco trial, it seemed unlikely that the jury was headed for a unanimous guilty verdict against CEO Dennis Kozlowski and CFO Mark Swartz. Despite mountains of evidence to support the state's claims the executives stole $600 million from the company and spent it on, among other things, a $6,000 shower curtain and museum-quality artwork for their homes, a guilty verdict apparently wasn't on the horizon. Jordan announced the prosecution had not proved criminal intent. The defense can only hope another enamored juror winds up as part of the jury pool in the new trial.

Although I rail against it, the truth is, the poor and uneducated are much more likely to be treated harshly. One popular theory is that the wealthy can afford to hire a better defense team. The other important factor is that jurors are wrongly predisposed to think that someone who is successful, white, and without a documented criminal history is less likely to commit a crime. Throw into the mix an individual on trial whom the jury believes they actually know, someone who has been in their homes many, many times—albeit on the television screen—and it's almost impossible to get a conviction.

The idea that any of these privileged defendants are less likely to commit wrongdoing than, say, a minority just slogging through the day like the rest of us, is simply not true. The famous, the beautiful, the well-educated, and the wealthy, with impossibly straight white teeth and sporting couture clothing at trial, are just as susceptible to greed, anger, and evildoing as anyone else. It's just tough sometimes to convince a jury of that.

GREED BY THE BOOK

When Chaucer wrote *The Canterbury Tales*, he put Greed on the list of the Seven Deadly Sins. Greed has been around since time began and now it has wormed its way into the jury deliberation room. Why? Because we as a society have made it possible. Centuries ago there was no *National Enquirer* offering big bucks for first-person accounts from jurors and no competition-crazed TV and movie producers wooing jurors to trade information for national notoriety. There was no *Dateline*, no local news that could make instant celebrities out of jurors addicted to the limelight. In the not-so-distant past, jurors may have gotten some semblance of notoriety within their communities, but they couldn't make any real money off it. Now they can, and they pose a serious threat to our justice system.

Today's jurors have discovered there's money to be made by sitting in the jury box. The public's hunger for information about high-profile trials—for the "inside story" that now must be secured at any or all cost—has spawned a distinctly contemporary phenomenon that's at the root of the problem we now face: juror greed. This disturbing new development is a many-tentacled monster. It hungrily reaches out from the courtroom steps to feed its insatiable appetite for fifteen minutes of fame and fortune, courtesy of the exposure and hefty checks offered by tabloids, television, and publishers hawking tell-all books.

A decade ago, the "trial of the century" ignited the juror–turned–literary cash cow phenomenon. The Simpson trial spawned scores of books, including *I Want to Tell You: My Response to Your Letters, Your Messages, Your Questions*, written by the defendant before the trial even started. Jurors quickly followed suit. First there was *The Private Diary of an O.J. Juror: Behind the Scenes of the Trial of the Century*, by Michael Knox, O.J. Juror Number 620. The book is a wordy tell-all from a juror who was thrown off the case for lying about his criminal record. Talk about tainting the jury! Knox's gossipy tome (cowritten with *National Enquirer* columnist Mike Walker) was published while the trial was still going on. Then came *Madam Foreman: A Rush to Judgment?* by Amanda Cooley, Carrie Bess, and Marsha Rubin-Jackson. Cooley, the foreperson on the Simpson criminal trial, united with two other jurors to defend the most infamous acquittal in recent history.

Of all the exploitive moves by the major players of the O. J. Simpson murder trial, this one takes the cake: Tracy Hampton, the twenty-six-year-old flight attendant who quit the jury early in the case claiming stress, posed for a layout in the March 1995 issue of *Playboy*. In keeping with the decorum of the trial, the spread was shot in a courtroom setting. My verdict? In the words of O. J. Simpson himself, Hampton is definitely "100 percent not guilty" of having too much class.

I learned firsthand how the Simpson trial forever changed the way jurors view their civic duty. In 1995, while I was still prosecuting felonies in Atlanta, Geraldo Rivera asked me to come to New York to do a show with Cooley and the other jurors who had written *Madam Foreman*.

Rivera had kindly featured me as a regular on his nightly legal show during the trial. This was my chance to finally get a look at this jury for myself. Their verdict had astounded me and disappointed me. I actually felt I had the wind knocked out of me when it was announced. I was completely intrigued with the idea of meeting some of the jurors responsible for Simpson's acquittal.

The jurors on the show were unfailingly pleasant to everyone. Regardless of what I threw at them, they either acted as if they had no idea that the damning evidence I brought up even existed or simply discounted it as not being persuasive enough. I realized that even if these ladies had a Technicolor movie playing in surround sound of Simpson doing the deed, they'd choose to believe it was a fake, doctored by police, and vote to acquit all over again. Trying to reason through the evidence with these ladies was like shrieking at a deaf man. After throwing numerous pointed questions about the evidence at them and minding my manners on air as best I could, I finally realized that nothing and nobody would ever get through to them. Even if they ever thought they were wrong, they'd never admit it. There was nothing left to prove. The trial was over.

After the show, we all walked out to the street together. It was a cold, gray day in Manhattan, and I had dressed for Atlanta weather, no coat, hat, or gloves. The women walked straight to a waiting white stretch limousine and started trundling in. I stood there saying my good-byes. As the last lady juror stepped into the car, she turned back and looked me straight in the eye. I'll never forget her words: "Nancy, you know, this trial has been the best thing that ever happened to me! I've been to the best restaurants, hotels, shopping, everything! It's really been something!" She got into the car, and the door slammed shut. I just stared at the car as they drove away.

I felt numb. As I watched the limo's taillights disappear east up the street, my eyes filled with tears. I thought of Nicole Brown and Ron Goldman lying dead outside Nicole's home in a river of their own blood. I pictured their families distraught and crying on the hard wooden pews of the courtroom the day the verdict was read. The best thing that ever happened? My own blood ran cold.

The Simpson case might have been the tipping point for jurors-turned-pseudojournalists, but the incidence of such unabashed greed isn't new. Before that case commandeered the title of "trial of the century," it had been assigned to many trials, including that of Jack Ruby, who was the unapologetic vigilante-justice killer of Lee Harvey Oswald, the accused assassin of John F. Kennedy. The 1964 trial spawned one of the first jury-service-for-profit novelists. Max Causey, a thirty-five-year-old administrative engineer, was elected foreperson on the trial. During jury selection and trial, he kept extensive notes. Those notes became the basis for his memoir, *The Trial of a Juror*, published two years later. In 2001, Causey's nephew, John Mark Dempsey, released the book with new material, including interviews with other jurors, under the title *The Jack Ruby Trial Revisited: The Diary of Jury Foreman Max Causey.*

The Charles Manson case was another major trial in which jurors realized they could capitalize on jury duty and take it straight to the bank. The Manson jury spawned several books, including *Trial by Your Peers* by juror William Zamora, whose book was later rereleased under the title *Blood Family.* Also from the Manson trial: *Witness to Evil* by juror George Bishop. It turns out everybody saw dollar signs after that trial. In a bizarre twist on the juror tell-all genre, even the spouse of a Manson juror penned a book. Rosemary Baer wrote *Reflections on the Manson Trial: Journal of a Pseudo-Juror.*

When I interviewed Bernhard Goetz after his trial, he told me in a quiet voice that the multiple shootings at the center of his "Subway Vigilante" case stood for more than the facts at trial. He explained that he saw himself as one man fighting back in his own deadly way against crime when no one else apparently would. His case now stands for the juror-gets-rich phenomenon as well. *The Subway Gunman: A Juror's Account of the Bernhard Goetz Trial* was written by Mark Lesly with Charles Shuttleworth. Lesly, a martial-arts instructor, along with other jurors, second-guessed postverdict and bent over backward to justify their decision to acquit. Cha-ching!!

Hung Jury: The Diary of a Menendez Juror, authored by juror Hazel Thornton, proved that a verdict wasn't a prerequisite for a juror looking to cash in on crime. I had no idea that someone would be so proud to be on a jury that couldn't reach a verdict on a case involving two adult sons accused of murdering their father and mother in cold blood. But the story of two spoiled young men who escaped justice for a short time after running through their parents' assets, drunk on money they would never have thought to go out and earn themselves, was just too sensational for publishers to pass up.

While the Tyco jurors made plenty of headlines just by being themselves, it was reported by *New York* magazine that one of them, a nurse named Parker Bosworth, planned to write a tome entitled *Tyco—The Trial: A Nurse's Diagnosis* but then reconsidered. Another one of the jurors, Peter McEntegart, a reporter for *Sports Illustrated,* wrote about the case for *Time* magazine. We'll have to wait and see if his story or those of others who were in the deliberation room with him turn into juror tell-alls.

This disturbing phenomenon cannot be blamed solely on the celebrity of the defendant. No one knew who Erik and Lyle Menendez or Charles Manson was before they committed their gruesome crimes. They became infamous because of their cases. What is most disturbing is not that books about high-profile murder cases are being written, but that the plan to write them may be born before or during voir dire. This concept is critical because, if true, it bears on the motives not only for jury service but for a particular verdict—the outcome of the trial itself. Most often a conviction sells the best, followed by an acquittal, with a hung jury placing a very distant third place. If it is ever shown that a book deal, plan, scheme, notes, or even concept existed pre–opening statement, there is a huge risk of mistrial hanging over what may otherwise be a valid true verdict.

TRIAL BY JURY

I was always intensely anxious during jury selection in cases I tried, because it was so pressure-filled. In my earliest days as a prosecutor, it was the part of the trial I looked forward to the least. While I came to really enjoy this aspect of trying a case, there were a few episodes along the way when I thought for sure I'd blown it.

While I had no problem prosecuting rapists and murderers, I found it very difficult to stand up and ask a hundred potential jurors, "Have any of you ever been arrested or been in trouble with the law in any way?" It felt so intrusive, even downright rude. Being from the South, I was raised to believe that good manners are all. I also knew that if a juror was rubbed the wrong way by that question, I could never have him or her on the jury. I was also sure that if I inadvertently got someone who'd had a brush with the law onto the jury, I'd pay for my mistake come verdict time.

In 1987, during my first bank-robbery case, *State v. Jones*, I found out just how wrong I was. It was a very difficult case to prove, because the defendant had been heavily disguised at the robbery. He wore a wig, mustache, beard, hat, and sunglasses. He'd even had a "break-away suit" that was basted lightly up the back so he could tear it off as soon as he ducked into the alley outside after the robbery. I desperately wanted to identify him from the still photos lifted off the bank's video camera—and even I couldn't make the ID.

I had my jury in the box after a few days of striking and was midway through the case when my investigator burst through the swinging doors of the courtroom one morning. The doors didn't make a sound when they opened, but I felt the rush of air when he entered the room. I was in the middle of a direct examination of a state's witness and felt mildly irritated because I didn't want anything to take the jury's focus off the witness stand. Despite every directive I had ever issued, my investigator started trying to talk to me during questioning. I could barely contain my frustration. When I ignored him, he actually pulled on my sleeve.

When I refused to speak to him in open court, he handed me a note. It read: "The juror in the back row wearing a plaid shirt is a convicted bank robber." Trying as best I could to look casual, I glanced at that juror, and—oh, yes, he was looking right at me. What could I do? It was my own fault. I hadn't asked these jurors if they'd ever been convicted of a crime, because I didn't want to offend them. I'd also assumed that because the jurors were pulled from voter-registration rolls and felons can't vote, I would never wind up with a convict on a jury panel. Man, was I ever wrong.

Since I'd never asked the right question, the juror had never lied, and I knew I had no grounds for complaining. The defense certainly didn't ask. They'd be thrilled to know he was there! I analyzed the situation overnight. I liked the man. I had originally wanted him on the jury. I got a good feeling from him during voir dire. The following morning, I went with my instinct. I argued directly to that juror during closing arguments, pointing out all the things the defendant had done wrong that resulted in his capture. For instance, the bank robbery note that reads: "Don't touch the alram. This is a robbey." (Translation: Don't touch the alarm. This is a robbery.) In addition to being a bank robber, Calvin Jones was also a very bad speller. That helped me immensely when I had him perform a writing comparison. He reversed letters in practically every word—the same way he did in the robbery note. The jury loved it.

I was lucky. The jury returned a guilty verdict. As the jurors filed out of the box to leave the courtroom, my bank robber juror stopped and our eyes met and he reached out his right hand to me. He quietly said, "Thank you." I will never forget him or what he taught me. Even though I had made the tactical error of not asking the jurors the tough questions on voir dire, he saved me. He also taught me this—rap sheets don't always reflect a man's character. To remember that, I keep the bank robbery note, "Don't touch the alram. This is a robbey," framed over my desk today.

The worst jury I ever got was in an aggravated-assault and armed-robbery case, *State v. Wilson*. In the 1988 trial, I tried the defendant for armed robbery and ended up getting a conviction on lesser charges. I made several mistakes in this case, but I blame not getting the verdict I wanted on my own error in jury selection. The victim was a stripper who was dressed in a cheerleader's outfit when she left a bar at four in the morning. For the trial, I made sure she looked prim and proper and actually had her mention what church she belonged to. I never made that mistake again. The jury could see straight through the "church lady." They could spot a stripper a mile away. That was one mistake I made during the trial—but it wasn't the biggest.

During jury selection, I noticed the behavior of one woman when the pool took the general juror oath. She stood stiffly with her hands by her sides and refused to raise her right one to swear on anything. She was the only person out of nearly one hundred who wouldn't raise her hand in solemn promise to uphold her duty. In my inexperience, it didn't send up a red flag like it should have.

At the time, I was still green enough that I would ask ridiculous questions during jury selection, like "What do you do in your spare time? What books do you read? What magazines do you like?" She was telling me loud and clear that she was trouble, but I was too blind to see it.

"What do you do in your spare time?"

"What do you mean by that?"

"Well, do you like to read, do you like to dance?"

She stiffened up at the mere suggestion she'd like to dance. "I don't dance." That struck me as odd, being the Macon Cotillion swing champion for my age category.

"You don't dance?"

"No."

"Oh, okay."

And I kept going. I had a woman who refused to dance, who wouldn't raise her hand and take the oath, and I put her on the jury. It turned out her religion disallowed her from passing judgment in any way on another person. Under any circumstance—even at a jury trial! It's a miracle I got a guilty verdict at all! And I thought the stripper was my problem! No way . . . it was the church lady!

I should have known. She struck me wrong and I should have gone with my gut. But I had plotted out strategically how I'd use my ten strikes, all the way back to Juror Number 50. If I had used the strike up front—she was one of the first twelve—I would have had to change my strategy. I saw the defense loading up the jury with defense-oriented jurors, so I had to strike carefully. Plus, I very rarely struck anybody off the jury. It always took a lot for me to strike anyone, if I did, and even then, I was profusely apologetic about the whole thing.

In this case, as I recall, we did open strikes, where you strike out loud in front of the jury. How that works is, you stand up and speak directly to that person, saying, "The state respectfully excuses the lady juror. Thank you," and you throw the person off. Everybody is seeing you reject people, which in my mind is not a good thing. So I accepted her onto the jury. While many jurors want to be rejected so they can go back to their homes and offices, there are those jurors who not only want to be on the jury but take the rejection as a personal slight.

There are also silent strikes, when lawyers write their decisions on a piece of paper. The state strikes, then the defense, and then they both take each strike decision up to the judge's bench. That way the panel never knows who's striking whom, just the lawyers and judge. Preemptory strikes are allowed—for instance, if someone is a cop or is acquainted with or related to a witness or a party in the case or one of the lawyers.

Another way lawyers strike a jury is to hold all their strikes until the end of the selection process, after general questions are posed to the entire panel and follow-up questions are asked to individual jurors. In all cases, the judge decides how a jury is selected, and in some jurisdictions it's a matter of tradition.

After I won a guilty verdict on a lesser charge in the case, I later discovered that my nonjudgmental juror had been the lone holdout causing a compromise verdict. I learned two lessons from these trials: One, always follow your instinct when you strike a jury, and two, if you get a bad vibe from a juror, they're out. It shouldn't matter if it's a nun, a priest, or a virgin—they're gone! In the case of the nonjudgmental juror, I ignored the all-too-obvious warning signs, and she nearly cost me a true verdict of guilty.

WHY SEQUESTRATION DOESN'T WORK

Sequestration embitters a jury. It's just too much of a hardship—especially in high-profile cases that go on forever. I think it's asking too much of people. Sequestration makes jury service, already inconvenient, much more difficult. As I explained before, a lot of people try desperately to get out of jury service. They will make up out-of-town flights, doctor's appointments, day-care problems, financial hardships, and medical emergencies if it will keep them off a jury. People's grandmothers will die five times during a trial. Can you imagine what the lawyers are left with if the jury pool knows they're going to be sequestered? You basically end up with a lot of jurors who don't have jobs—which is usually what the defense wants anyway.

I generally never agree with sequestration, because it doesn't work. Stories have circulated that sequestered jurors in high-profile cases are resentful and get news of the trial during allowed visits from family members. One possible remedy for that problem would be to question jurors in those cases on a daily basis as to the possible tainting that may have occurred during those visits, in addition to directing them each afternoon at the close of court not to engage in such conversations. I believe that jurors should be repeatedly instructed to guard against tainting the case in any way that could result in their removal from the jury or, even worse, a mistrial. Where there's a will there's a way. If jurors are going to ask their families about news reports on the case during visits, there's really no way to prevent it. Either jurors are going to take their oath seriously and follow the law or they're not.

Here's a perfect example of why, in my view, sequestration is useless. It is not always the answer because no matter how much a judge tries, like an overprotective parent, to safeguard a jury, the world still gets in, as in the murder trial in 2000 in Las Vegas of Sandy Murphy and Rick Tabish, charged with the murder of mogul Ted Binion. One day, the jury went to lunch at a buffet and a hotel worker named Richard Sueno called out, "Not Guilty!" in a room where the jurors had gathered. That could have been grounds for a mistrial, but one wasn't granted. (Murphy and Tabish were found guilty of the crime and sentenced to life in prison, but the verdict was ultimately reversed because of the admission of hearsay into evidence.) This makes the case that sequestering a jury is like being an overprotective parent. As much as you try to prevent it from happening, the jury is going to scrape their knees. Lawyers simply have to be prepared to deal with it—and sequestration isn't the way. It just makes everybody angry and surly.

In the Scott Peterson trial, Judge Alfred Delucchi had the right idea. Concerned about media taint of the Peterson jury, yet not a fan of jury sequestration, Delucchi allowed the jury to come and go freely during the evidentiary phase of the trial, then sequestered them for deliberations and verdict. It worked!

WRITE THAT DOWN!

In many jurisdictions, jurors are not allowed to take notes. Some judges favor it, some don't. It's all a function of the local rules. The thinking behind banning note taking is that the jury's supposed to render a true verdict based on their collective memory—not on a specific set of notes. Lawyers aren't expected to keep track of everything without notes, so why should a jury? It's very hard to take in all the evidence without them.

To be fair, on the other hand, you also have the glaring example of the doctor-lawyer released from the Scott Peterson trial. He was even voted foreperson of the jury until he departed the courthouse. We were all knocked out by his multiple degrees, but I guess the weight of the *nineteen notebooks* of notes he took during trial was just too much baggage for the Peterson jury. In the end, though, I think disallowing juries from taking notes is tantamount to treating them like children.

Another nonsensical courtroom practice is withholding a written copy of the law from the jury. These are the laws and the instructions by which jurors judge the facts of the case. The thinking here is extremely condescending as well. The rationale is, most jurors are not lawyers and they shouldn't get hung up on legal definitions. Excuse me? They are the sole judge of the facts and the law of the case. I say give juries all the tools they need to do their job properly. Have you ever heard anything so ridiculous? No pen, no paper? No way.

A WORD ON JURY CONSULTANTS

Jury consultants have become a thriving cottage industry thanks to defendants with bottomless bank accounts and grandstanding defense lawyers. Jayson Williams's defense team had jury consultants. Mark Geragos used them in Winona Ryder's trial, the Susan McDougal case, and the Scott Peterson case. Johnnie Cochran sought their advice in the Simpson case, although Cochran could strike a jury with both eyes closed and his hands tied behind his back.

Conventional wisdom at the defense table is that two or more heads are better than one. Jury consultants hired by the state are very, very rare, because prosecutors can't afford them. Jo-Ellan Dimitrius, who has worked on the trials of Scott Peterson and Kobe Bryant as well as on the Robert Blake case, is one of this country's best-known jury consultants because of her work in the Simpson trial. According to *People* magazine, she charges $350 an hour for her services. The defense pays through the nose for Dimitrius and other like-minded colleagues for their "expert" opinion on who should sit in the jury box.

I've done battle with her on *Larry King Live* and we rarely agree. She swore the Scott Peterson jury was pro-defense until the bitter end. The night of the guilty verdict, she was notably absent on the air waves.

Call me old-fashioned, but I still contend that the practice of using jury consultants is pure psycho-babble. Many consultants are psychologists or sociologists who have developed an expertise in jury selection. They work with defense teams to create "juror profiles" for cases by determining the ideal age, sex, median income, and background each juror should have, in part by looking at statistics. I find the process way off base, because in my mind it all boils down to common sense. I don't need a psychology degree or a highly paid "expert" to tell me the obvious.

Defense attorneys typically want the same kind of person: somebody who mistrusts cops, who doesn't like the system, who has been "taken advantage of by the government"—audited, arrested, convicted, or investigated. Simply put, they want jurors as much like their clients as possible. The defense doesn't want military personnel, government workers, or pensioned retirees who have worked hard their whole lives sitting on the jury. They basically want gullible, unemployed individuals. If they happen to have a rap sheet—all the better! The more like the defendant a juror is, the happier the defense is. If you look closely at a case, you'll see that, whenever possible, defense attorneys do their best to strike a mirror image of the defendant within the jury box when it comes to race, age, gender, background, and belief system. In referring to "gullible" jurors, I'm taking about people who would actually buy into a defense like "A satanic cult did it" or "There's a serial killer loose in Modesto!" or "A Colombian drug lord is responsible." An extraterrestrial *may* have landed and done the deed, but a jury's verdict should be grounded in reason, not fantasy.

I just don't see why a lawyer needs to hire someone to tell them that a guy with a DUI history should not serve on a DUI case. I certainly never needed anybody to tell me that a guy who's been arrested for domestic abuse shouldn't sit on an aggravated-assault case. As I've said before, the single most important part of any case, following trial preparation, is jury selection. The case is won or lost when you put those twelve people in the box. Everything else hinges on that. It was true for me, because I always had my cases ready before jury selection. I'd decided who the witnesses were going to be. I'd found and interviewed them and had written their questions in my trial notes. It was all very technically laid out before the trial even started for me. The only variable was my jury. Why would you put something so important in someone else's hands?

Whether you're a defense or prosecuting attorney, it's your jury, not the consultant's. The lawyers are the ones who have to live with that jury, so the lawyers must follow their instincts. I always struck my juries with my investigator in my ear, because he would have insights that I may have missed. At that point, we would have worked together long and hard on the case. He was the only one I would listen to during jury selection, because we shared the same goal—a true verdict—and could best determine who would be most receptive to our case.

If an attorney wants or needs a jury consultant or a client is happy to foot the bill for a consultant's advice, then more power to them. But when the rubber meets the road, it's the victims, the defendant, and the lawyers who have to live with the verdict—not the jury consultant. They have no stake in the outcome of the trial and will be on to their next paycheck in no time.

RENDERING A TRUE VERDICT

Even with all the challenges our jury system faces, don't throw out the baby with the bath water just yet. A trial by a jury of one's peers—the foundation of the American judicial system—is the last line of defense for ensuring that the truth comes out in court. The jury is the final arbiter of the facts and the law of every case that works its way to the courthouse. Landlord-tenant disputes, car accidents, contract issues, child molestations, rapes, and murders all go to a jury for the "ultimate issue" as it is called in the law—the truth of the case. Yes, the current assaults on the jury process are imperiling the system. They present obstacles we must overcome to ensure justice. But those twelve people sitting in the jury box are all we have, so they must be handled with great care.

There is no question there has to be a better screening process for striking a jury, which should start with having more intensive jury questionnaires. The questions on the forms that are currently used generally fall along these lines: Are you a resident of this jurisdiction? How long have you lived here? Are you married? Where do you work? That's usually the extent of it. A lot of jurisdictions don't even ask that much. That's crazy. For a start, questions about whether a potential juror has a criminal history certainly need to be asked. An enhanced jury questionnaire, along with a sermon on the sanctity of the juror oath—complete with both an oral and written rendition—would certainly help weed out "stealth jurors"—those who would somehow profit from service.

Newly added written questions must also address the issue of potential book-for-profit schemes and any other offers floating around, such as money for television and radio interviews, exclusive magazine stories, and, of course, last but not least, *Playboy* "pictorials." If, after a juror has answered all these inquiries, serious questions persist, I advocate a full investigation as to dates of any such offers and the production of phone records, interview notes, and contract-signing dates to support proof of "deal-free jurors." The potential for tainting is enormous as a result of these impediments to justice and must be avoided at all costs.

I also advocate the radical concept of contempt-of-court findings and substantial money levies against jurors who indulge in such schemes pretrial or during trial. In this instance, contempt-of-court findings should go hand in hand with jail time and the loss of voting rights, as occurs in felony cases. Jurors who seek to gain from jury service before or during trial should be kept forever off the voting roster and, consequently, out of future jury boxes. My fear, though, is that the draw of profiteering and fame is as old as time itself, and to cure it is to cure human nature.

The answer? The First Amendment right to free speech guarantees individuals, be they United States citizens, immigrants, the president, or an ex-con, the God-given right to speak out. That includes television and book deals. But for jurors, I firmly believe, the only way to secure a true verdict is to allow them to speak and write about the case all they want with a condition: They do so only well after the trial. I predict that will help solve the problem pretty quickly.

Another important preventive measure that should be taken to keep starstruck jurors out of the courtroom is to carefully screen them according to their media consumption in all forms: television, newspapers, magazines, and the Internet. I recommend the inclusion of detailed questions covering jurors' television-viewing habits: number of hours per week viewed; general and specific programs or genres viewed; shows and reading materials that were their favorites in childhood, teen years, and adulthood. The media plays such a big role in our lives today; it is pure folly to exclude it as a factor in voir dire. Red-flagged jurors could then be questioned during individual voir dire as a follow-up to the jury questionnaires. It would be relatively simple to have media-related inquiries added, with the input of psychologists, trial lawyers, and judges in order to more carefully prescreen the jurors before they even enter the jury pool, much less the jury box.

If one or both lawyers fail to cover the bases when faced with jurors serving on a trial with a celebrity defendant, the onus should be on the judge to ensure a fair-minded jury. While many judges have a hands-off approach to trying cases, in this peculiar instance they must inject their own questioning of jurors regarding their views toward celebrity defendants in general and specifically to the one on trial. I would also encourage the incorporation of celebrity-oriented questions on jury questionnaires. In order to be effective, these questions must be standard operating procedure and not subject to the whim of counsel's memory or diligence in filing the right motion.

Another way to prevent juror misconduct is to run rap sheets and arrest records on jurors. This isn't usually done—I never used them—but it's something that must seriously be considered now, especially in light of the Martha Stewart juror Chappell Hartridge. While all such information is public record, these documents must be obtained through law enforcement or court personnel, because they have to be researched and electronically produced. It's a computer search that doesn't take long to get, provided the lawyer has the right date of birth, race, and gender for the potential juror. The bad news: It's more work for already overtaxed prosecutors, who then have to hand over their results to the defense. It's only fair the defense get a copy of the report. (And naturally the defense would be thrilled to get ex-cons in the jury box!) One caveat: The defense should at the very least share the work that goes into getting this information. Better yet, the court's administrators should run the rap-sheet search prior to jury selection and provide the results to both sides.

I also foresee the looming possibility of credit checks run on jurors to discover any civil suits pending against them that would bear on the case. But here's the problem: If this becomes common practice, it would almost certainly dissuade people from sitting on juries. Would you want to sit on a jury if it was going to be made public that you were sued for nonpayment on a bounced check in 1991? How about if your credit-card problems or brush with bankruptcy were uncovered? I wouldn't.

The bottom line: Penalties for juror misconduct must be instituted and enforced. Those who violate the oath and taint the jury should find themselves back in court again, seated behind the defense table facing charges of their own. That is how valuable the jury system is. We must be prepared to deal harshly with those who abuse it. For those who slip through the cracks for whatever reason, justice needs to come down hard and fast. There must be repercussions for juror wrongdoing. People who lie to get on juries or lie during the trial must be prosecuted to the fullest extent of the law. I have a firm belief in the jury system, and to the people who violate the integrity of the court I say, "Hang 'em high."

CHAPTER THREE

JACKPOT JUSTICE

I HAVE A WAKING NIGHTMARE EVERY TIME I HEAR about another abuse of the justice system that's fueled by greed. I see a courthouse—as grimy and gritty as it can get after decades of use, millions of cases and defendants civil and criminal, all passing through its courts. Despite its worn appearance, I envision snapshots of what's gone on inside. Juries have been struck. Defendants and witnesses have been sworn under oath to tell the truth. Victims' families have sat in its halls praying for justice. But then, the building begins to swell and strain at the corners—twisting and trembling. The structure seems to be collapsing on itself. As the wind whips around and the sky turns black, the courthouse groans. Lightning strikes. Court documents, desks, and law books fly out the windows as people come running down the courthouse steps. While I stand frozen, watching, the building morphs into one of those fantastic ATM machines you read about but never see for yourself, one of those wacky ATMs that randomly dispense thousands to whoever happens to be there. The courthouse-turned-ATM is spitting out an endless stream of twenty-dollar bills. Money flies through the air, covering the streets, landing in the trees. Suddenly people run toward the building from every direction and begin cramming their pockets with their ill-gotten gains. Loaded down in cash, they run away, no one looking back.

That's when it dawns on me—the courthouse has become one big, huge, malfunctioning ATM machine—a jackpot at the expense of justice.

We've borne a culture of courthouse vultures. Yes, of course there are wrongs that are at least partially righted by money awards. These judgments are well deserved but can never totally set things right. As fantastical as the scenario in my waking nightmare may seem, it is rooted in reality. This wholesale manipulation driven by greed is hell-bent on turning Lady Justice into a whore and lawyers, witnesses, and assorted courtroom hangers-on into her pimps. Don't believe me? Read on.

CHECKBOOK JOURNALISM

It's become SOP—standard operating procedure—for prosecutors to warn victims and witnesses not to give interviews, much less accept money for them, before trial. The reason behind these admonitions isn't just a moral one—it's born out of stark fear that witnesses who trade information for cash will destroy the state's case. Most often, those who value money over justice are destroyed on cross-examination when it is revealed that they have a financial interest in the outcome of trial. The ammunition that paid interviews provide on cross-exam is a serious threat to a true verdict. Additionally, if the state or a state's witness taints the jury pool with public pretrial statements, the defense can—and will—ask for a change of venue. Not so for the state, as prosecutors have fewer remedies against defense witness or defense lawyer misconduct.

Prosecutors nationwide learned a valuable lesson from the William Kennedy Smith rape trial in 1991. Anne Mercer, a critical witness for the prosecution, should have been the perfect "outcry" witness for the state. At trial, the outcry witness is typically the first person to whom a rape victim tells what happened, most often in a distraught state. Such witnesses are invaluable to the state because they can either corroborate or discredit a victim's credibility.

Anne Mercer drove Patricia Bowman, the alleged rape victim, home from the Kennedy mansion in Palm Beach that night, immediately after the reported rape. At trial, Mercer underwent a vicious attack by the defense, led by attorney Roy Black, and with good reason—Mercer had to admit under oath that she was paid $40,000 for an appearance on the television show *A Current Affair*.

The defense rests.

Another high-profile defendant nearly walked free when a key state's witness sold his story to the *National Enquirer*.

Michael Markhasev went to trial for the 1997 murder of twenty-seven-year-old Ennis Cosby, son of the beloved entertainer Bill Cosby. The young, unarmed Cosby was ambushed and shot as he was changing a flat on a freeway exit ramp. The state's star witness, Christopher So, testified in no uncertain terms that he overheard Markhasev confess to the shooting. The defense launched its case with an assault on So's credibility after it was uncovered he had contacted the *Enquirer* about their offer of a reward in the case. It turns out So pocketed $40,000 for interviews and was promised another $100,000 if Markhasev was convicted. To make matters worse, the detective who investigated Cosby's case testified under oath that when he interviewed So, the witness actually asked the cop, "Does my story sound good?"

Luckily, Markhasev was convicted and sentenced to mandatory life behind bars in 1998—no thanks to So, whose greed nearly tilted the scales of justice the wrong way.

O. J. Simpson's trial serves as a textbook primer on what is wrong with the justice system on so many, many levels, this one included. Does the name Jose Camacho ring a bell? It should. This guy was sliced up like a Thanksgiving turkey on cross-examination by the defense in the O. J. Simpson case. In what should have been strong testimony for the state, Camacho said Simpson bought a knife in the store where he worked a few weeks before the double murders. But the witness's damning words turned into every prosecutor's worst nightmare come true. Camacho had to confess that he accepted $12,500 from the *Enquirer* after *Hard Copy* had offered him "peanuts." Prosecutors tried their best to salvage Camacho's credibility by stressing that he sold his story only after his testimony at grand jury. Obviously, the strategy didn't work.

Jill Shively, another star witness in the case, testified in front of the grand jury that she saw Simpson driving like a madman near the scene of the murders. Prosecutors had no alternative but to to scuttle her testimony after she sold her story to *Hard Copy* for a reported $5,000.

This blatant brokering for the "dirt" on a sensational case isn't even done in secret. The *Enquirer*'s editor appeared on *Larry King Live* to show off the $1 million check the tabloid had offered to Al Cowlings to tell what really happened in the white Bronco during the chase seen around the world. In one of the only displays of restraint shown by the major players in that case at the time, the Simpson insider opted not to jump on the trial's gravy train. Cowlings did wind up cashing in, however, selling autographed photos of the infamous Bronco chase online.

This phenomenon of witnesses selling out to the media isn't a by-product of our 24/7 media age—it only seems that way because the number of outlets vying for "exclusives" has grown exponentially in the last few years. Paying for stories is a dangerous and destructive tradition. And it's not just scandal-mongering tabloids and TV shows that shell out big bucks for salacious stories to sell. A 1994 issue of that *Columbia Journalism Review* reported that the revered *60 Minutes* paid Richard Nixon's henchman H. R. Haldeman $25,000 for his story in 1975. G. Gordon Liddy went for the reduced rate of $15,000. Nixon himself brought in the biggest haul. Swifty Lazar, the late Hollywood über-agent, brokered a $600,000 deal for Nixon's interview with David

Frost that aired in 1977. Frost defended himself on CNN in 2002, saying at least he got to quiz Nixon on television, as opposed to the watered-down version the disgraced ex-president offered in his book—for which he received $2.3 million.

Clearly, the shady practice is alive and well today. In January 2004, the *New York Times* reported that CBS news magazine *60 Minutes* paid Michael Jackson $1 million for an exclusive interview after he'd been charged with child molestation. While the network called the allegations "categorically false," a CBS spokeswoman acknowledged that there was another deal that had been struck with the King of Pop. Jackson had to deny the charges on air during the *60 Minutes* interview in order for the network to consider broadcasting his musical special, pulled from CBS's schedule after Jackson's arrest in November 2003. Another television icon bites the dust.

JUST SHUT UP!

Legislation could easily be passed in each state to outlaw payment or anticipated payment of witnesses and other participants in criminal cases before trials. The First Amendment protects free speech—not storytelling for fame and profit. To witnesses who just can't shut up, I say tell your story for free before trial if you absolutely must—if jeopardizing the case means nothing to you—but do not pass go, do not broker a deal, and do not collect any cash until after the trial. Judge Alfred DeLucchi implemented a great idea after the Scott Peterson guilty verdict. He disallowed any form of payment, not so much as a fruit basket, to Peterson jurors in exchange for talking until ninety days following Peterson's sentencing.

This way everybody's happy: loose-lipped witnesses, the prosecution, the victim, and the victim's family. There's one sad face in the crowd: the defense attorney who just got robbed of a potentially explosive cross-examination. But I'm not using up all my energy blaming greedy witnesses. There are plenty of other pigs gorging themselves at the jury rail.

TO SERVE AND PROTECT— THEIR OWN INTERESTS

Police investigations often take months, even years, to complete. The reality is that cops are lucky if somebody even says thank you when they're done. I can't count the number of bear hugs, handshakes, and letters that were written to me by cops after I uttered those two painfully obvious words. I saw it as a small gesture of appreciation after they put in extra hours to work a case, gave testimony on the stand, or undertook additional investigation at my request. Sadly, it's more than most officers are accustomed to getting. To me, it's the heart and soul of what law enforcement is all about . . . to serve and protect a grateful public.

They may be few and far between, but unfortunately there are bad apples, officers who are looking for a lot more than a simple thank-you or the personal satisfaction of a job well done. Montgomery County police chief Charles Moose, who headed the investigation into the Washington, D.C., sniper case in 2002, is one of them.

During the shootings in the fall of that year, people in the D.C. area were afraid to pump gas, let their children walk from bus to classroom, or stop by the grocery store. Fear gripped those who lived in or around the nation's capital as the body count around the Beltway rose by the day. Just one year earlier, the nation had lived through the September 11 terrorist attacks. Many feared terrorists had returned and were now unleashing their hatred on individuals. But now, unlike in most serial killings, there was no tie linking the victims to either each other or their killers.

Moose quickly emerged as a hero while the horrific scenario played out in newspapers and on television around the country. He presented a calm, competent front to the nation, assuring everyone the killers would be caught and justice would be served. Eventually, John Allen Muhammad and Lee Boyd Malvo were arrested and charged with thirteen shootings and ten murders in Maryland, Virginia, and Washington, D.C. The killers' path of death and destruction extended all the way south to Alabama.

Now, long after the mystery has been solved, Moose's bid to cash in on the case continues its ripple effect. The idea of a police officer succumbing to unbridled greed before a case even goes to trial gives being a police offer, formerly an honorable profession, a big black eye. And for what? A book deal. Moose signed with publisher E. P. Dutton in January 2003 to deliver *Three Weeks in October: The Manhunt for the Serial Sniper.* His story was based on the suffering of the ten innocent people who lost their lives at the whim of two nomadic killers as the victims went about the day-to-day business of living. Moose's deal was reportedly $170,000, a little more than his annual salary. He claimed the book was a once-in-a-lifetime chance.

Once in a lifetime? Sonny Buchanan, a thirty-nine-year-old landscaper, was shot dead from behind while he was cutting grass in Maryland. Linda Franklin, an FBI analyst, was shot in the head in the parking lot of a Virginia Home Depot after she and her husband shopped inside. They and the snipers' eight other victims had their "lifetimes" brutally cut short by these random acts of violence.

After a Montgomery County ethics panel refused to let Moose cash in on his office, he resigned from law enforcement. Not content simply to go off and pen his tell-all, he promptly sued his former employer in federal court, claiming that the county had violated his civil rights and denied him free speech. When it looked as if he wasn't getting anywhere with that self-serving argument, he changed his story and announced that his book would be a work of fiction in which the lead character just happens to investigate sniper killers who gun down victims at random.

Robert F. Horan, the prosecutor for Fairfax County, Virginia, who oversaw the prosecution of Malvo, said in an interview before the book's release in 2003 that Moose could have caused irreparable damage to the case. "If it gets into evidence—what they did, how they did it—then you get into an area where the argument can be made that anybody who read the book would be unfairly prejudiced," he said. Moose didn't even give prosecutors an advance look at the book. He defended himself by claiming that he'd never said he would do so.

The same ethics panel stopped Moose from collecting a paycheck for a movie deal. But this wasn't just about becoming a media celebrity. Only weeks after the snipers were arrested, Moose and his wife, Sandy Herman-Moose, applied to run a private consulting firm, setting themselves up as "keynote presenters, workshop leaders and facilitators." Maybe they can lecture on the loss of ethics.

Moose's book created a potential field day for the defense on cross-examination—and they didn't even have to work for it. Moose served it up to them on a silver platter! It's shocking to me that the deal was being struck before the killers even went to trial, giving legs to the argument that Moose drove the investigation in a manner most suited to upping future book sales, amounting to an incredible violation of trust. So go ahead, trash Simpson-case detectives Vannatter, Lange, and Fuhrman for their books all you want (more on them later)—at least they had the decency to wait until after the verdict to write their memoirs.

THERE'S A REASON THEY'RE CALLED AMBULANCE CHASERS

Lawyers hate lawyer jokes, but we have to admit there's a reason people love to hate us. The actions of my unscrupulous "colleagues" have tainted the profession and fueled the widely held belief that we're all prostitutes who will do anything for a dollar. *Webster's* defines an "ambulance chaser" as "a lawyer or lawyer's agent who incites accident victims to sue for damages." Webster was too kind.

Ambulance chasers are just like roaches—when you stomp one, another pokes its head out of a crack. If you've never encountered one, drop by the critical-care unit, trauma ward, or emergency room of your local hospital. Peek down the corridors of the courthouse just after a courtroom calendar call and keep your eyes on defendants, petitioners, and respondents who are "pro se"—momentarily without counsel. Even mortuaries and funeral homes aren't off-limits. And if you think the one place you'd least expect to find whores of the court is the police station, think again. The truth is, police precincts are among their favorite spots!

That's right. It's called "solicitation" of clients and it's unethical. After every car crash, domestic disturbance, bar brawl, or Little League dukefest, a 911 police report is generated. A "connection" inside the police station supplies a "runner" who works for the ambulance chaser with fresh police reports, and the chase is on! The information in a police report includes the complainant's name and address, Social Security number, and date of birth, the location of the incident, witnesses' names and contact information, full police accounts, and statements made on the scene—even helpful diagrams are included. Score!

Later in this book, I'll tell you the story of a car crash I was involved in one morning on my way to court to start a murder case. When I got home from court late that evening, I got right into bed with all my files, ready to work until I fell asleep. My phone rang just as I settled in. Because my number's unlisted, I expected either a cop due up on the stand the next day calling about his subpoena or my investigator. Wrong. On the other end of the line was a silky-smooth voice, like those deejays on late-night jazz stations.

"Hello, Nancy?"

No niceties on my part with unnamed callers. "Who is this?"

After a brief pause the caller continued, "I'm calling about your accident this morning. How do you feel? Any discomfort?"

"Who is this?"

"Just a friend inquiring if you have a lawyer?"

"Who is this? Because you're talking to a felony prosecutor who'd love to nail you and the sleazebag lawyer you work for. I know you're a runner. You give the law a bad name. Speaking of names, what's yours?"

Click. If I hadn't been headed into day two of a major felony prosecution, I may have actually tracked the call and busted him. That night, I was already worn out after day one of a murder trial and didn't have time to stomp roaches. I had a jury to convince.

It's not just the ambulance chasers who belly up to the trough. Respectable, silk-stocking lawyers can be just as bad. I won't compare them to common streetwalkers, though. They've got more in common with the well-dressed hooker sitting at the bar in the Ritz nursing a Cosmo. Same profession, different uniform. Personal-injury lawyers take up to 40 percent of a client's jury award or settlement. They're those guys who represent litigants in car crashes, slip-and-falls, dog bites, medical malpractice, and emotional-distress cases. Think about it: Would you pay your real-estate agent, a headhunter, or even a waiter 40 percent of the tab? No way!

TAMING THE BEAST

I support a grass-roots movement to stamp out exorbitant "contingency fees." The two main objectives of this worthwhile mission: limiting how much clients must pay for an appeal of their case and placing caps on how much lawyers can make off pain-and-suffering awards. To date, such laws have passed in eleven states and are pending in twenty others. There has also been talk of tort reform that would lessen the incentive for ambulance chasing by limiting lawyers' percentage of a client's jury-verdict award. I'm fully behind reducing the lawyer's cut to a reasonable 10 to 20 percent of the gross award, as opposed to the whopping 33 to 40 percent they get now. In 1999, the top ten jury awards totaled almost $9 billion, up from $750 million two years before. Under the current contingency-fee framework, the lawyers took around $3 billion of that. The total of the top one hundred jury verdicts in 2002 was three and a half times greater than in 2001. Do the math—if you can stomach it.

Contingency lawyers claim in their own defense that without them, there's no one left to protect the so-called little guy. That could be a convincing argument if they, the lawyers, weren't pickpocketing the little guy to grab huge fees for themselves!

Then there are cases that affect thousands of people: the massive class-action suits in cases like the phen-fen disaster, certain breast-implant cases, drug- and product-recall tragedies. In these instances, individuals join together in a single cause of action. Unfortunately, the truth is that the individual often gets a very small settlement while the lawyer gets a percentage of the overall award, often reaching into the millions. There's something very wrong with that picture. The solution? The law must put caps on class-action lawyers' fees. I'm not holding my breath waiting for that to happen, though, because the deep-pocket plaintiff's lobby have a sympathetic ear in Congress and the state legislatures, because both bodies are populated by—you guessed it—lawyers!

Please don't misunderstand me. There are serious, life-changing injuries, both physical and emotional, that call out for down-and-dirty lawsuits. Money awards in those cases serve justice in their own way. More power to those hauling the well-deserving to court and in front of a jury! My disgust is reserved for the others who slither into court—the gluttons dining out on what Lady Justice blindly offers to everyone. They need to be stopped, as do those who believe the civil system is their own private piggy bank, their lucky lottery ticket. They are fueled by the avarice of lawyers who've traded in their law degrees for dollar signs. They give all lawyers a bad name. Forget those sorry excuses for lawyers—they use and abuse Lady Justice as if she were a cheap one-night stand.

AUTHOR! AUTHOR!

Jurors aren't the only ones who cash in by writing courtroom exposés. After Louise Woodward's "nanny trial," I was reading through a mountain of court documents and found some civil plaintiff's filings. One was a motion to stop Woodward from selling her story and making a profit. In a footnote, I was stunned to see all the books spawned from the Simpson trial offered as proof that everybody and their house cat is making money off the misery of others. The authors include old girlfriends, ex-wives of lawyers, a niece of Simpson's, lawyers who had nothing at all to do with the case, of course jurors, witnesses, and detectives. Let's not forget that Simpson himself did a pretrial book and an audio version in which he "answered" questions from fans who had written to him while he sat in jail. Take a look at the text from the footnote:

Baker, Terry (with Kenneth Ross & Mary Jane Ross), *I'm Not Dancing Anymore: O. J. Simpson's Niece Breaks the Silence* (1997), New York: Kensington; Barbieri, Paula, *The Other Woman: My Years with O. J. Simpson. A Story of Love, Trust, and Betrayal* (1997), New York: Little, Brown & Co.; Berry, Barbara Cochran (with Joanne Parrent), *Life After Johnnie Cochran: Why I Left the Sweetest-Talking, Most Successful Black Lawyer in L.A.* (1995), New York: Basic Books; Clark, Marcia (with Teresa Carpenter), *Without a Doubt* (1997), New York: Viking Penguin; Cochran, Johnnie L. (with Tim Rutten), *Journey to Justice* (1996), New York: Ballantine Books; Cooley, Armanda; Bess, Carrie; & Rubin-Jackson, Marsha (as told to Tom Byrnes with Mike Walker), *Madam Foreman: A Rush to Judgment?* (1995), Beverly Hills, CA: Dove Books; Darden, Christopher (with Jess Walter), *In Contempt*

(1996), New York: ReganBooks; Dershowitz, Alan M., *Reasonable Doubts: The O. J. Simpson Case and the Criminal Justice System* (1996), New York: Simon & Schuster; Eliot, Marc, *Kato Kaelin: The Whole Truth. The Real Story of O.J., Nicole, and Kato, from the Actual Tape* (1995), New York: Harper Paperbacks; Fuhrman, Mark, *Murder in Brentwood* (1997), Washington, D.C.: Regnery Pub.; Goldberg, Hank M., *The Prosecution Responds: An O. J. Simpson Trial Prosecutor Reveals What Really Happened* (1996), Secaucus, NJ: Birch Lane Press; Goldman, The Family of Ron (with William and Marily Hoffer) *His Name Is Ron: Our Search for Justice* (1997), New York: William Morrow & Co.; Kennedy, Tracy, & Kennedy, Judith (with Alan Abrahamson), *Mistrial of the Century: A Private Diary of the Jury System on Trial* (1995), Beverly Hills, CA: Dove Books; Knox, Michael (with Mike Walker), *The Private Diary of an O.J. Juror: Behind the Scenes of the Trial of the Century* (1995), Beverly Hills, CA: Dove Books; Lange, Tom, & Vannatter, Phillip (as told to Dan E. Moldea), *Evidence Dismissed. The Inside Story of the Police Investigation of O. J. Simpson* (1997), New York: Pocket Books; Persaud, Tara (with Lewis Smith), *O. J. Simpson Murder Case: The Story of the Mystery Woman* (1997), Shippensburg, PA: Destiny Image Pub.; Resnick, Faye D. (with Mike Walker), *Nicole Brown Simpson: The Private Diary of a Life Interrupted* (1994), Beverly Hills, CA: Dove Books; Resnick, Faye D. (with Jeanne V. Bell), *Shattered: In the Eye of the Storm* (1996), Beverly Hills, CA: Dove Books; Shapiro, Robert L. (with Warren Larkin), *The Search for Justice: A Defense Attorney's Brief on the O. J. Simpson Case* (1996), New York: Warner Books; Simpson, O. J. (with Lawrence Schiller), *I Want to Tell You: My Response to Your Letters, Your Messages, Your Questions* (1995), New York: Warner Books; Thomas, Marguerite Simpson, *Life with O.J.* (1996), Avenal: Random House; Uelman, Gerald F., *Lessons from the Trial: The People v. O. J. Simpson* (1996), Kansas City, MO: Andrews and McMeel.

It's amazing that so many people are suddenly inspired by a literary muse after somebody else gets murdered. Although the Simpson defense team holds the record for killing the most trees, plenty of other defense attorneys have gotten into the publishing business. Timothy McVeigh and his lead defense attorney, Stephen Jones, locked horns in a bitter lawsuit when the condemned Oklahoma City bomber learned a week before his 1998 sentencing that his own lawyer had signed a deal with Doubleday to write a book about the trial. Jones landed a nonreturnable advance of $600,000. McVeigh's appeal attorneys argued Jones had violated Colorado (the trial was held in Denver) and Oklahoma rules of conduct for lawyers. For his part, McVeigh said in a court filing that the book deal added a "sense of betrayal" to a "deep feeling of distrust" that he already had for Jones.

OUTRAGEOUS FORTUNES

Looking to make a quick buck? Hang out at the courthouse or, better yet, take the witness stand. Brian "Kato" Kaelin became the nation's most famous houseguest during the Simpson trial. A day on the witness stand became the basis for an entire career. Using his newfound fame as a springboard, the shaggy-haired aspiring actor scored a morning radio show in L.A. and acting gigs on shows like *Roseanne* and Showtime's *Beggars and Choosers*, where he had a two-year stint. He even popped up in several B movies on the big screen. Now, there's a witness who went far. I wonder how the families of Nicole Brown and Ron Goldman feel about his celebrity status—especially since he saved his real impressions on who murdered Brown and Goldman for after the trial. Years later, he told Barbara Walters, "I believe in my heart [Simpson] is guilty." He did, however, make sure to set the story straight when the *National Examiner* proclaimed in a cover story during the trial that "Cops Think Kato Did It!" Kaelin filed a $15 million libel lawsuit against the tabloid and settled for an undisclosed amount. Cha-ching!

Speaking of pseudocelebrities fleecing the courthouse, remember Jessica Hahn? She's the former church secretary who shot to fame after her affair with PTL televangelist Jim Bakker was exposed in 1987. She received $265,000 in hush money taken from the preacher's ministry to keep quiet about their tryst. Bakker was booted from his TV ministry and indicted on charges of fraud and conspiracy. In 1989, he was convicted and sentenced to a forty-five-year prison term. His sentence was later reduced to eight years.

For her part, Hahn seized the media moment and capitalized on her infamy. *People* magazine inexplicably named her as one of the 25 Most Intriguing People of 1987. The following year, she bared all in *Playboy*. The Long Island native went on to launch her own 900-number phone line and popped up on television programs like *The Howard Stern Show* and *Married . . . with Children*. While Bakker's sexual shenanigans and tearful apology failed to ignite a tinderbox of television deals, Hahn milked her pop-culture curiosity status as long as she could.

To find one of the most blatant examples of cashing in on legal proceedings, you need look no further than the White House's most infamous intern, Monica Lewinsky, whose affair with former president Bill Clinton resulted in his 1998 impeachment and made headlines around the world. In exchange for cooperation with special prosecutor Kenneth Starr's investigation, she was granted immunity. Rather than maintain a low profile (heaven forbid!), Lewinsky grabbed on to her newfound celebrity and began showing up at glitzy parties, including *Vanity Fair*'s annual Oscar bash in Los Angeles. She's been dining out on her role as "the other woman" ever since. She was reportedly paid $700,000 for an interview with Britain's Channel 4, where she recounted her version of her affair with the former president.

Lewinsky also told her side of the soap opera in the 1999 book *Monica's Story* and launched a career designing handbags sold in a few stores and on her own Web site. HBO coughed up plenty for her first-person account in a special entitled *Monica in Black and White*. In

1999, she landed a contract as a public spokesperson for Jenny Craig but was dropped by the weight-loss company just a few months later, after the public made clear they weren't buying her as a role model even if it was just for a diet program. Undeterred, in 2003, Lewinsky signed on to host the reality show *Mr. Personality* on Fox, where she handed out—believe it or not—advice on dating.

Lewinsky is still wringing every last penny out of an experience from which most people would desperately try to distance themselves. In 2004, reports surfaced that Lewinsky was selling her story to Hollywood and wanted actress Mandy Moore to star in the film. Stories circulated that two different movies would be made: a racy one for foreign audiences and a tamer version to be shown here on U.S. cable television. A momentary lapse of good taste? Stay tuned.

The woman just doesn't give up. Lewinsky extolled checkbook journalism at a seminar in Scotland that summer, where she boldly told the crowd she had no regrets about her kiss-and-sell approach. "You'd be an idiot not to get the money," she exclaimed. "Your story is a commodity."

Linda Tripp, the gabby tattletale who secretly taped her phone calls with Lewinsky, also cashed in. The woman who stood on her driveway and told us, "I'm you," learned the hard way that less-than-telegenic players in a made-for-television scandal can be ruthlessly criticized for a lot more than questionable ethics. Apparently stung by barbs about her appearance, Tripp underwent her own "extreme makeover" with a reported $30,000 worth of plastic surgery, including face- and eye-lifts, nose and chin jobs, and neck liposuction performed by a celebrated Beverly Hills plastic surgeon. A press release on Tripp's Web site stated that the surgery was paid for by an anonymous "benefactor." The statement from the trustee of the Linda R. Tripp Defense Fund boasted that no money from her defense fund, which helped "defend against the Clinton machine," had been tapped for her makeover.

Tripp prettied-up the package, but the stench of her role in Kenneth Starr's investigation of the former president stuck. She claimed she was given only menial tasks for the duration of her tenure at the Pentagon after she became a figure in Monicagate. Still, she kept her $88,000-a-year job, despite her newfound infamy, until 2001, when she was swept out by the incoming Bush administration along with the rest of the previous administration's appointees, as is customary. But that was the least of her problems. After receiving an anonymous tip from inside the Pentagon in 1998, the *New Yorker* reported that Tripp had failed to disclose an arrest for grand larceny when she was a teenager applying for a job. After a plea bargain, the charges had been reduced to loitering.

Tripp sued the Department of Defense for an alleged violation of the federal Privacy Act, which prohibits the government from releasing personal information about individuals without their consent. She alleged that the information was leaked to embarrass her in retaliation for her role in Starr's investigation. In 2003, the lawsuit was settled, and she received a payment of $595,000 and other "financial benefits" courtesy of the taxpayers. That's what I call a witness fee.

AND ALL I GOT WAS THIS LOUSY T-SHIRT

While human drama plays out inside the courthouse over life-and-death issues, there are parasites that have virtually attached themselves to the walls of the building and are working hard to suck the last drop of decency out of the proceedings within. Merchandising the pathos of high-profile court cases makes light of the weighty events of a trial and turns it into a sideshow worthy of equally repellent souvenirs. From T-shirts and placards that read FREE WINONA to FRY MCVEIGH to GO JUICE, the courthouse takes on a carnival-like atmosphere and the true purpose of the trial—to seek justice—gets lost.

Spectators on either side of the fence who participate in these spectacles seem to have a hard time separating the truth in court from what they see on the TV screen. In many ways, I think a lot of people have simply given up trying. I guess it's just easier to buy a FREE KOBE T-shirt than it is to fairly consider the accusations of the nineteen-year-old alleged victim in the case. There's even a Web site dedicated to "freeing Kobe" that cautions its readers that Bryant is innocent until proven guilty—then offers a whole host of "Free Kobe" merchandise.

Unfortunately, in Bryant's case, the prosecution got in on the act of trivializing a serious felony. The defense grabbed the ball and ran with it. Attorneys on both sides of the aisle swapped accusations of malfeasance, reducing wrenching evidence and complicated legal issues down to a sideshow starring—what else?—tasteless souvenir T-shirts. Allegations flew when employees of the Eagle, Colorado, district attorney's and sheriff's offices ordered T-shirts depicting a stick figure being hanged and displaying derogatory statements about the NBA star.

Although the defense routinely smeared the alleged rape victim, they also lobbed a volley of insults against the state over the T-shirt allegation. "This shows the bias of the investigators and prosecutors toward my client," claimed defense attorney Pamela Mackey. Krista Flannigan, a spokesperson for the district attorney's office, said prosecutors had forgotten about the T-shirt business "until it became an issue." Ultimately the district attorney had to give a formal apology over the T-shirt debacle. "I apologize for being misleading. It was not at all intentional. It was done without my knowledge or authorization," said Eagle County, Colorado, district attorney Mark Hurlbert. "The shirts may be inappropriate, but they are certainly not racist. I have taken action within my office to address this matter." It didn't end there, the two sides attacked each other until the Kobe Bryant case came to an unpredictable, upsetting, and dissatisfying close.

In the end, whoever's T-shirt is at issue, this is not a game where either side is supposed to wear a uniform emblazoned with its particular mascot. It's the law. This is the courthouse. Come on, people, show some respect.

LOSING GROUND

In the wake of all the pain caused by the death and disappearance of Laci Peterson, local Redwood City, California, authorities wanted their own piece of the pie. In February 2004, city officials issued a press release announcing that the trial venue in San Mateo County would charge television stations $51,000 to rent a coveted slice of asphalt near the courthouse. The announcement was met with shocked silence from reporters. The county spokesperson was then shouted down by reporters and producers who accused the county of blatant price-gouging. Several media outlets feared losing their spots and their court coverage because they couldn't pay up. Finally, after being exposed by the media, local officials backed down from their money-grubbing scheme.

MURDER GOES GLOSSY

In the fashion industry, image is everything. Eye-catching advertisements that create "buzz" are part of many big companies' marketing strategies. The Italian conglomerate United Colors of Benetton went to sickening lengths to get attention in 2000, with a controversial ad campaign that ran in magazines and newspapers all over the country. The ads weren't about the year's new styles or anything to do with fashion at all. The campaign centered on convicted murderers sitting on death row for heinous crimes, featured in glossy, professional photos portraying the "plights" of twenty-six death-row inmates. In the ads, inmates talk about their childhoods, their dreams, and their heroes. There is, of course, no mention of their victims. There's no sign of the company's trademark sweaters, just stories glamorizing the convicted killers. Benetton says that the campaign—called "Looking Death in the Face"—was designed to show the human cost of capital punishment. One such "face" was that of Missouri native Jerome Mallett, who has sat on death row since 1986 for the brutal murder of an unsuspecting highway trooper. There was no sign of Mallett's victim or the trooper's family left behind to mourn him anywhere in Benetton's ad.

Apparently Benetton forgot about that part of the "human cost" of the crimes these men committed. Just like a courthouse T-shirt merchant (albeit with much more expensive wares), this corporation made money off murder. Benetton used death-row inmates and the justice system itself to improve its market share. The manufacturer of warm and fuzzy sweaters worn worldwide also caused intense pain to the families of innocent people killed by the men the campaign "humanizes."

Sears, Roebuck & Co., God bless them, decided to take action. In the wake of Benetton's death-row ad campaign, the retailer announced it would immediately pull Benetton-designed clothes from all four hundred of its stores. The ad was just too significant for Sears to ignore after receiving hundreds of consumer complaints. *Advertising Age* wrote that Sears believed "the whole episode is tragic, for the victims, for Sears and for Benetton."

Sears wasn't alone in their anger at Benetton's attempt to turn justice on its ear in hopes of hitting the jackpot. The state of Missouri sued Benetton for featuring death-row inmates housed in their prisons, claiming the company deceived prison officials into believing the inmates were being interviewed for a project sponsored by the National Association of Criminal Defense Lawyers. Another nauseating revelation about the campaign: The Associated Press reported some of the inmates received up to $1,000 for their participation. During a television interview on CNN's *Insight* in March 2000, Benetton's creative director, Oliviero Toscani, didn't deny the claim. Instead he defended his actions, saying, "You get angry when you think. Already this is not bad. . . . You must look at something, think about it and react. So they got angry. That means they talk about the image."

You'd imagine that Benetton already makes enough off the sales of its overpriced clothing hawked in malls all over the country. Most of all, you'd imagine that the pain of the victims themselves, now dead in their graves and unable to raise their voices in protest, would stop them. I guess not. If you're looking for me, I'll be shopping at Sears.

GRAVE ROBBING
FOR PROFIT

Even the investigation of crime scenes has become a lottery ticket of sorts—a potential jackpot for profiteering. Here's the single worst example I know of: In the midst of our nation's sorrow over the terrorist attacks of September 11, 2001, profiteers exploited the World Trade Center attack with fervor. They discovered there was money to be made by selling everything from chunks of debris to buckets of ashes to bereaved families of the dead. Tourists jostled each other to take snapshots of twisted metal and sooty concrete dust. It turns out many of the photos had a price.

Within days of the attacks, a macabre "souvenir" row sprang up, hawking relics from the disaster. Naturally, T-shirts were among the first items for sale. Then the grave robbers came up with the idea of clipping images from the newspapers and magazines and enlarging some of the most upsetting shots, including ones of trapped office workers at the windows agonizing over whether to die by fire or to jump. Next, it was reported that the Mafia also wanted a piece of the action. Several people with alleged connections to organized crime were accused of looting and stealing 250 tons of scrap metal from the Towers to be resold.

By far, the worst offense to arise out of the tragedy was when hawkers contacted victims' families after their phone numbers were posted on leaflets begging for information about their missing family members. Many were solicited by phone to purchase debris and dirt from Ground Zero, where their loved ones had died.

I can't condemn only the sleazy barkers selling T-shirts and enhanced photos of the scene. Even the "good guys" went bad on this one.

FBI agents from around the country were sent to New York to sift through debris from the attack to locate any shreds of evidence for the investigation. Some of the four hundred agents working at the mass burial ground who were supposed to be looking for evidence actually took some. The feds themselves later admitted some of their own people who combed through the rubble actually swiped "souvenirs."

Several agents took items that would break your heart, including the American flags that had topped the buildings, patches from World Trade Center security uniforms, and marble chunks that had once been the Towers. The agents in question claimed that the items were harmless mementos of all their hard work, but the Twin Towers site is a mass grave for thousands of innocent people. To many families who lost their beloved relatives that morning, Ground Zero is hallowed earth, and there's no such thing as a "harmless" memento. It's like stealing from a cemetery.

Even the special agent who managed the recovery job at Fresh Kills Landfill in Staten Island, New York, was accused of giving items taken from the ashes as gifts. When questioned later, the agent "had no recollection." Civilians who looted were prosecuted—not so for the federal agents who did the same thing.

To make matters worse, the agent who reported the stolen "souvenirs" was then attacked for having "tarnished" the FBI. It's true. To add insult to injury, the special agent/souvenir seeker remains with the agency, having faced no demotion or penalty, while the reporting agent, Jane Turner, was dismissed. Of course the FBI claims that Turner was not dismissed for blowing the whistle. They say she'd been a problem employee for many years. Somehow, I don't think *she's* the problem.

WITH FRIENDS LIKE THESE...

In an interview that aired in 2004, before Kobe Bryant's rape case, a "friend" of the woman accusing the NBA star of sexual assault said the alleged victim had told her that Bryant "went the whole way." This "friend" explained that the alleged victim did not elaborate and that she did not press for details. Another "friend" revealed that the young woman had gone into hiding, upset over reports of her "emotional difficulties" and over the media stakeout outside her home. This trusted confidante then disclosed that the alleged victim was hiding in Denver.

The *Vail Daily News* didn't have to look far to confirm a story reporting that the young woman had previously sought a doctor's care for emotional problems. "She did seek some medical help," another acquaintance blurted out on a network morning show. "She knew she needed it, so she went and got it. She was definitely emotionally fragile, but I don't think it had anything to do with what happened." Other "friends" let it slip that the woman accusing Bryant of rape had attempted suicide twice. The *Orange County Register* also reported she overdosed on drugs a few weeks before the alleged sexual assault. The story was corroborated by several helpful pals. While one friend said she thought "it was just a cry for help," others blamed the accuser's bizarre behavior on her being distraught over a tumultuous breakup with a boyfriend and the death of her best friend in an automobile accident.

Who are these people? The whole parade is disturbing.

They're the same people who disclosed that the alleged victim had unsuccessfully tried out for the talent show *American Idol*, which helped bolster the defense's claim that she saw Bryant as a ticket to celebrity. These helpful "friends" are the ones who have shown themselves to be in love with the limelight and the perks that come with it. They might not be paid outright for their interviews, but they've been flown to New York City for some of their television appearances, put up in the best hotels, taken to fantastic dinners, and chauffeured to Broadway shows.

Television shows that claim they would never pay for stories get around the literal definition of cash for information by showering guests connected to victims and defendants in high-profile cases with perks that would make a Hollywood celebrity jealous. If people are traveling to New York from Anytown, U.S.A., to make an appearance on a morning show, of course they need a hotel room, but what's wrong with the Holiday Inn? I'd say a stay at a five-star New York City hotel, complete with the A-list treatment, makes these coveted insiders more inclined to try to "please" their hosts by making headline-grabbing comments on air. Producers know this. It's a cynical practice by the media that should be reined in. It may be unrealistic to expect the law to set limits on media conglomerates, but, like the unwritten agreement that has until very recently kept outlets from making the names of rape victims public, an agreement to set limits on "perks" is desperately needed now more than ever.

Why? Because every word uttered by these attention-hungry "friends" is available for the defense in these cases to twist and misconstrue. In the Bryant case, it was impossible to miss them, as these chatty chums were everywhere—on morning talk shows and nighttime news programs. Early in the case, the photo ops on every major news channel became all about them—not about the alleged victim and certainly not the case. What's next? A spot on *Fear Factor* or *The Bachelor*? I wouldn't be surprised.

ALL IN THE FAMILY

Didn't Martha Stewart have enough to worry about after she was convicted for lying to investigators last year? Then came the icing on the cake. Shortly after, Stewart's youngest brother, Frank Kostyra, announced his plans to sell over two hundred items that had once belonged to Stewart on eBay. Among the items up for sale: the Singer sewing machine the embattled domestic diva used to sew her own wedding dress back in 1961. He also hocked the double boiler she once used for melting chocolate, cuttings from the Stewart family fig tree, and an oak rocker that belonged to the family's grandparents. Obviously he's not the sentimental type. At least the money is going to a good cause. Kostyra said proceeds from the sale will go toward his self-published book, entitled *My Life with Martha: The Making of Martha Stewart*.

Couldn't he have left the woman alone as she headed off to Alderson Women's Correctional Facility to deal with her severely damaged reputation and business ventures? Isn't going to jail and living with the label "convicted felon" enough? Kostyra made no apologies for exploiting the most famous member of his family, saying the sale was for "people who want a piece of the Martha legacy." My sentence for a greedy brother who's guilty of selling out his own sister in the first degree: a lifetime of shame.

THERE'S GOLD IN THOSE ARCHES

Not every instance of jackpot justice is born out of high-profile cases. Some cases become infamous because of the outrageous court claims by greedy plaintiffs looking to up their income with frivolous lawsuits. There are countless stories of physicians who give up the practice of medicine, claiming frivolous lawsuits price medical malpractice insurance out of their reach. What about the zany claims that gun manufacturers are responsible for crimes? But the mother of all laughable lawsuits is the McDonald's hot coffee case. In 1992, a seventy-nine-year-old New Mexico woman spilled coffee on herself after picking it up at the drive-through window and got burned. The jury awarded her $2.7 million—a judge later reduced it somewhat, and on appeal the case was settled for an undisclosed amount. Ronald McDonald must look like a giant piggy bank to a lot of people. The chain has been a popular target for customers with an appetite for more than fast food. In 2001, a class-action lawsuit was filed by vegans against the restaurant for failing to disclose that McDonald's fries were made with beef tallow oil. In recent years, the chain has been sued because its customers get fat. They're fat because they eat too much fast food! It's deadly to the courts, the way these frivolous lawsuits bloat the system, choking Lady Justice.

A real way to curtail outrageous court claims that suck the system dry is to institute higher standards of proof in personal-injury cases as well as to have trial judges charge the jury in more detail. There is a theory of contributory negligence that should be taken into consideration. Our legislatures must enact more conservative statutes so as to reduce the number of ridiculous claims in which the complainant is actually at fault. If you're harmed by eating french fries, prove it! Another measure to stop frivolous lawsuits would be to levy a punitive fine against attorneys who encourage money-grabbing clients to file suit. Instituting ethical reprimands isn't an unreasonable solution either.

Another simple solution would be to allow the jury to consider an alternative within the same trial. If the jury first finds no liability on behalf of the respondent, it should then consider awarding not only attorneys' fees to the respondent, but punitive damages as well, without needing a separate lawsuit based on the complainant's bogus claims.

In many jurisdictions, when these shameful lawsuits are filed and the respondent is forced to hire lawyers to defend against the claim, punitive damages can and should be ordered by the court as punishment for the misuse of the system. Those parties who glut the system with false claims should be ready to face the fact that if they are found out, the court will come down on them with major-league punitive awards to the other side—that come out of their own pockets.

CHAPTER FOUR

BLOOD MONEY

AT THE END OF EVERY FELONY TRIAL, WHEN I read out the word "guilty" in open court, I felt no jubilation. But at least I drove home those nights believing, naïvely, that I had helped set things right in some way. I believed that the system had given a small degree of peace to a family torn apart by violent crime. I had no idea that the persecution of innocent victims, once avenged by a jury verdict of guilty, continues on in a very real sense. I was shocked to discover there is a whole new meaning to revictimization—a whole new universe, in fact—in which that same family can be victimized over and over again, and at the moment there is not a darn thing we can do about it.

I'm talking about "murderabilia." Sold through the Internet.

SICKNESS FOR SALE

Get yourself some ginger ale and soda crackers, because I predict you'll soon be as nauseated as I was when I discovered the truth. The marketing of "murderabilia," as it has been coined, is a business that's not only alive and well on the Internet, but actually thriving. It's a marketplace growing fat and happy off the intense pain and suffering of others. On any given day, you can log on and, for the right price, become the owner of disturbing and gruesome mementos from crime scenes. A frightening number of personal items once belonging to evil monsters—many of them convicted killers who are sitting on death row—are for sale.

Items like autographed, killer-owned, prison-issued socks, autographed photos, and letters, as well as other items from California serial killers Lawrence "Pliers" Bittaker, Roy Norris, William Suff, and Charles Manson are hawked online. "Railway Killer" Angel Resendez-Ramirez is believed to have started killing innocent victims while still in his twenties, and at the time of his 1999 arrest, he was a suspect in at least fourteen murders. This monster is so confident of his marketability that he refuses to autograph any item behind bars for less than $25.00.

The online bloodsuckers hawking murderabilia aren't to be underestimated. They are not only innovative, but creative as well. As soon as they realized the legal loophole left open by the U.S. Supreme Court's reversal of Son of Sam laws, they got busy—but there was a problem. They weren't smart enough to write a book or a screenplay, which is now allowed thanks to that same Supreme Court. The alternative moneymaking scheme gaining popularity among criminals in recent years is the online sale of articles related in any way to the most disturbing, the goriest, and the most emotionally racking criminal cases on the books. What happens when they run out of variety and the clientele wants something more than nail clippings, hair samples, autographs, or photos? An online auction hawking Resendez-Ramirez's foot scrapings had opening bids that started at $9.99. Visa, MasterCard, and money orders accepted.

The movie *Psycho* has a cultlike following. Now the inspiration for the movie, Wisconsin farmer Ed Gein, is immortalized online through a range of bizarre items such as a wood fragment from his farmhouse and a crucifix Gein made in a mental hospital. A scrapbook of newspaper clippings detailing his murders dating back to 1957 sold online for nearly $200.

In this macabre online shopping mall, one item that stands out in its bizarre nature involves one of the most evil serial killers in U.S. history, the sadistic "Killer Clown." John Wayne Gacy's case is disturbing on so many levels. The number of known victims is an astonishing thirty-three. A little-publicized fact is that Gacy "slipped" through the fingers of the justice system shortly before his murder spree began. But for that miscalculation, how many lives would have been saved?

In 1968, Gacy was indicted by a Black Hawk County grand jury for forcible sodomy on a teen, for tying up and violently raping the boy while he was visiting Gacy's home. Four months later, Gacy was hit with additional charges for hiring a man to beat up the rape victim in retribution for going to police. After court-ordered psychiatric testing, Gacy pled guilty to sodomy and got ten years behind bars at the Iowa State Reformatory for men. Thinking he had put Gacy away for years, the sentencing judge probably rested easy that night. But in a horrific error in judgment, prison and parole authorities overrode the judge's intentions and paroled Gacy just eighteen short months later.

On June 18, 1970, Gacy walked out of Iowa prison gates a free man and immediately relocated to his hometown of Chicago. By 1976, the first of Gacy's known murder victims was missing.

Gacy was ultimately convicted on all thirty-three murders after a hard-fought courtroom battle in which he mounted, complete with psychiatric "experts," a formidable insanity defense. Among the more horrifying facts uncovered during the trial: Many of Gacy's young victims were found buried beneath the foundation of his home with their underwear stuffed down their throats. Their deaths were due to asphyxiation. Then to add insult to injury, the very dirt from Gacy's crawl space was made available for purchase online.

It is inconceivable to me that the dirt purchased online may have come in contact with one of the poor victims—some snatched unaware and then chloroformed once in Gacy's car. Parents of those who were killed by Gacy were left to wonder who bought the dirt that covered the body of their son.

The "dirt for sale" phenomenon isn't just an aberrant flash in the pan. As of September 2004, the soil from the deadly disaster at David Koresh's compound was still being hawked online. The raid on the Waco compound led to a fifty-one-day siege, a fiery inferno, and the deaths of eighty-five people, including four ATF agents and seventeen children. The Branch Davidians believed that God communicated with them through Koresh. In addition to stockpiling an arsenal of weapons and ammunition, Koresh preached that he was the "Lamb of God," and only his "seed" was pure, meaning that only he could have sex with girls and women in the compound.

Not interested in dirt? How about fingernail clippings from the hands of an honest-to-God serial killer? Nails from the very hands that murdered as their victims begged for their lives. They're yours if you know how to point and click online at a disgusting array of ghoulishly named sites. California serial killer Lawrence Bittaker is one of the cruelest serial killers ever known. He was ultimately convicted for the abductions, sex tortures, and murders of five known teenage girls. Bittaker and his codefendant, Roy Norris, conspired to outfit the "Murder Mack," as they called it, a van with tinted windows and devices on board to transform it into a mobile torture chamber. Literally snatching young girls off the street, one en route home from a prayer meeting, Bittaker and Norris delighted in raping, torturing, beating, and attacking their victims with pliers. With the music blaring to muffle any cries for help, the two often videotaped their tortures. Now in line for death by lethal injection, Bittaker spends his time on death row playing bridge and filing hundreds of frivolous lawsuits. One suit complained of cruel treatment because of a broken cookie on his lunch tray—and it wound up costing the state thousands of dollars in legal fees to defend. Bittaker often signs letters to fans with his pseudonym, "Pliers."

Keep all the above in mind and get ready for this: an auction Web site once listed Bittaker's fingernail clippings, with bids starting at $9.99, and described them as being "direct from the murdering hands of this fiendish killer." The description of the item featured this enticing sales pitch: "Collect 'em or use them in rituals to summon the dead. . . . Own some pieces of Larry now, 'cause once they execute him, there won't be enough of Larry left to go around."

Another disturbing online offer involves cannibal serial killer Arthur Shawcross, now serving 250 years behind bars for the murders of eleven women in Rochester, New York. In just one more instance of justice gone wrong, Shawcross was released from prison in New York after serving fifteen years for the murders of two young children. After his inexplicable early release, Shawcross relocated to Rochester in the 1980s. He went on to murder and cannibalize eleven victims. As of this writing, a sample of Shawcross's hair goes for $20 online.

Some of the most popular "killer" items for sale online are from Jeffrey Dahmer, convicted and sentenced to life for raping and murdering boys (some as young as thirteen) before cannibalizing them. Once in prison, Dahmer died at the hands of a fellow inmate, causing his murderabilia to skyrocket in price.

Actual crime-scene photos are linked online as well, complete with shots of murdered victims in various stages of undress. Morgue photos are not exempt. Web sites list the Charles Manson–Sharon Tate murder-scene photos, apparently laser-copied from the originals taken of the August 1969 slayings. As of September 2004, even copies of the autopsy report of murder victim Nicole Brown Simpson could be purchased online. Can you imagine how powerless the Browns feel, now forced to sit by, helpless, as a cold-blooded predator makes money off their daughter, their sister?

THE WORLD'S MOST
TWISTED TOY STORE

There is also a whole new genre of action figures available online, and I'm not referring to G.I. Joes or Power Rangers. I'm talking about serial-killer action figures, sold in toy stores and online. Ted Bundy, John Wayne Gacy, Jeffrey Dahmer, and Ed Gein are some of the serial-killer action figures created by Dave Johnson of Denver. They start at $39.99 apiece, and one site promises that the Columbine killers will soon be available.

Speaking of Columbine, last year I learned that a Texas man was peddling a card game based on the Columbine shootings, with players enacting the sickening roles of teenage shooters Eric Harris and Dylan Klebold. The goal is to achieve "divine retribution" against high-school classmates and teachers. Harris and Klebold murdered a dozen students and a teacher, wounding more than twenty others at Columbine's local high school on April 20, 1999. The two then killed themselves in the school library. Although the game's creator insists he's not trying to get rich, his Web site sells the game for $20. The box cover bears a shot of Klebold that was taken by a Columbine security camera. In it, Klebold is wielding the TEC-DC9 pistol he used at the school. The game states, "You are armed with guns and bombs . . . and your goal is to kill everyone, for that ultimate goal of immortality in the minds of men, with nothing more to sacrifice than a life with which you would have never done anything bigger than this, anyway."

Serial-killer trading cards are available online, much like a kid's baseball cards, offering the killer's vital stats, photos, correctional facility, and body count. Can you bring yourself to consider the pain this will cause the families of innocent victims? To live through the death and the funeral of their loved ones, and then the trial of their killer, only to endure a slap in the face from an online huckster in league with

OBJECTION! 99

a murderer? Serial-killer cards are offered by companies in New Jersey and California and by many other online sites.

The purpose of sites that promote their wares with phrases like "death," "dementia," or "serial killer," complete with sponsors listed, is clear: to profit from the pain of others. In that vein, a serial-killer museum is set to open soon. The band Korn's front man, Jonathan Davis, wants to put his collection of serial-killer murderabilia on display. According to MTV online, Korn is working with archivist Arthur Rosenblatt to create a museum in Los Angeles to display his extensive collection of items from convicted mass murderers. Items include the Volkswagen that Ted Bundy used to search for his victims, clown suits worn by John Wayne Gacy, and drawings by "Night Stalker" Richard Ramirez. Another site proudly announces that it "deal[s] with the devil himself" and hawks, among other things, T-shirts featuring Railway Killer Rafael Resendez-Ramirez's own artwork created in his cell at San Quentin.

If I hadn't seen the glorification and marketing of killers online with my own eyes, I would never have believed it. I can't help but wonder just who would buy fingernail clippings or hair samples of killers, knowing full well that victims' families have only photographs, high-school yearbooks, and memories to remember them by. The level of victimization is so intense it is sickening, yet it is allowed to thrive under the current laws of nearly every state in this country.

You may, as I do, wonder not only who buys these items but who sells them as well. They go by monikers like Supernaught and Drfixator. Others have more gruesome, crime-obsessed names that I won't list here because I refuse to give these ghouls the attention they crave. The names, created by the sellers as their online pseudonyms, reveal these people's aspirations and in themselves, speak volumes. You may be surprised that anyone would visit such a Web site, much less spend money on such repulsive offerings, but the reality is that bidding is lively. I was horrified to learn sales double at Christmastime.

Killers and their online pimps are reaping a windfall off the lives of murder victims. The general consensus among website purveyors is that they are not the morality police, and until the law stops them, they will continue. In my mind, that makes them accessories to the further victimization of those now dead, unable to speak for themselves.

These sites take no responsibility and refuse to shut down the serial-killer auction site, blaming the marketplace. Remember, the dealers, their advertisers, and their buyers/enablers profit from every online sale, including sales of murderabilia. If these entrepreneurs won't close down their sites, why won't they give the proceeds from these sales to victims'-rights groups? When asked this question by various victims'-rights advocates and others, they declined to respond.

Believe it or not, it's all legal.

LITERARY LOOPHOLES

Not so long ago, it appeared that crime victims were protected by the Son of Sam laws. David Berkowitz got that moniker when he became known as one of the most feared killers in New York City in the 1970s. His pent-up rage and frustration culminated in the murders of six people, injuries to seven others, and resulted in the largest manhunt in New York City history. During his reign of terror, he stalked lovers' lanes looking for victims and held the entire city hostage. When he was finally captured, the country was shocked to learn that the evil madman terrorizing the city was a chubby-cheeked postal worker with a deceptively sweet smile. Once in police custody, Berkowitz confessed to all the crimes and begged a trial judge to lock him away forever so he could never kill again. He is currently serving a 365-year sentence at the Sullivan Correctional Facility in Fallsburg, New York.

The possibility Berkowitz might write a screenplay and capitalize on the terror he'd caused galvanized the country. The Son of Sam laws went into effect in New York in 1977 and were originally enacted to stop

Berkowitz from profiting by selling his story. The laws prevent criminals from receiving profits for recounting their crime, including books, movies, screenplays, and television deals. The laws also require that the contracting party pay any proceeds directly to the actual victims or, as an alternative, to a state victims'-compensation fund. Following New York's lead, forty-two additional states and the federal government enacted similar legislation.

Since then, the country has been lulled into the belief that our justice system would never allow criminals and their "dealers" to make money off the suffering of crime victims. Not so.

The Son of Sam laws were actually reversed by the Supreme Court back in the case of *Simon & Schuster, Inc. v. New York Crime Victims' Board*, 112 S.Ct. 501 (1991). The case arose after convicted gangster Henry Hill detailed his life of crime with the mob in a book titled *Wiseguy*. New York columnist Jimmy Breslin praised the book, which became the basis for the movie *Goodfellas*, calling it the "best book on crime ever written in America."

The Supreme Court allowed *Wiseguy* to be published. They declared the Son of Sam laws unconstitutional, claiming they violated criminals' First Amendment right to free speech. The Court held that the laws must be narrower because they included those charged with a crime in addition to those convicted. The justices wrote in their decision that the laws did not distinguish between works substantially about the crime versus those that mentioned the crime tangentially. For instance, Malcolm X had been behind bars, yet his works were not about his crimes but about his vision for societal change. Under the original Son of Sam laws, those works would have been banned.

Amazingly, after the reversal of the Son of Sam laws made criminal profiteering easy, few states took action. Most have not revised their laws to address the Court's *Wiseguy* ruling.

In 2000, Mary Kay Letourneau—the former elementary-school teacher from Seattle, Washington, who had a sexual relationship with one of her sixth-grade students, then-twelve-year-old Vili Fualaau—was legally allowed to help publish a book chronicling the "affair" despite being sentenced to jail in 1997 on a statutory-rape charge.

The State of Washington's State Court of Appeals ruled that Letourneau could not be barred from profiting from her story as part of her sentence, despite a Washington State law that allows for the confiscation of profits made by criminals in describing their crimes. At the time, attorney James Lobsenz cited the U.S. Supreme Court's decision ruling that convicts have a constitutional right to profit from book sales and movie rights, saying, "Is there any possible way we can argue with a straight face that our law is meaningfully different than the Son of Sam law in New York that was struck down?"

A French publishing house contacted Letourneau's attorney, who brokered his client and her underage lover a $200,000 advance for their story. The title of this page-turner? *Un Seul Crime, L'amour— Mary Kay Letourneau & Vili Fualaau*, which translates into—buckle your seat belt—"Only One Crime—Love." The book even included a defense of Letourneau penned as a prologue by Fualaau's mother, Soona.

The opportunity for criminals to cash in on their crimes must be stopped once and for all. The fix? Address the Supreme Court reversal in the *Wiseguy* case and carefully specify what is allowed and what is not. Works that deal with a crime and profit from that crime specifically would be allowed—but all the money would go to the victims. The revised law would not suppress criminals' right to speak but would prevent them from making money off a work that is substantially about the crime. This is a sane and sensible solution.

The issue came to the forefront again when a California judge ruled against Sharon Rocha, the mother of Laci Rocha Peterson, in 2004. Spurred on by reports that Scott Peterson was planning to profit from his own account surrounding the events of the murders of Laci and their unborn son, Conner, Rocha filed a lawsuit in Stanislaus County Superior Court. She asked for an injunction to transfer any income Peterson may receive from books or movies to a protected trust until a verdict in the case was reached.

In the lawsuit, Rocha claimed that Peterson and unnamed others "have solicited, arranged payment for, received or will in the future receive 'proceeds' from the sale of rights to or materials that include or are based on the story of a felony for which Peterson is charged . . . and [of which he] may ultimately be convicted."

With no Son of Sam protections, such civil lawsuits must be filed by relatives of a homicide victim to block defendants from profiting in the case through lucrative media interviews and movie and book deals. California also had a Son of Sam law, ordering outright that felons pay their victims any money they got from selling their stories. Since the *Wiseguy* reversal, victims' families must now go to civil court at great personal cost and file an additional wrongful-death suit against criminals, as the Brown and Goldman families did against O. J. Simpson. A jury awarded the families $33.5 million in judgment, but they've seen precious little of it.

This isn't unusual. Efforts to collect from defendants in such cases are usually fruitless. In order to do so, victims' families have to track a defendant's moneymaking activities themselves or pay someone else to do it. The process costs them inordinate amounts of time, money, and effort. The cases can drag on forever, allowing the accused time to dispose of or hide the assets. It's no secret that O. J. Simpson made plenty of money signing sports memorabilia at various fairs around the country. In the summer of 2004, during interviews that commemorated the ten-year anniversary of Nicole Brown's murder, he even announced on national television that he's in "talks" to star in his own reality show, called *Juiced*. The premise: Simpson pulls stunts on unsuspecting people. Sound familiar? Believe you me, if Simpson does wind up doing this disgusting show, he won't be doing it for free. If he does profit from this ridiculous scenario, even if it's just one dollar, that money belongs to the Browns and the Goldmans.

In the Rocha case, Sharon Rocha was initially denied the injunction under a legal technicality, as no money had yet been earned by Peterson and, at the time of the filing, he had not been convicted of any crime. According to the Associated Press, Peterson's attorneys argued that he should be allowed to pursue movie and book deals even if he *is* found guilty. Incredible.

VICTORY FOR VICTIMS — NO BULL!

I will never forget the case of mob underboss Salvatore "Sammy the Bull" Gravano. As part of a sweetheart plea deal—sweet for Gravano anyway—he sang like a bird against John Gotti of the notorious Gambino crime family. "The Bull" confessed to planning or committing nineteen murders nearly ten years earlier as part of a deal with federal prosecutors to implicate Gotti and over three dozen other mobsters. Even with nineteen murders under his belt, Gravano did just five years behind bars on racketeering charges and then went underground as part of the Witness Protection Program. Unable to live a straight life, he left the program and chose to live openly in Arizona, a free man until he was charged with running an ecstasy drug ring with his wife, children, and a group of white supremists.

To make matters worse and heap additional heartache on his victims' families, Gravano wrote a book detailing his life with the mob—and it sold. Gravano inked a 1996 deal with author Peter Maas to write the book on Gravano's lifetime of crime, including murders. Maas then struck a subsequent deal with HarperCollins Publishers to publish the book and 20th Century Fox to do the movie. A victims' board tried to force Gravano, Maas and his company, T.J.M. Productions Inc., HarperCollins, and Maas's agent all to give the book's proceeds to the murder victims' families.

On appeal, New York's appellate division ruled that the state's Son of Sam laws do not allow the Crime Victims' Board to seize Gravano's book proceeds, claiming that the laws do not apply to the federal crimes to which he pled guilty. Gravano's lawyer, Larry H. Krantz, called the ruling "correct." Michael Dowd, attorney for Maas and T.J.M., said, "It's a wonderful decision for anyone who'll ever put pen to paper." Harper-Collins issued a news release saying that the decision "makes clear that authors and publishers can publish accounts of criminal activity without fear of interference from the Crime Victims' Board." So everybody was happy—except the victims' families. Their only recourse was to hire lawyers and file civil wrongful-death suits against Gravano.

But then, in a stunning turn of events, the state of Arizona did what New York claimed couldn't be done. New York claimed that its laws didn't protect the victims. Arizona's restitution law does, even when the crime takes place outside of Arizona. Ads placed in East Coast newspapers sought out Gravano's victims and offered a portion of royalties from his book. The ads were run by the Arizona attorney general's office and were allowed after Arizona prosecutors won a court fight over proceeds from the book *Underboss: Sammy the Bull Gravano's Story of Life in the Mafia.*

Although Gravano's Phoenix attorney disagreed with the decision, his argument didn't hold water with Maricopa County Superior Court judge Mark Santana. The defense lawyer claimed that "it was a violation of the First Amendment."

The fight didn't end in the trial court; Gravano took it on appeal all the way up to the U.S. Supreme Court. And why not? The New York appellate court had sided with Gravano. He rolled the dice again—this time with a different result. The Supremes refused to hear his appeal, an alternative they often choose when they either agree with the lower decision or simply do not want to rule on the case. Ironically, on the very day the Supreme Court made its announcement, another court had a sentencing hearing on Thomas "Huck" Carbonaro, a reputed hit man who had schemed to kill Gravano with a remote-control bomb for betraying the Gambino crime family. In the end, Gravano is still behind bars doing a twenty-year sentence for running a massive ecstasy ring, and the victims won their right to his book proceeds, thanks to an Arizona judge. It was a victory, true, but bittersweet. Power to the Grand Canyon State!

VICTIMS TAKE ACTION

When I researched the background of Senate Bill 1887, the California Son of Sam 2 legislation, I discovered that California's Senator McPherson was a big proponent of the bill. McPherson had read an article in the paper about the Supreme Court's declaring the Son of Sam legislation unconstitutional, and was pained. McPherson's own son was murdered a couple of years ago in San Francisco, so this deeply touched him. McPherson contacted the state attorney general's office, and they coauthored the Son of Sam 2 legislation. Two crime-victims' organizations, Crime Victims United of California and the Carole Sund/Carrington Foundation, got behind the bill as well. After a long struggle, the bill was signed into law by Governor Gray Davis on September 17, 2002.

While a revised federal Son of Sam law is still needed to stop criminals from getting rich off their own tales, an effective legislative solution has been enacted in a few states that is helping to end online criminal profiteering.

Richard Allen Davis, the kidnapper who killed a beautiful little twelve-year-old girl, Polly Klaas, in 1993, was hawking handwritten letters and photos of himself wearing only underwear online. Polly's father, Marc Klaas, reacted, taking aim at the California legislature. He joined forces with Texas victims'-rights crusader Andy Kahan to champion a revolutionary idea: the Notoriety for Profit Law, often referred to as the "Murderabilia Law." Klaas and Kahan learned from the cracks in the Son of Sam laws and threw in a new twist to foil the profiteering. Largely through their efforts, the Notoriety for Profit Law has been in effect in California since 2002 and in Texas since 2001, putting the kibosh on sales of murderabilia online as well as on other outlets.

A few months before Kahan planned to go public on ABC's *20/20* to expose Internet sleaze and his plans for the new law, he had already scored a major victory against online ghouls. The auction site eBay got wind of what Kahan was doing and in May 2001 made the stunning announcement that eBay would prohibit further murderabilia sales. There are, however, many other outlets that refuse to stop trading in terror.

Kahan's "Murderabilia Law" is a great start. In California and Texas, where it is on the books, criminals can still sell their hair and fingernails online, but here's the good news: The state may seize any money generated above and beyond the fair market value of the item itself, based on notoriety. The new version allows police to seize profits, notably those earned from Internet sales, if it can be shown that the value of an item is enhanced by its connection to crime. For instance, a human hair sample sells for little or nothing online, and its fair market value in most cases is next to zero. If the price of a hair sample is enhanced because of the infamy of its owner, the additional profit is seizable by the courts in those jurisdictions that have passed the Notoriety for Profit Law.

The law, which makes the watchdogs the state and local authorities, will also stop third-party brokers like Ghoul-Chaser from profiting from murderabilia, sending proceeds from such sales into the same fund for victims' families or directly into the state's Crime Victims' Compensation Fund. It's hoped that similar models will find their way onto the floors of state legislatures and assemblies across the United States. There is no reason the federal government shouldn't follow suit.

Some people may call this draconian, but I strongly advocate jail time for third-party dealers who either work in conjunction with a murderer behind bars or otherwise get their hands on "the goods." In my mind, these online brokers are aiding and abetting in furtherance of the original crime by profiting from a victim's pain. They should be charged with a misdemeanor crime that carries a penalty including not only a fine, but jail time for the crime. And for those detractors who cry that this would restrict free commerce, I say that the very same reason we don't sell cocaine at the supermarket should apply to the sale of Bittaker's fingernails online. It's wrong. It's just plain wrong. If people really want to stop this disgusting business, this is the way to do it. What possible impact could a twelve-month misdemeanor charge have on a defendant doing life without parole? The law has to go after those who will be most affected by its implementation . . . the dealers/brokers. I say book 'em!

When I consider the power of the Internet combined with the evil of those who take joy in murder, I feel like David doing battle against Goliath. The "Murderabilia Law" is an important step in stopping the injustices perpetrated by online ghouls and others seeking to cash in on crime and its pain and suffering. I believe that an important goal of our country's justice system should be to protect a victim's family from seeing their loved one's killer profit from heartache. The only notice grieving families should ever receive regarding criminals who took away their loved ones should be an execution announcement from the state's death row, not a "for sale" ad on the Internet.

CHAPTER FIVE

AIRBRUSHING THE AWFUL TRUTH

IN MOVIES AND ON TELEVISION, EVERYBODY IN the courtroom is beautiful. Hollywood's glamorized version of our justice system depicts lawyers who are always dressed to the hilt, with flawless hair and makeup. Thanks to smartly written scripts, counsel always provides the perfect response to every question. The victims are usually actors with great bodies and porcelain smiles. Occasionally their hair is a little messy. A few fake cuts and bruises are sometimes thrown in, in keeping with the "gritty" mood of the drama. Even the defendants look great and are often characterized as misunderstood.

By the closing credits, everything is wrapped up neatly and the good guy wins out. I wish that were true in real life. The actual struggle against crime, whether it's violent or white-collar, bears little or no resemblance to what audiences are shown. The stark truth of what goes down in courtrooms across the country when prosecutors are fighting for the rights of victims is just that—a struggle. It's hand-to-hand mutual combat between state and defense. Kidnapping, murder, rape, and child molestation reveal the ugliest sides of human nature. Prosecuting the violent offenders who commit these crimes is dirty business— dirtier than the casual courtroom observer, much less a TV audience, can ever know.

When a case finally wends its way into a courtroom, to a jury of twelve in the box with alternate jurors waiting in the wings, nothing is as it was when the crime was first committed. By the time the state delivers an opening statement, the truth has been "packaged," whittled down by defense lawyers, trial judges, and appellate courts to a perfunctory presentation. Here are just a few things most juries never see: images of the victim in life, a majority of crime-scene photos, autopsy photos and reports, the dying words of the deceased, and the suspect's extensive criminal history. Also disallowed: fingerprint crimes called "similar transactions," motive evidence, rap sheets, and sometimes even the suspect's confession. It's all gone. I'll explain why later in this chapter.

By the time a trial begins, the defendant's testimony becomes a "script" that sounds canned and practiced. The evidence seems surreal, dated, and strangely detached from reality. With the passing of time and the repackaging allowed by the system, the enormity of a violent crime translates into muted voices, soft and tiny, in a cavernous courtroom. Lost is the moment of the act and the events that followed: the subsequent investigation, backbreaking hours of preparation by investigators and lawyers, and the raw grief of the victim's loved ones. What is left for the jury is a sanitized, cleaned-up, objection-free version of the facts—just the way defense lawyers want it. By twisting the rules of evidence, the defense can score a myriad of pretrial victories, including the exclusion of state's witnesses, suppression of crime-scene and autopsy photos, and obscuration of the true nature of the defendant. All of these things aid in helping achieve their ultimate goal: airbrushing the awful truth.

I still remember the first triple-homicide case I tried, in 1990. It made headlines at the time because it involved a major cartel's drug trail from Miami to New York. Because of the case's enormous implications, I was sure I'd be passed over in favor of an older, more experienced prosecutor. It didn't happen that way. The case came to my courtroom by random assignment, and I kept it. That's how indictments in metropolitan jurisdictions are disbursed among the trial judges. A computer assigns each case a number up into the tens of thousands. The numbers are assigned randomly and evenly to each of the dozens of judges in each jurisdiction. The computer could assign one prosecutor forty cases in one week with only one murder, the rest being car thefts, burglaries, and rapes. The next week could land you another forty cases, fifteen of them being brand-new murder files. The computer understands only the ordered case number assigned to the file—it's blind to the nature of the case. This is so defense lawyers can't accuse the state of "judge shopping"—in other words, expressly assigning specific cases to tough judges or strong prosecutors versus the weak links that invariably exist on the bench and in the courtroom.

This particular triple homicide had evolved out of an ongoing turf battle that took place midway along the direct route from Miami, where narcotics of all types flood into the United States and are then "muled"—transported—up Interstate 75 toward New York City, one of the country's main drug-distribution hubs. Atlanta is the first major stop for traffickers as they flee Miami to escape the city's heavy DEA presence.

The most vicious drug-related gang violence goes down in clusters of inner-city Atlanta's housing projects. This particular housing project, home to thousands of people, was easily one of the most violent. The apartments were configured in a horseshoe shape, with entrances at either end. Because of the huge number of drive-by shootings and drug-related activities that occurred there, one entrance had actually been barricaded closed by police. They cordoned it off with barbed wire so suspects couldn't elude them during chases. I didn't know that when I went to investigate the crime, but I learned pretty quickly.

The first time I drove there, I did so naïvely believing that witnesses would actually talk to me just because I asked. The murders went down on a Sunday night at about ten past eleven, on the project's playground, which was at the center of the U-shaped apartment configuration. Any people who happened to be looking out their windows that night would have had to have seen what happened, but no one would come forward. People broke down into two camps: those who were afraid of retaliation, which was a given, and addicts who couldn't care less about murders that took place on their own kids' playground.

Airbrushing the awful truth in this case was the primary goal of the defense. The crux of the case was that three young black men had been gunned down, execution-style. The youngest one had tried to run when he realized what was happening. He took off, attempted to jump over a chain-link fence, and was shot multiple times in the back. In the first crime-scene photo I saw of him, he was lying flat on his back. I couldn't make out the unusual markings on his face until I drove to the medical examiner's headquarters and questioned the doctor who had performed the autopsy. He explained that when the victim was murdered, he was in the midst of climbing over the chain-link fence surrounding part of the playground in his effort to escape. That's when he was shot, and that's where he died. His cheek, jaw, and neck were smashed into the fence, and he hung there dead until police took him down. Another shot also took me a while to figure out, until I interviewed one of the crime-scene techs who took the photos. Under the fence was a cement gutter. I didn't even realize what I was looking at until he explained that it was blood from the body of the teenager literally running down the gutter. The defense team objected to the photos' coming into evidence, claiming they were prejudicial and would incite the jury. I argued they symbolized the intense level of violence that night.

The jury never saw them.

BEARING WITNESS

No witnesses? No case.

The defense is always thrilled when a state's witness fails to show, is too afraid to come to court, or can't be located or convinced to get involved. After being named as the district attorney in the triple-homicide case I went to the scene at many different times of the day and night to try to get witnesses to testify. Because my name had been in the local papers as the prosecutor in the case, no one would answer the door when I came around. I'm sure I stuck out like a sore thumb, dressed in my court clothes and rumbling up in a huge, county-issued Crown Victoria— widely known in practically every state in the country as *the* unmarked government vehicle. My investigator and I would sneak around the back of the apartments so that the neighbors of potential witnesses wouldn't see us and word wouldn't spread that they were cooperating. We would knock on every door and occasionally talk ourselves into someone's apartment. We were literally begging people to testify if they had seen anything.

One apartment we made it into had absolutely no furniture except one sofa lying lopsided, feet missing, in the middle of the den floor. It looked as if someone had set it on fire but not finished the job. The place was filthy. Everyone in the apartment was either already high, smoking pot, or doing lines. It was the first crack house I'd ever been in.

Although I knew that my investigator packed at least two guns at all times, I, as usual, was unarmed. We knew instinctively that everyone in this place was armed to the hilt. After we "badged" our way in, we asked about the shootout. Everything went silent, and they all looked at each other. I knew they knew more, but nobody spoke. Then they visibly began shrinking away from us and fumbling for words. The end result of our visit: no witnesses.

I was having a tough time digesting the conditions under which this community (including the little children) lived. I had just witnessed a felony crime right in front of my eyes. In my mind, that called for action. When we got to the car, I picked up the walkie-talkie to report the cocaine. My investigator yanked it away before I could finish. He told me in no uncertain terms that there was no way we could report it or stop it. They'd be out on bond two days after arrest, back in the same dope house, and our chance of a conviction in the triple murder would be shot. Reporting the crack house would certainly have stopped any potential witnesses from ever cooperating. I felt helpless, but I knew I couldn't do anything to jeopardize the case. I had to find witnesses. To this day, I think of the little kids who lived there. Their clothes were dirty, and they had nothing. I didn't report the crack house and continued to work the case.

I finally heard about a witness who allegedly drove a school bus during the day. I knew she would have avoided me if she had any idea I was coming. Late one afternoon, I went back to the projects to try to approach her with a subpoena as she came in from work. I never told people when I was coming, because if they had even an inkling I was on my way, they'd definitely vanish by the time I showed up.

As odd as it sounds, by this time I had seen many, many crime scenes and never shed a tear. I'd stayed dry-eyed through countless reviews of autopsy findings, bloodstains, dead bodies. All that mattered was getting a true verdict from the jury, putting violent offenders behind bars and away from innocent people, and then tackling the next case. At the time, Atlanta's crime level was so high that I sometimes tried three cases in one week. My Monday mornings usually started with a murder or rape trial. The minute a jury left the courtroom to begin deliberations, the sheriff would usher in the next panel of sixty to eighty jurors, who'd been waiting in the hall to be struck for the petit jury (twelve people). The second case would usually be something along the lines of a drug possession or trafficking case calling for only five to ten witnesses. After that, a simple burglary or car-theft jury could easily be struck, with only a few witnesses needed to prove the case. When all the cases had been given to the jury, my investigator and I would haunt the courtroom, subsisting on Diet Cokes and crackers until the verdicts came in. I thought I was steeled against emotions that would cloud my focus.

But the day I went looking for my bus-driver witness, something was different. I had scoured the playground where the crime occurred for weeks, digging for ballistics evidence the police might have missed. This was the first time I'd been there in the light of day, and the scene stunned me. All over the playground—even under the swing sets and monkey bars—was broken glass, cigarette butts, used condoms, bullets, bullet casings, discarded miniature glassine bags for holding crack. There were even used syringes everywhere.

I sat there in my car, hunched over the wheel, waiting. And then came the children. I watched in horror as dozens of kids poured off two school buses and onto that playground, running and laughing. I still don't know why, but suddenly it was too much. I put my head on the steering wheel and cried and cried. I couldn't stop. Watching those children grow up in that world, swinging high on a swing set over broken glass and glassine bags—it was just too much. All I could see was a whole new generation immune to crime, literally growing up right on top of it. I had seen a million crime-scene photos and not felt a thing. But seeing those children living in that world and never having a chance was more than I could take.

That night at home, and for days afterward, I tried to figure out why I was still prosecuting. What was the point? After this case, there would just be more—a never-ending stream of violent crime. I wanted desperately to quit. I felt lost. My mission had run aground. Everything about the case left me with a horrible feeling of hopelessness. Then I heard about a possible witness, a hooker named Shorty, who I'm sure is dead by now. She had been on the edge of the playground that night but was afraid to speak out. Somehow we talked her into it. I'll never forget what awaited me when I went to her apartment. When she opened the front door, I saw what had to be about twenty babies lying on the floor in front of a television. They were all infants, some wrapped in blankets, some not—but not one ever cried out for care or affection. I discovered she made extra money as a part-time baby-sitter. I tiptoed around them on the way to the kitchen, where she asked me if I wanted something to drink. She gave me some green Kool-Aid. While I was sitting there, I happened to look up at the clock on the wall behind me. It took all I had not to shriek and leap out of my chair. There had to have been eighty roaches running up and down the wall like ants. I set the glass down, opened up my file to work, and pretended to drink so I wouldn't be rude.

On the day Shorty was to take the stand, things dragged on and on. Suddenly it was five o'clock. I could see that the jury was drawn and tired. My investigator thought we should stop, but my gut told me we had to get this woman on the stand now. The jury had to be there, in that moment, on the playground the night of the killings, before they went home for the day. Up until this point, the day had been filled with one "expert" after another, plus a couple of cops.

On the stand, Shorty described what she had seen that night, and she was growing more and more agitated as she went on. She testified that all of a sudden she heard the shouting, and when she looked over through the darkness, she saw the three young men gunned down. Her fear was a palpable presence in the courtroom. Before I could stop her, she half stood at the witness stand and screamed at the top of her lungs, "He shot them! Shot them dead!" She then pointed to the defendant as she cried out in the courtroom, "I looked and saw him! He turned and looked at me in the dark, and I was so afraid that I ran."

You could have heard a pin drop in the courtroom. The jury finally got it. The truth was raw, and it hurt. I stopped and turned to the judge. We were done. The jury went home with Shorty's cries ringing in their ears. As much evidence as the defense had managed to keep away from them, this was one witness it couldn't airbrush.

When the jury delivered their verdict, they found the triggerman guilty on all three counts of malice murder. I forced myself to look directly at him to "publish the verdict"—read it aloud in open court. After leaving the courthouse that afternoon, I was standing at a crosswalk waiting for the light to change when I turned and saw that a member of the jury had come up next to me. He was a tall black man in his early fifties. During the trial, I had connected with this juror and directed much of my argument and questioning of witnesses directly at him. He didn't speak but held out his hand to shake mine. My eyes filled with tears as we gripped hands. He disappeared into the crowd crossing the street, and I never saw him again. The defendant in the case remains behind bars serving three consecutive life sentences.

The level of violence and lack of regard for human life displayed during that case, combined with tactics used by the defense, were just plain wrong. I needed an armed escort to take me to my car every night after court. My tires were slashed in the county court's parking deck, and my back door was kicked in. My mailbox was run over and knocked down three times. Things grew worse as the investigation and trial wore on. I finally had to stop staying at my own home during the trial.

In the course of prosecuting this case, it all became overwhelming. The ugliness of the truth exposed an intense level of violence and hatred that was saturating my life. It's impossible to slog hip-deep through mud every day without tracking some back home with you. I felt lost, and I wanted to quit. In my closing statements to the jury, I argued with all my heart that they were the voice of those who have no voice—the victims who are all too often the poor and uneducated. If they didn't speak out against injustice, I reasoned, then who would? As I argued to the jury, my own words rang in my head. I knew at the time that I was just weary, weary with the weight of the trial. I knew I wasn't ready to stop fighting the only way I knew how—as a prosecutor. After the trial, my mother gave me a ring with three rows of diamonds: one for each of the three victims. I wear it to this day.

A PICTURE SPEAKS A THOUSAND (UNHEARD) WORDS

I was reminded of that triple-homicide case when I learned that the trial judge in the Laci Peterson murder case had warned potential jurors that they would likely see graphic and upsetting crime-scene photos. There would likely be photos of Laci—or what was left of her, which was her bones with a little flesh on them, wearing a maternity bra, washed up against a rocky beach. Her skull and portions of her limbs were never found. Compared to the vibrant images of the smiling and happy young brunette we came to recognize from television, the contrast is nearly impossible to erase from your mind.

As awful as the crime-scene photos are, they depict the truth. Murder is an unsettling and gory reality. Crime-scene and autopsy photos are the closest things attorneys have when it comes to sharing that truth with the jury. Words alone cannot do the truth justice. The jurors, however, never learn the harsh reality of crime, and they never will under the current rules of evidence. I believe that all crime-scene and autopsy photos showing the victim's injuries must be admissible. It has been ruled repeatedly by appellate courts that such photos would inflame and prejudice the jury. Of course a jury will be inflamed. Of course jurors will be prejudiced to the extent that the evidence of the murder itself is inflammatory and shocking. Is there a way to pretend that the violent taking of a human life isn't shocking? All evidence pointing to murder is prejudicial. The defense argument that evidence in a murder trial is prejudicial to the jury is a ridiculous and disingenuous game played with words.

I have gotten certain autopsy photos in under very limited circumstances. I prosecuted the kidnapping, rape, and murder of an unknown woman whose body was found dumped in an empty field. We didn't have much to go on, but part of the proof that made it to the jury was an autopsy photo of the victim's skull showing violent bruising under the skin. Because the wound was apparent to the naked eye only in the autopsy photo, it was allowed. And it was in fact inflammatory. When I first saw the photo, I didn't even realize what I was looking at. All you could see was blurry pinkish tissue, bordered in black. The medical examiner pointed out, "That's her head. This is her hair." It didn't really hit me then, because I was looking at a discoloration of tissue just beneath her skull. In that context, the photo came in to show the nature and degree of a blow to the head and the subdural (beneath the skull) bleeding. Autopsy photos are often the only method to explain certain injuries, but more than that, they are the only way in which the true horror of the crime is ever known to a jury. The stark reality is that this victim ended up at the county morgue with her body dissected. Harsh? Yes. True? Yes. It is part of the nature of the crime and must not be hidden from the jury.

THE SCENE OF THE CRIME

I also firmly believe that *all* crime-scene photos must be admissible. Defense attorneys try their best to have as many as possible excluded from evidence, so as to distance the jury from the reality of the crime. It's much better from the defense's point of view to reduce the murder, rape, or child molestation to a clinical evaluation as reported in the notes of a doctor, nurse, or medical examiner. I say, "No!" Crime has nothing to do with a black-and-white, printed version of injuries and analysis. It is all about the assault on human dignity, on the human psyche—and it's about the victim. The human equation must not be airbrushed out of the courtroom.

The courtroom is no place for the weak-kneed, and the jury must see the reality and intensity of crime. To show the truth to a jury, prosecutors must know the rules of evidence backward and forward, using those rules as their swords and their shields. A superior knowledge of the application of law is the only hope for the reality of crime to make its way to a jury. Being able to use those rules to your advantage, to lay the groundwork as to why photos must be admitted, is essential. Reviewing the crime scene and victim and autopsy photos with a fine-tooth comb often reveals strategies to allow the truth before the jury. Arguments such as depicting the trajectory path of bullets, the severity of deep-tissue wounds, the number of blows or lacerations are examples of why autopsy photos should be allowed. The depictions of distances, heights, lighting conditions, positions of bodies, furniture, cars, and other objects shown only in crime-scene photos are examples of why those photos should be allowed. For every exhibit entered into evidence, there must be a reason for its admittance. The only way to win the battle to reveal the awful truth is through the expert use of the facts of the case and the expert application of the rules of law.

The same holds true when jurors visit a crime scene. If and when (it's rare) a jury ever does get to see the crime scene, you could put a bow on it and sell it at Bloomingdale's. It's been cleaned up and stripped of the evidence that reflected the horrors the victim suffered in his last moments of life. It's Crime Lite. At the time of a crime, there is more to the scene than simply what you see. Its what you feel, what you smell, what you sense. It's an overpowering presence, as if someone is there.

An incredible example of crime-scene manipulation occurred during the O. J. Simpson trial. Love him or hate him, Johnnie Cochran is a criminal defendant's knight in shining armor. A field trip to Simpson's home included the judge, the jury, lawyers for both sides, a fleet of reporters, photographers, and videographers—and Simpson himself. The purpose of the trip to Nicole Brown's home on Bundy Avenue and Simpson's home on Rockingham was to give the jury a chance to see things for themselves. The prosecution had intended for jurors to focus on viewing the locations of Brown's and Ron Goldman's bodies, the spot where the infamous bloody glove was found, and the bedroom where police had collected Simpson's blood-spattered socks.

The defense, however, seized upon the viewing of the scene as their opportunity for spin control, painting Simpson as a kind, benevolent family man. Before the jury motored over to Simpson's home on chartered buses, the defense allegedly did some redecorating. A print of Norman Rockwell's famous painting of a beautiful little black girl being escorted to school by federal marshals was borrowed from Johnnie Cochran's office and positioned at the top of the home's center staircase. Pictures of Simpson standing with white golfing buddies disappeared. A glamour shot of Simpson's white girlfriend, Paula Barbieri, was stashed away. They were replaced with photos of Simpson's elderly mother. A Bible was planted in the living room. Since Simpson's house was not a crime scene, this bit of redecorating was perfectly legal. The tour was a great success for the defense. Simpson even got the unprecedented chance to speak to the jury outside the courtroom, not under oath and without the benefit of cross-examination. At one point, it was reported, he declared proudly while gesturing toward the backyard, "That's where I practiced my golf swing."

On the tenth anniversary of Nicole's and Ron's murders, I interviewed a Simpson juror and asked her how, in the presence of so much evidence, the jury rendered a not-guilty verdict. She answered, "The state didn't carry its burden." Then I asked, What about the blood evidence? How do you reconcile that? Her response: "I don't have to reconcile it."

The manipulation of the crime scene by the defense in many different cases is well documented. In October 2003, during the murder trial of novelist Michael Peterson in North Carolina, the defense fought hard for a jury viewing of the showpiece of a home in Durham perfected by its owner, Peterson's wife, Kathleen. Her novelist husband was caught up in a web of online gay dating sites, financial hardship, and a secret past that included the death of a woman connected to him. Kathleen had been found dead at the foot of the stairs in her own home, with seven lacerations to the back of the head. According to her husband, he was alone outside smoking a cigarette by the pool, and when he went back inside, he discovered his wife dead at the base of the stairs.

At trial, it was revealed that approximately eighteen years before, Michael Peterson's "close friend" Elizabeth Ratliff had been found dead at the foot of *her* stairs with numerous lacerations to the back of the head after Peterson had taken her home that night.

Police had searched the Petersons' North Carolina home exhaustively for a murder weapon, which was believed to have been a missing blowpoke that normally stood by the fireplace in their home.

By the time the jury finally got their view of the Peterson home, the bloodstained stairs and walls had been cleaned and to a certain extent boarded off. Every room was polished up to look like a page out of *House Beautiful*, complete with fresh-cut flowers and the smell of Lemon Pledge!

There were no signs of the blood that had spattered onto the ceiling, suggesting a blow to the head as opposed to a fall down steps as the mode of death.

Incredibly, the long-missing blowpoke was finally "found" by the defense. Of course, by the time they produced their "discovery," it was fingerprint-free. Clearly, as time passes, there is more and more opportunity to doctor the scene. In the high-stakes gamble of a trial, that motive to airbrush the awful truth is overwhelming. In this case, the jury didn't buy it. Peterson was convicted of murder one.

During Scott Peterson's trial I was concerned Judge Delucchi would allow the jury to go out on the San Francisco Bay, where Laci and Conner were disposed. In my nightmares, they would go out on a bright, sunny day and be surrounded by recreational crafts while imagining Scott Peterson enjoying himself on the water the day Laci went missing. What a miscarriage of justice that would have been. I went onto the bay myself to see where Laci was thrown overboard. In December, the water would have been choppy, the air cold and windy. No way was Peterson out fishing for fun on Christmas Eve. Thank God Delucchi understood the changing nature of a crime scene.

Before crime-scene visits are sanctioned by the court, I advocate that a two-pronged test be incorporated into the rules of evidence and met. First, whichever side wants the visit must proffer to the trial judge the reason for the visit, grounded in evidence and supported by rationale as to why photos or video of the scene would not suffice. Second, whoever has had supervision and control over the scene must show, under oath, that the scene has not been manipulated in any way. Any manipulation of the scene is grounds for a contempt-of-court charge that should come with jail time and should be made known to the jury. That way, it will be up to them to decide why a party would choose to rearrange history and what, if any, bearing that manipulation has on the guilt or innocence of the accused. Why give anyone an excuse for a sneaky reshaping of a crime scene?

THE NAMELESS,
FACELESS VICTIM

It's odd that as a prosecutor, you invest so much time and effort to bringing a victim's case to a jury, only to have that victim wind up largely anonymous. In murder cases, the jury never gets to know the victims in life, their joys, their concerns, their fears, their triumphs—or their pain even in death. In our system, victims are reduced to case numbers. What I mean by that is that a number is given to each case indicted, a different number is attached by the police, a number is given at the crime lab, a different one at the hospital, yet another at the medical examiner's office and the morgue. Even in court, the defense refers to the victim by a number. Prosecutors can sometimes fall into the same trap, even though they don't have to. During Scott Peterson's preliminary hearings, the defense attorneys constantly referred to specimen numbers, ID numbers, and exhibit numbers rather than to the name of the victim. They didn't say, "Where did you find Laci's pants?" Instead they asked, "Where did you locate State's Exhibit 43?" The more impersonal, the better the defense likes it. Whether it's the victim's clothing or belongings, her voice on an answering machine, photos of him in life, or his dying words—the defense scores big when evidence like this is suppressed.

I've seen other prosecutors play the number games, too. I don't understand why. Maybe they get caught up in all the legalese. I've also watched as lawyers on both sides snap on plastic gloves in court, covering themselves, protecting themselves from getting dirty in court, as if the dried blood on a victim's clothes could somehow infect them. It's all so sanitized, so clinical, so removed from the reality of the victim's suffering.

All these years later, I remember how my fiancé's bloody clothes were laid out at trial as an exhibit for the jury to see. They had a numbered tag attached to them on the defense table. I can remember him driving away that morning wearing those clothes, his blue eyes smiling, his arm waving out the car window as he left. Of course the jury never knew that. They also never saw the interior of the Jeep he was driving just before his murder. Blood had splattered on the roof and the doors. I'm sure the defense objected to their seeing that. It was too real and, of course, too prejudicial.

IN LIVING COLOR

It's even more difficult to allow a jury to get the smallest glimpse of the victim in life. Photos like high-school or college graduation portraits or family snapshots are rarely allowed, because the defense will argue they have no bearing on the guilt or innocence of the accused. True, perhaps, but that doesn't make it right. The only legal alternative is to find a solid evidentiary reason to allow photos showing victims in life to be brought in. Rick Distaso managed to get in evidence a video of Laci Peterson in life, puttering around her kitchen. He wisely found an evidentiary basis. Another alternative I often used in my opening statement was to describe the victim in as much detail as possible, so as to have those images fresh in the jury's mind.

I was determined to have the jury get a picture of the young victim in a murder case I tried. He was a thirteen-year-old boy nicknamed "Moonbeam," who was a good student and played in his school band. He wore a huge pair of glasses and, to me, was just precious. He was gunned down as part of a revenge killing. Revenge on a high-school band member? It was a case of mistaken identity. The two perps who shot Moonbeam had intended to shoot someone else, allegedly over a drug deal gone bad. As if *anyone* were the "right" person. So, from a distance, they murdered a thirteen-year-old boy walking along the sidewalk near the apartments where he lived. Testimony from the stand described the boy crawling along after the first round of fire, begging for his life and calling out for his mother as the rounds from an AK-47 continued to be pumped into him.

I had Moonbeam's class photo and I wanted to show it to the jury. Pursuant to defense argument, the judge disallowed it because it would "inflame the jury" if they saw the smiling young victim in his school photo. It would have made them think about how young, how innocent, he was. In the end, I managed to get the photo in. Moonbeam had on the same shirt in his photo as he did the night he was shot. For that evidentiary reason, it came into evidence as corroboration for eyewitness testimony. Throughout the state's case and until the defense team dramatically removed it, I kept it on display in front of the jury, so they would not forget that this case was about a little boy. A boy who played in the band and had a life before him. The jury rendered a guilty verdict.

From then on, I devised ways to get photos of the victims admitted into evidence so they would not end up as faceless numbers on a police report or a coroner's injury sketch on a diagram. In most cases, juries learn little if anything about a victim's life, but when a defendant takes the stand, they learn what a great guy he is, how much money he gives to charity, how he's involved with his community, and what a good father he is.

FAMILY TIES

Belongings or photos of a murder victim in court can definitely come back to haunt the defendant. But a defense lawyer's worst nightmare is seeing loving family members seated in court before the jury. This was especially true during the Scott Peterson murder trial, as Sharon Rocha and her family sat practically each and every day in row one, closest to the jury. The fact that people grieve and mourn a victim's death is an extremely undesirable notion to the defense. So with much twisting of tail and gnashing of teeth, a plan of counterattack was developed. Now it's standard operating procedure to kick the victims and their families out of the jury's view. Often a "Motion to Enjoin the Victim's Family and Friends from Sitting Directly Before the Jury and Showing Emotion in the Courtroom During the Trial" is filed. In fact, it is so often used that there's even a form for it accessible online, lifted directly from "A Capital Defender's Toolbox for Criminal Defense and Death-Penalty Litigation."

Another method to dehumanize the victim during trial involves a cynical and increasingly common practice employed by the defense, especially in high-profile cases: using the rule of sequestration to keep the victim's family members out of the courtroom. The rule of sequestration states that witnesses are not allowed to sit in the court while others testify. It was created for one valid reason: to prevent one witness's testimony from shading that of another.

Not surprisingly, this valid rule has been perverted into a dirty trick by attorneys. Victims' families are routinely thrown out of court under false pretenses—ostensibly because they are going to be called as witnesses for the defense. The tactic was employed by the defense in the case of Danielle van Dam, a bubbly seven-year-old who loved Mickey Mouse. In February 2002, van Dam was abducted from her own home in San Diego during the night as her family slept nearby, down the hall from her room. The little girl's blood and blond hair were later found in a neighbor's RV. Her left palm print was found, located as if she were reaching out to a built-in table beside the grown man's bed. Her blood was also found on the jacket of that same neighbor, David Westerfield. Danielle's nude body was finally discovered by a volunteer in the nearby desert, a few weeks after her disappearance. The badly decomposed body was identified partially by the little Mickey Mouse earring she still wore. At trial, the van Dam family was subpoenaed. Westerfield's attorney, Steven Feldman, actually claimed that the defendant felt threatened by Danielle's father and managed to have him thrown out of court. Danielle's mother, Brenda, had to sit there without her husband, listening to devastating testimony about the murder of her child. She was also ordered not to look directly at the jury, not to make any eye contact with them whatsoever. Danielle's grief-stricken mom was also forbidden by the court to wear a photo pin over her heart with the image of her dead daughter.

In August of that year, after the trial was over and Westerfield had been convicted of Danielle's kidnapping and murder, I met with her parents. I will never forget Brenda's lifeless voice that night at dinner. Her eyes welled with tears as she described to me the way she and her husband were treated in court. The revictimization of the family that was allowed to take place throughout the trial was devastating to them. Not only did they lose their daughter, they were mistreated by the justice system as well.

The same kind of battle loomed large in the Oklahoma City bombing trial in 1997—but with a twist. The defense for Timothy McVeigh objected to survivors' simply gathering together to watch the trial—which was moved to Denver—on closed-circuit television set up specifically to accommodate hundreds of crime victims and families. McVeigh's defense vowed they would ban survivors who could conceivably be called as witnesses from attending the trial as well. While cameras have traditionally been banned from federal courtrooms, survivors petitioned the court to allow the closed-circuit hookup. Thousands were up in arms over the possibility that survivors would be excluded from seeing the trial. After a major court battle, the closed-circuit viewings were ultimately allowed, although most victims and their families are not so lucky. McVeigh got the death penalty and was executed in 2001.

One answer I have devised to address this issue is to force the defense to make a proffer, an evidentiary showing before the judge and outside the presence of the jury, as to why a family member or friend of the victim is under defense subpoena. If that purpose is deemed "trial strategy" by the defense and therefore properly kept from the state, the showing could even be made in camera, or behind closed doors in the judge's chambers, and taken down by a court reporter. I believe the same rules should apply to the defense and the state. For instance, in the preliminary hearing for the Scott Peterson trial, Peterson's father, Lee, was called to the stand by the state in part to testify to the fact that he knew nothing of his son's purchase of a boat until after Laci went missing. That is legitimate grounds to call a family member from the other camp. Lee Peterson was allowed to sit in the courtroom afterward. His testimony, once given, could not taint or be tainted by later witnesses. The same reasoning applied to the Rocha family, who was also allowed in court during trial, seated in row one.

The attorneys' feet should be held to the fire as to the cause of the subpoena. In other words, hold them to their proffer. A simple way for prosecutors to avoid this whole issue is to call the family member or friend up front in their own case to allow cross-examination by the defense and then release the person as a witness. At that point, since the defense has had its chance to question the person at the beginning of the case, there is no reason to keep the friend or family member from the courtroom. The person should then be free to sit up front and center. If the defense's stated reason for calling the witness turns out to be false, I firmly believe a contempt order for the lawyers is in order. The defendant is not biased and the outcome of the trial is not tainted, but the lawyer is reprimanded and punished for mistreating the victim's family. Only when courts begin to protect victims' families will their mistreatment at the hands of the justice system come to an end. Until then, the airbrushing continues.

EXTREME MAKEOVERS

While the victim is all but airbrushed straight out of the courtroom, defendants get a little helpful airbrushing themselves. There's a world of difference between the scowling perpetrator in his mug shot and that well-groomed, nice-looking guy seated between a phalanx of defense attorneys. It's a transformation straight out of that creepy reality show *The Swan*, where contestants have tons of plastic surgery and then compete in a freaky "beauty pageant."

The murderous Menendez brothers got quite a makeover before their first trial in 1993. The two tennis-playing, sports-car-driving, silver-spoon-fed brats who brutally murdered their mother and father couldn't have looked more wholesome at trial than if they were posing for a Brooks Brothers catalog. Think they looked all *GQ* when they were spattered with blood, dreaming up a story for the cops? To see them in court in their preppy getups, complete with pullover sweaters and button-down shirts, you'd think they were coming straight out of an accounting class at Yale. The icing on the cake was supplied by defense attorney Leslie Abramson, who was constantly petting and patting them while picking imaginary lint off their cashmere sweaters, as if she were comforting two little lost boys. Hello! This was their parents' murder trial! You have to wonder how these nauseating displays of manufactured wholesomeness affected the jury. Obviously something worked, because the jury deadlocked in 1994. A year later, when their second trial began, the brothers grim weren't so lucky. In 1996, they were convicted of murder.

A FAMILY AFFAIR

The Menendez trial still has not been put to rest.

The brothers' convictions are on appeal in the Ninth U.S. Circuit Court of Appeals, a federal appeals court that reviews select cases out of state courts within their jurisdiction. Cases in state court are appealed directly to that state's appeal's court, such as the California Supreme Court. After that decision, either side can take the verdict up to a higher court, that being the district court of appeals. There are usually one to three federal district courts in each state, depending on the population. After making it through the district-court level, the lowest federal appeals court, the case goes on up to the circuit court. There are eleven circuits in the country, divided geographically. California is governed by the Ninth Circuit, well-known as kooky all around. Just so you get a sense of the jurists who will make the decision, keep this in mind: The judges reviewing the Menendezes' verdicts are part of the same court that declared it illegal for a little girl in public school to utter the words "under God" in the morning Pledge of Allegiance. The Menendez appeal will, no doubt, rely heavily on the "mistreatment" of the brother defendants. I got an earful of their story on July 15, 2004, when I interviewed Tammi Menendez, the wife of jailed double murderer Erik Menendez, on *Larry King Live*. She married Erik in prison after his conviction and sentence to life without parole.

She started writing him when the first trial started. Naturally Menendez wrote back. During our interview, she told me that while watching the first trial, her "heart went out to him. I felt sorry for what he was going through. And I wanted to reach out and say I supported him. Then he wrote back, so . . ."

So she married him! She also moved her young daughter, around five years old at the time, all the way from her home in a small town in Minnesota to just around the corner from the maximum-security prison in California that Menendez calls home. It's a family affair—she takes her little daughter to the prison for jailhouse visits in the family room with the other convicts.

In her mind, Tammi has managed to convince herself that the blame rests at the feet of Menedez's partner in evil, his brother, Lyle, with this rationale: "He [Erik] was the younger brother. . . . I know that Erik wouldn't have committed the crimes without [Lyle]. . . ."

Although Tammi doesn't think so, the truth about Erik's role in his parents' murders is hard to swallow. That night we played a portion of the testimony at trial for her. Here's what she heard:

UNIDENTIFIED FEMALE: *Did you empty the gun?*

ERIK MENENDEZ: *Every shell I had.*

UNIDENTIFIED FEMALE: *And what did you do after you reloaded?*

MENENDEZ: *I ran around and shot my mom. I was just firing as I went into the room, I just started firing.*

UNIDENTIFIED FEMALE: *In what direction?*

MENENDEZ: *In front of me.*

UNIDENTIFIED FEMALE: *What was in front of you?*

MENENDEZ: *My parents.*

UNIDENTIFIED FEMALE: *So you were firing at your parents?*

MENENDEZ: *Yes.*

I have a hard time dealing with the idea that it is so simple for someone who has heard the truth to gloss over it. Erik Menendez makes no bones about it—he shot his own mother in cold blood. I know he claims his father molested him, but no claims were ever made about his mother. I take his abuse claims about his father with a big box of salt. I wondered about Tammi's personal ability to ignore her husband's brutal ambush of his own mom. I wanted to try to get inside the mind of someone who professed to love a man who admits to savagely killing his mother.

Our conversation continued:

GRACE: *It's my understanding they've got life without parole. I would like to ask Mrs. Menendez a question. I just— The dichotomy of shooting your mother dead and then*

going out and hiring a private tennis coach. You know,
when I was that age, I was working two jobs and going
to school. A private tennis coach. Your mother is dead?
I just have a real problem with that. I know that you
say your husband is sensitive, and I believe you, but do
you ever allow yourself—I know love is blind, but do
you ever allow yourself to think about the brutal nature
of the murder of Mrs. Menendez, Kitty Menendez?

TAMMI MENENDEZ: *I think about it a lot, and I think*
about the crimes, and I think about
what happened. But there again, I
understand the abuse that he went
through. And—

LARRY KING: *But the mother didn't do any of the abuse, did*
she?

MENENDEZ: *No. But psychologically, you know . . .*

KING: *She supported the father.*

MENENDEZ: *Very bizarre. Very bizarre house. A lot going on.*
Very dominant father. There were many witnesses
that testified to that.

I was obviously confounded at her decision to uproot her little girl
to be closer to Erik Menendez. I asked about the effect the relationship
may have on her daughter.

GRACE: *I respect Mrs. Menendez, she seems like a kind and*
gentle person. But I worry about the little girl and

*what possessed Mrs. Menendez to uproot her little girl
and move her down the street from a jail.*

MENENDEZ: *That's a difficult question to answer. You know, for
a while, I did not bring her into the prison system.
I kept her away from being subjected to that. But I
brought her a few times for holidays, and she—
It's not as bad as what people think, as far as the
visiting room. She loves to go, and she doesn't have
problems with it right now.*

KING: *But she's going to grow up with some understanding of
who her stepfather is.*

MENENDEZ: *She will. She sees him on TV every now and
then. I don't let her watch anything that's on,
but she knows that he's, you know, popular, and
she deals with it very well. Psychologically, she
seems to be fine with it.*

KING: *Do you have any worries about Erik with her?*

MENENDEZ: *Not at all.*

KING: *Bad influence and the lot?*

MENENDEZ: *He's so good with her. He's taught her a lot of
good. He's very gentle. He has more patience
than I do.*

This exchange proved to me that not all airbrushing begins and
ends in the courtroom. When I think back on the interview with Erik

Menendez's wife, I extend her mind-set to potential jurors. It strikes fear in my heart—a fear that those in a search for truth, responsible for the implementation of justice, could be like Tammi Menendez. Blind by choice. I pray it isn't so.

UNFAITHFUL

I watched every minute of former NBA star Jayson Williams's manslaughter trial on my Court TV show, *Closing Arguments.* We learned during the trial that on the night he shot Gus Christofi, Williams had made fun of and derided Christofi for being hired help. The limousine driver was far too starstruck to respond, much less walk off the job. Christofi had even brought along an instant camera, hoping to get a shot of himself with Williams. That never happened. Instead of a photo, Christofi got a gunshot to the chest that left him dead on the floor of Williams's multimillion-dollar mansion.

That night, after a party with his posse, Williams had a snootful of booze and brought everybody back to his place for a "tour" of his mansion. Once in his bedroom, Williams took down a loaded shotgun from his gun case and cracked it open, then shut, while pointing it directly at Christofi, who stood only two feet away. The gun "went off," although a witness testified he saw Williams pull the trigger. As Gus Christofi lay dying on the floor, there were no prayers, no last rites, no comfort or solace for him by Williams. Instead, before the man was even dead, Williams wiped his own prints from the gun and grabbed the dying man's hand, placing it on the gun to make it look as if Christofi had committed suicide.

During the trial, I watched Williams in court. It was an Oscar-winning performance. The serious and subdued defendant sported a huge silver cross on his lapel. I'm all for wearing crosses, but not when the crucifix is being used to sway a jury. Think about it: In all the years Williams played ball, do you recall ever seeing him wear a cross around his neck, boast a Christian bumper sticker on his Mercedes, or even sport a tiny crucifix tie tack? Did he ever mention his religion on air during all the time he was an NBC sports analyst? No. But when push came to shove, Williams pulled out a giant cross lapel pin for his trial. After the jury acquitted him for the shooting death of Mr. Christofi, a photograph was taken the next day of Williams on a patio of his mansion, where he and his wife were enjoying a big bottle of champagne. He wasn't wearing his cross.

DOG BITE

When the Williams jury spoke, court watchers were stunned to hear they acquitted on the top count of aggravated manslaughter, deadlocked on simple manslaughter, only finding culpability on lesser charges like tampering with and fabricating evidence. But don't worry, it ain't over yet. After the stunning decision by the New Jersey jury, a jury that included one lady juror who reportedly had eyes only for Williams throughout the trial, the state swears they will retry the deadlocked counts. But that's not the end of the story. In the first trial, trial judge Edward Coleman refused to allow prosecutors to introduce the similar transaction evidence regarding Williams's dog, Zeus. The alleged incident happened in August 2001, six months before Christofi died in Williams's bedroom after being shot in the chest.

In early 2004, in the midst of jury selection, a handwritten, anonymous letter made its way to the prosecutor's office. The letter directed state investigators to locate and question Williams's former teammate "Dwayne somebody." After investigators identified and tracked down the former Nets player Dwayne Schintzius, he told a shocking story about an August 8, 2001, incident when he, Williams, and another friend, Chris Duckery, went to dinner at the Mountain View Chalet. According to court papers, after returning to Williams's home, Schintzius said he bet $100 that he could drag Zeus, a Rottweiler and reportedly a trained attack dog, out of the house. Well, Schintzius said he did in fact get the dog out of the house, and when he won the bet, he told Williams to pay up. According to Schintzius an angry Williams stalked inside his multimillion-dollar pad, returned with a shotgun, and shot Zeus point-blank, killing him.

As if that weren't enough, Williams's ex-teammate reported that after shooting his own dog, Williams pointed the gun at Schintzius and told him to clean up the dog's dead body "or you're next." Zeus's remains were never found by investigators.

When the story got out, animal lovers went berserk, and rightfully so. It almost seemed as if more people were enraged over the shooting of the dog than of the person, Gus Christofi. As of this writing, the former NBA star now faces a full-court press by an animal-cruelty complaint for allegedly killing his dog with a shotgun. The New Jersey Society for the Prevention of Cruelty to Animals filed the complaint within months of the deadlock over the alleged incident with his pet, Zeus. By that time, of course, the statute of limitations for criminal charges on animal cruelty had expired, so the SPCA opted for civil charges carrying a maximum fine of $250.

At the time, Williams's camp responded when Judy Smith, a spokeswoman for Williams, suggested that Jersey prosecutors had cooked up the whole thing and stated, "This is a blatant attempt to pile on and create publicity about an issue that a judge had already ruled has no place in the trial."

As of this writing, prosecutors are asking the trial judge not only to retry Williams's manslaughter case in Hunterdon County, the original trial venue and where the Christofi killing took place, but also to reconsider his earlier decision not to let the jury in the manslaughter trial hear about the alleged dog killing and yet another dangerous alleged shooting incident in the parking lot of the Meadowlands Sports Complex. Williams is currently scheduled to be retried on the remaining reckless-manslaughter charge.

MODEL MOMS

Could anybody ever forget Pam Smart, who arranged to have her husband murdered by a teenaged lover? Or Susan Smith, who buckled her two boys into their car seats before drowning them and blaming an "unknown black man" for the crime? Those two presented like school librarians in court.

A review of "airbrushed" defendants just wouldn't be complete without Sara Jane Olson, the doctor's wife and mother of three who in a former life was known as Kathleen Soliah, a member of the terrorist group Symbionese Liberation Army. Authorities had been looking for Soliah for years because of her involvement in the terrorist group's plot to plant bombs under two police cruisers in 1975 as revenge for the killing of six SLA members earlier that year. Before Olson was indicted in 1976, she left California, changed her name, and started a new life.

The woman who eluded authorities for over two decades had recast herself as a church volunteer and soccer mom. During an interview with ABC News after her arrest, she described herself as "just an average American woman." Not exactly. Her photo had appeared on the television show *America's Most Wanted* in a segment on the twenty-fifth anniversary of the deadly activities of the group. The FBI was offering $20,000 for information leading to her arrest.

In June 1999, while she was on her way to teach a citizenship class to recently arrived immigrants in St. Paul, Minnesota, she was pulled over by police. At the time she was arrested, she was also wanted in connection with a 1975 bank robbery in which Myrna Opsahl, a forty-two-year-old mother of four, was murdered. "She can change her name, and she can pretend to be a model citizen," said Jon Opsahl, whose mom was gunned down at the bank where she had gone to deposit the money from her church's offering plate. "But I just want her and everyone else to know that she really can't earn that status, because twenty-five years ago she helped murder a true model citizen: my mother." Opsahl could see through the airbrushing.

Worried that a jury might see through it, too, Olson derailed plans for what was sure to be a sensational trial and took a plea bargain in October 2001, pleading guilty to two counts of possessing explosive devices with intent to murder police officers. Moments later, she denied her guilt to reporters, saying she feared she couldn't get a fair trial in the wake of the September 11 terrorist attacks. The judge handed down two mandatory sentences of ten years to life, which Olson accepted on the condition that she would serve only five years and four months. But that wasn't the end of it. The Board of Prison Terms stepped in and amended her sentence to fourteen years to life. The saga continued in 2002, when Olson's lawyers appealed that decision. Ultimately, Sacramento Superior Court judge Thomas Cecil agreed that the board had ruled improperly. Despite pleas for leniency, Olson wound up getting thirteen years in prison. Olson couldn't airbrush away her past, but she did rack up a pretty steep bill for the taxpayers while trying.

Speaking of soccer moms, the ultimate acting award should probably go to Betty Broderick. Meredith Baxter portrayed Broderick in a made-for-TV movie that chilled viewers to the bone. Broderick basically lived in a jealous rage after her husband, Dan Broderick, a prominent California lawyer, divorced her and married a younger woman. Being angry about the turn of events is understandable, but leaving hundreds of obscene messages on the newlyweds' answering machine and then plowing her car through their front door was a little over the top. On November 5, 1989, Broderick broke into their home late one night and executed the couple as they slept in their bed. She was a woman seething with out-of-control rage.

To see Broderick in court, though, with her sensible blond bob, understated makeup, and classic sweater set, you'd think she was on her way to volunteer as a pink lady at the hospital. Broderick stood trial for the murders twice. The first trial, in October 1990, ended in a hung jury. Twelve months later, the jury from the second trial convicted on two counts of second-degree murder. I believe one of the reasons the jury ultimately saw through her facade was that the prosecution had managed to introduce some of those hateful answering-machine messages to legally show Broderick's frame of mind. In doing so, they exposed her for what she really was—an angry and hateful monster.

There are only a few ways for the jury to get to see the real defendant. Mug-shot photos and videotaped statements made at the time of the search or arrest can offer a glimpse of the person as he or she was at the time of the alleged crime. Mug shots are often kept out of evidence under the claim that they are of little evidentiary value. Not so. I once had a mug shot taken of a drug offender wearing the same easily identifiable thousand-dollar workout suit at the time of arrest that matched the eyewitness description of another drug deal that had gone down a few days before. How much more relevant can a mug shot get?

Remember those mug shots of a drunken Nick Nolte, Diana Ross, and Glen Campbell? They may look pretty buttoned up and straitlaced in court, but the police photos tell the jury the real story about the night of the arrest—they were drunk and they were driving! Those mug shots and those videotaped statements should be admitted into evidence. They enhance the testimony of cops and eyewitnesses like nothing else. Don't believe me? Go online and check out Nick Nolte's mug shot. I rest my case.

IT'S A RAP (SHEET)

A defendants' makeover doesn't end with a few cosmetic changes. The defense is allowed to rewrite history and pretend in front of the jurors that the case they are trying represents the defendant's very first brush with the law. To hear it in court, most defendants are as pure as the driven snow and land in court due to a huge misunderstanding or poor policing. What the jury doesn't know is that a large percentage of defendants on trial are repeat offenders. Under our justice system, a jury may not be told that the defendant has a rap sheet as long as a football field, a propensity for crime, and a knack for working the system. The reasoning behind this ruling is so the jury will decide the case on the facts, not on the defendant's track record. Even more disturbing is that more often than not, similar transactions are disallowed from evidence. It's true—when defendants have committed a "fingerprint crime" before—same scheme, same design, same MO, same jurisdiction even—the jury rarely knows about it.

In the Jayson Williams trial, even though Williams faced charges stemming from a deadly mix of guns and violence, the jury never heard evidence that this was by no means his first encounter with either. Although the jury did learn that the athlete had shot and killed the unarmed Christofi, the judge tossed out evidence that the defendant had brutally shot his dog in the head when the animal didn't behave as Williams wanted. He even threatened to shoot the friend who'd witnessed the dog's cold-blooded shooting. We knew that Williams had grabbed a gun and shot out the tires of a security van parked in a public parking lot at the Meadowlands Sports Complex, but the jury didn't. The charges were dropped after Williams agreed to enter a pretrial intervention program. Instead, the jury heard in opening statements that Williams was just a big "teddy bear" who's all about love. The jury never had a clue, and that's how the judge wanted it. The most shocking exclusion: The judge ruled out evidence that the former NBA star was intoxicated at the time he shot Christofi to death. It's downright baffling, especially when you consider that Williams had run up a $600-plus bar tab with his friends that night and registered a blood-alcohol level of 0.12 a full eight hours after the shooting. (The state's standard for intoxication in 2002 was 0.10).

The rules regarding similar transactions are extremely draconian at present, often including time limits as to how far back the state can go to show prior bad acts. Such time limits thwart the system. For instance, that type of time limit could conceivably preclude Michael Jackson's 1993 civil settlement arising out of alleged child molestation from being heard by a jury, as it is over ten years old. It's likely a jury will never hear the actual number of young boys who claim Michael Jackson fondled or molested them.

In the Scott Peterson case, there was partial suppression of bloodhound evidence indicating that Laci's body, not Laci in life, had been in Peterson's office storage unit. In the Jack Kevorkian trials in 1999, the jury never knew exactly how many people he had "assisted" in their own deaths.

I call for past bad acts to be allowed into evidence, especially when they are probative as to the motive or state of mind of the defendant or the victim. Until the courts relax the rules, toss out inappropriate time limits, and allow the jury to know the truth, the whole truth, and nothing but the truth, the airbrushing of defendants' true nature will continue.

THE DEAD CAN TELL
NO TALES

They're called dying declarations—the last words uttered in life by victims. Defense teams in courtrooms across the country stay up nights trying to find ways around letting these words make their way to a jury. Now, under a U.S. Supreme Court ruling made in 2004, *U.S. v. Crawford*, calling for the cross-examination of such a statement before it can come into court, it is highly unlikely they ever will. When Ted Binion was murdered, the crime scene was set up to look as if Binion had overdosed on heroin. After Binion was found dead, Rick Tabish, the lover of Binion's girlfriend, Sandy Murphy, was discovered out in a secret location in the desert digging up Binion's buried silver bullion. The night before the millionaire's murder, Binion called his lawyer. In that call, Binion said he wanted to change his will to cut Murphy out of it. At the time, he stated, "If I'm dead, you'll know what happened." He didn't make it through the night. After a jury conviction, an appeals court ruled that Binion's last words were inadmissible because of a hearsay challenge, and the case was reversed.

In 1999, Rae Carruth, the former NFL wide receiver for the Carolina Panthers, was charged with masterminding the murder of his girlfriend, Cherica Adams. The couple had gone to a movie one evening in South Charlotte, North Carolina, and left the theater in separate cars. The twenty-four-year-old Adams told a hospital nurse that while Carruth's white Ford Expedition hit the brakes in front of her black BMW, another car pulled up directly beside her. The driver opened fire on her. Four bullets hit her in the back, damaging her stomach, liver, and right lung. Despite her injuries, Adams was able to call 911 on her cell phone.

According to court papers, Adams became immediately suspicious that Carruth was behind the shooting. During the trial, one prosecution witness said he heard police ask the victim who she thought was responsible for the shooting and she replied, "My husband, I mean, my boyfriend."

Adams was rushed to the hospital, where she delivered her and Carruth's son ten weeks early. She managed to hang on, slipping in and out of consciousness for a month. During that time, she recounted three pages of notes filled with her recollections about the shooting. In December of that year, Adams died. Her baby was stricken with cerebral palsy for life as a result of the shooting. Adams's mother is left to raise her grandson now that her daughter is dead.

What could possibly be the motive in such a hideous crime? In 2000, at the beginning of the trial, prosecutors said Carruth set up Adams's murder because he didn't want the baby and had no desire to pay child support. The dying words of Cherica Adams lived on and were allowed into evidence, over the strenuous objections of the Carruth defense. This instance firmly supports a change in the law to more freely admit dying declarations and spoken fears by the murder victim.

Will similar evidence be admitted in the Robert Blake murder trial? I have spoken many times with Bonny Lee Bakley's sister, Margerry Bakley. She described in chilling detail how her sister was afraid of

Blake even after giving birth to his child, Rose. Margerry Bakley told me Bonny Lee stated that she feared Blake would murder her and claimed that he had even shown her a bullet and said, "This has your name on it." In my assessment of the pretrial rulings Judge Darlene Schempp has made so far, including completely dismissing the case of Blake's codefendant, Earle Caldwell, in 2003, I find Schempp incredibly defense-oriented. I pray that Bakely's own words of premonition and warning as to her own murder will not be suppressed in court by the judge at the request of the defense. The victim, Bonny Lee Bakley, must be heard.

CHAPTER SIX

THE POWER OF THE STATE IS A MYTH

IF YOU BELIEVE IN SIGNS–AND I DO–CONSIDER that Lady Justice gave us a powerful one around the time of the manslaughter trial of former NBA star Jayson Williams. High up on the roof of the Somerville, New Jersey, courthouse where the case was heard, she stood blindfolded with her sword in one hand, the scales of justice in the other. For decades, that statue has proudly presided over the courthouse and all that has gone on within its walls. But as the Williams acquittal and mistrial approached, a windstorm brewed outside and ultimately the powerful winds tore the scales from Lady Justice's hands and robbed her of her ability to weigh the truth.

Throughout the trial, Williams's well-known defense attorney, Billy Martin, constantly referred to all the "power" of the state's investigators and police that had come down on his client. The truth, in fact, was quite different. Before Costas "Gus" Christofi was gunned down with Williams's twelve-gauge shotgun, the police had admired the athlete. When they arrived on the scene after the shooting, they certainly were not there to frame him. But that didn't stop his attorneys from referring to all the state's witnesses as part of one big plot out to get Williams. It simply wasn't true. There was, in fact, a conspiracy going on—the one Williams and his posse had orchestrated. Williams was acquitted of the most serious charge of aggravated manslaughter, and the jury dead-locked on the lesser count of reckless manslaughter. So much for the all-powerful state railroading an innocent man.

Another athlete—O. J. Simpson—claimed police had framed him, as did David Westerfield, the convicted killer of seven-year-old Danielle van Dam. Westerfield also claims that the girl's family was in on the plot to get him. During Winona Ryder's shoplifting trial, her defense attorney, Mark Geragos, claimed that the security guards at Saks Fifth Avenue in Beverly Hills were part of a plot to set up one of America's most popular celebrities. As defenses go, it's a pretty common argument: The state is always out to get its client. The thinking behind the claim is, the state will do anything and everything in order to secure a conviction—as if a conviction will somehow get that prosecutor a raise or a promotion or a big fat bonus check. That's not the way it happens. The morning after a trial, prosecutors go back to their offices to wade through their mountains of unopened mail and all the new files that have piled up on their desks while they were in court. They settle in and begin all over again. There is no raise. There is no promotion. There is no big fat bonus for a convic-tion. There is, however, a new set of crime victims calling out for help.

The reality is that "the state" is the individual prosecutor mak-ing the case and taking the heat. In order to buy the defense's conspir-acy theory, you must believe that the individual—the local county prosecutor—wants desperately to send the wrong person to jail and that the prosecutor is somehow morally dedicated to a conviction re-gardless of whether it's right or wrong. That's completely absurd.

I have great faith in the Constitution, which was conceived and created in part to protect the accused—the defendant—on trial from the power of the state. The trial-related personal freedoms in the Bill of Rights protect the defendant—not the victim and certainly not the prosecution. The defendant has the right to trial by jury, not the state. In many jurisdictions, if a defendant wants a bench trial (with no jury), he gets one, whether the state agrees or not. It is the defendant who has the right to appeal over many issues, not the state. Practically every conviction at trial is appealed, be it a shoplifting or a murder one case. And if the defendant can't afford an appellate lawyer, he doesn't have to worry! We pay for the appeals process for him!

When a jury acquits, however, that's it for the state. The prosecution normally doesn't get to appeal. The case is over. The state bears the burden of proof and must go forward with evidence at trial while the defendant has the Fifth Amendment right to remain silent. The accused quite often neither takes the stand nor puts up a single shred of evidence or a single witness. It's all okay under our Constitution.

The burden is also heavily on the state during the pre-trial "discovery" phase. The state must hand over evidence to the defense well before trial, including witness lists and scientific or crime-lab evidence such as fingerprint and DNA results, statements, and police information. The defense, even in states that tout reciprocal discovery, hands over far less to the state, and when it doesn't, either by accident or by design, there are few or no repercussions when the defense disobeys the rules. Here's why: If the defense hands over the name of an "expert" just before that witness is to be called, theoretically, under the rules, the defense can't call the expert because it didn't play fair and allow the state time to prepare. The reality: If the defense is in fact stopped from calling the witness, there will likely be a reversal on appeal, because the accused was not allowed to present his entire defense. The state would have to start all over with a new trial, from square one. Rarely does the state choose that option. If the reverse happens, the witness or evidence will be excluded or a long delay in trial granted in order for the defense to prepare for the new evidence. We saw this scenario play out several times in the Scott Peterson trial, each time resulting in an extended delay. Delays such as that traditionally work strongly against the state during a trial.

When it comes down to what goes on in the courtroom, it's the state versus the massive power of the defendant's constitutional protections. But the defense, even with multimillion-dollar pockets for investigators and experts, will argue to a jury that the prosecution's the one with un-limited resources and manpower to prosecute the "little guy." We also saw this argument in the Peterson case. In truth, Geragos ended up with some of the world's most renowned experts, like Dr. Henry Lee and Cyril Wecht, at his beck and call.

In practically every case I've ever covered or tried, I've heard the defense refer to the overwhelming power of the state. In doing so, the lawyers suggest to a jury that at trial everything was stacked against the lone defendant seated at the counsel table. When I was prosecut-ing, I felt that the exact opposite was true—and still do.

I never know whether to laugh or cry when I hear defense attorneys attack the all-powerful state. It reminds me of something that happened early in my career. I was on my way to answer a calendar call where the first case of the day was a murder trial. The shooting had left one man dead and another with a colostomy bag for life. All over a handful of "dope ropes"—gold chains—on display in the showcase of a pawnshop. En route, I had to wait at a red light several miles away from the court-house. While my car was stopped, dark, foul-smelling smoke began pouring out from under the hood of my Honda. I didn't have the time or the money to fix the thing, so I just kept driving, hoping it would keep running. That morning, I sat there thinking about the trial, wondering if I would end up smelling like exhaust fumes when I got to the courtroom. I looked over to the left, expecting to see another driver staring at my smoking hood and holding his nose, but instead there was a huge tractor-trailer sitting there. He could either go straight or turn left—I could only turn right. But when the light changed, he took a right turn, his giant wheels literally rolling over on top of my car. Guess what? The "state" screeched to a halt that morning because I wasn't there to pre-sent its case. The "state" was stuck at a red light with a tractor-trailer on its hood. The state that is spoken of so anonymously, as if it's this secret agency, is really a collection of people who are public servants pursuing justice. In this case, the state was a person standing in front of the jury with big dark circles under her eyes and resoled shoes. That is the state, okay? That is the state. And that's what people really don't get.

Another popular strategy among defense attorneys is to characterize the prosecutor as this Darth Vader–ish figure whose limitless power is hell-bent on persecuting and destroying helpless defendants with a single motion. I promise you, I never felt that sense of invincibility trudging through housing projects in my $39 dress from Chadwick's, trying to deliver subpoenas to witnesses who weren't exactly happy to see me at their front door. I did, though, always draw great strength from believing deeply that I had right on my side. I felt the same way every time I entered a courtroom. Speaking directly to a jury as I began my opening statement at trial, I would always be reminded that the real power of the state is the power of right, the power to do right. That is the one real power of the state.

MONEY TALKS...
JUSTICE WALKS

The defense frequently and easily outspends the state—especially in high-profile cases. I have no problem with a high-priced defense, as long as a jury is not tricked into an acquittal. The defense likely outspent the state in the Jayson Williams trial as well as in the O. J. Simpson "trial of the century." Here's a little-known fact: Often when defendants don't have the money to outspend the state, the defense can get public funds by petitioning the court for money to compensate experts. We the taxpayers pay for that. Our system guarantees a free lawyer if a defendant cannot pay for one, and at trial that is extended to include defense investigators and experts as well. Keep in mind that when the trial is over, if it ends in a conviction, the taxpayer also pays for the lawyers on appeal; and in some cases appeals go on for ten to fifteen years and wind their way all the way up to the U.S. Supreme Court.

We have recently passed the fortieth anniversary of the landmark case that made it possible for the likes of Timothy McVeigh, Terry Nichols, the Menendez brothers, the D.C. snipers, and countless others to rack up exorbitant costs at trial and hand the taxpayers the bill. Before the case of *Gideon v. Wainwright,* indigent defendants who were accused of crimes could be convicted and sent to jail without the benefit of a lawyer. The Supreme Court reformed that practice in 1963, ruling that the Sixth and Fourteenth Amendment rights to counsel and to equal protection under the law apply to poor and rich alike.

The kicker is that we, the taxpayers, foot the bill for both the local public defenders appointed to criminal cases and private, high-priced defense lawyers, as well as their posse of consultants, experts, and investigators. In California, David Westerfield and killer brothers Erik and Lyle Menendez hired private lawyers initially. But when the well runs dry, as it did in those cases, the public pays. The rationale is that defendants who have built up a relationship with a specific attorney can likely keep the attorney even if they cannot afford to because there's always us—people like my parents, who worked all their lives—to foot the bill.

The costs incurred with these cases are immense. Lawyers' fees in capital cases range from $500,000 to $1 million. In the Menendez case, Leslie Abramson represented the defendants in their first trial, which ended with a hung jury. At retrial, when the two had run through all their dead parents' money, the judge appointed the high-paid lawyer to the case because she knew the case thoroughly. The same thing happened with Westerfield's defense. Renowned lawyers Steven Feldman and Robert Boyce represented him at trial for huge fees. They later advised the court that they had used up all their client's money, including nearly $500,000 realized from the sale of his house. The judge booted them from the case in favor of cheaper counsel. An appellate court later reversed that decision, and the much more expensive team was reinstated. Check your tax bill for the damage.

The defense of the Washington, D.C., sniper John Allen Muhammad and teenage gunman Lee Boyd Malvo cost Virginia taxpayers more than $1 million. The defense bill for Muhammad was up to $900,000 as of spring 2004. The cost of their appeals will drive the tab even higher. Virginia doesn't put a cap on lawyers' fees in capital cases, where their hourly rate hovers around $150 per hour. Taxpayers paid nearly $60,000 on expert witnesses for Malvo alone. The total for his defense as of May 2004: $1,021,337. And before you choke on the $4 million defense we provided for Oklahoma City bomber Terry Nichols, compare it to the outrageous $13.8 million bill we paid for the defense of his confederate, convicted mass murderer Timothy McVeigh.

Consider this tidbit from our legal system's strange but frighteningly true files: North Carolina residents picked up part of the tab for the defense of Rae Carruth during his trial on the murder-for-hire case of his pregnant girlfriend, Cherica Adams. The cost of paying defense attorneys David Rudolph and Christopher Fialko proved too much for the wide receiver who was paid a reported $40,000 a game. The state picked up the slack. Rudolph justified the state-funded end run around justice at the time by saying, "The only important thing is that Rae Carruth is receiving a competent, caring defense."

Under North Carolina law, defendants in capital (death-penalty) cases have the right to two publicly funded attorneys who are supposed to be paid $85 an hour, but the final compensation is up to the trial judge. In high-profile cases like Carruth's, where the attorneys are savvy and aggressive, judges will grant extra money for experts and even jury consultants. Residents wound up paying more than $100,000 for Carruth, who was found guilty of conspiracy to commit murder but walked on the first-degree murder charge. I wonder who will pay for the care and feeding of his son, who was born with cerebral palsy because of the hit he ordered on his baby's mother?

Now consider this: How did a California fertilizer salesman pay for attorney-to-the-stars Mark Geragos's services? It's a mystery. At the time of his arrest, Scott Peterson stated he could not afford a lawyer, and the court appointed a public defender. In an interview with *People* magazine, the Petersons refused to comment on what they were paying Geragos to defend their son, but did say he wasn't doing it pro bono.

Estimates put his fee at $1 million. Forensic expert Henry Lee and medical expert Cyril Wecht, who are also part of Team Peterson, don't come cheap either. Reports indicated that many members of the Peterson family (including Scott's siblings) have taken out second mortgages on their homes and run through a good chunk of their savings—and that was before the trial even started!

As discussed in an earlier chapter, I strongly suspect the state footed at least part of the bill. The alternative would have been to appoint a new, court-appointed legal team midway through trial, like the local public defenders who had the case to begin with. This is tantamount to starting over from square one. You can almost guarantee that it would be argued that such a move would slow down the trial and put Peterson at a disadvantage, having a new lawyer unfamiliar with the case now trying to play catch-up. Both are true. Although a public-defender-based team would not incur legal fees, as PDs are already paid a salary by the state, it is highly likely the court would have left Geragos on the case at a reduced fee. On appeal, the Peterson tab continues to mount.

YOUR TAX DOLLARS AT WORK

Another misconception about "the power of the state" is the myth that the government—the evil empire—is taking in billions and billions of dollars in taxes that somehow go to help in convicting innocent people of crimes they didn't commit. That's simply ridiculous! I've often wondered what happens to all the money I've been paying in taxes all these years. What I see is Congress spending millions and millions of dollars on an outrageous list of projects that are nothing more than political boondoggles.

As I write this, I have just learned that Oregon prisoners now have flat-screen TVs to enjoy in the privacy of their own jail cells! Although the Oregon State Correctional Institution's administrator, Randy Geer, contends that the televisions are "not a luxury item," the fact is, the Salem prisoners now get to kick back on their bunks and enjoy brand-new flat-screen TVs that most of us on the outside don't have. The seven-inch sets are copies of flat-screen models in cars and airplanes. The inmates contribute to the cost of the sets from money they've earned while working in prison, but related costs are all paid for by the taxpayer. Oregon is not alone in making prisoners feel at home behind bars. Fifteen other states allow in-cell televisions.

Still a skeptic? When I think of all the rehabilitation programs, probation officers, and investigators currently needed around the country, the following is even more disturbing. Take a look at this short list of the government's pork project initiated after 2001. These are your tax dollars at work:

$50 million to build an indoor rain forest in Iowa

$1.5 million for a statue of the Roman god Vulcan in Birmingham, Alabama

$489,000 for swine-waste management in North Carolina

$273,000 to help Missouri combat "Goth culture"

$50,000 for a tattoo-removal program in California

$26,000 to study how thoroughly Americans rinse their dishes

$4,572 given to Las Vegas Helicopters, a company that performs airborne weddings officiated by Elvis Presley impersonators as part of a post–September 11, 2001, aid-to-airlines package

Those are just a few examples of the government's penchant to spend money on just about everything—except the justice system.

These are funds that could be used to staff hotlines, hire victims' counselors, and add desperately needed child-welfare workers, prosecutors, investigators, public defenders, or additional state court judges. The search for justice is shortchanged once again.

SLAVE WAGES

Cops and prosecutors are underpaid and overworked. I know that many people in many walks of life can make the same claim, but it strikes me that nobody is calling most of them out onto the street at 3:00 A.M. to stop a gunfight, a drug deal, or a domestic dispute. I can't even count the number of times police officers came in on their free time to go out with me to take crime-scene photos and help me work cases.

When the bank alarm goes off down the block, everybody in the diner doesn't look at each other to hop in their cars and run over and shoot the robbers—we all look to the cops. When our kids go missing or the house is burgled or the car is stolen, they answer the call. And the fact that they live on such low pay for such dangerous and important work is shocking.

It's much the same for prosecutors. In my case, coming off *Law Review,* I started out at $31,000 and after ten years of hard litigation, never got past $50,000. After prosecuting all day, I held down two different night jobs to make ends meet. I taught law classes at a downtown university in Atlanta, one in the law school and one in the undergraduate school. Many prosecutors have second jobs because state and federal salaries are so low. Lawyers in private practice make double or even triple what prosecutors do. I'm not complaining—I continued to prosecute because it was what I wanted to do and why I had gone to law school in the first place.

I'm not saying it wasn't hard, though. I can still remember coming home after class at nearly 10:00 P.M. and cutting my grass because I couldn't afford a lawn service to do it. The neighbors were so good; they never complained. I wondered—and still wonder—how cops do it. They have families to feed and second jobs to work through the night after they finish their shifts.

Low pay is a problem on the federal level also, to the extent that it's actually causing a defection within the FBI. It also raises the risk of corruption and espionage. FBI officials have been quoted as saying high debt resulting from low pay could make agents more vulnerable to offers of spying on the United States for cash. Taking the oath of public service is more like taking a vow of poverty.

According to an April 2004 report in *USA Today*, the base salary for new FBI agents is about $39,000. Houston cops start at $28,000. Chicago weighs in at $37,000, and in the capital of the world, New York City, rookies start at $44,000. Okay, Officers, rush out of the police station and stop a bullet for that!

Aside from rudimentary cost-of-living raises, salaries have not changed appreciably for the last decade. Think about it: Within that short time span, two U.S. counterintelligence agents were convicted of selling secrets to the Russians. Earl Pitts and Robert Hanssen both went down in history as traitors, making money off the sale of U.S. security secrets. Those are the two we know of.

Forget what you've seen in the movies. Prosecutors, unlike their silk-stocking opponents on the other side of the courtroom, very often do not have an army of flunkies and assistants. To prepare for a morning calendar call of, say, a hundred cases, I would sit in my office and dig through five or six boxes sent from the district attorney's office trying to find the eighty files I needed for the next day's arraignment. Without fail they'd be in the wrong offices or lost in the filing room. Hours would be spent just gathering cases for a calendar call—much less preparing for trial. There were no secretaries, no assistants, no paralegals. I wish I had a nickel for every time I had to go to the crime lab to drop something off or pick something up. I'd be rich if I had a dollar for all the days I had to drive to the police station, where I'd be hassled about where I parked when I was there to pick up fingerprint cards or a police report or simply to drop off a subpoena.

I can't even guess how many times I would go to the local 7-Eleven to get two or three packs of film for my Polaroid camera. It would kill me, because at the time they were $8 a pack. I needed the film to take additional crime-scene photos to show to the jury the next day. If something came up during the trial that I wanted the jury to see, I would drive over to take pictures and tromp around in my high heels getting whatever I could. I kept my camera in the backseat of my car until it was stolen (twice) during a trial. Thieves busted out the back window of my Honda to get the cameras or the car phone (they were installed then), and the office threatened not to give me another one. I started locking it in the trunk when I went to scenes.

I often bought my own supplies to use for visual aids at trial and never turned in my receipts because I was convinced that the district attorney would think I'd been extravagant in buying markers and artist's poster board—the big, thick kind a jury could see from a distance. Before closing arguments in a case, I would go to a local crafts store to pick up what I needed, then stay up half the night, crouched on the floor, listing summation points in blue marker on the boards from my trial notes. I can still hear them squeaking across the matte white surface. I'll never forget the sharp smell of the ink that always seemed to wind up all over the sides of my palms. That was the extent of the high-tech razzle-dazzle *I* used to wow juries.

My state-of-the-art visuals threatened to break the bank in *State v. David Lindsey Cook*, in which the defendant was accused of murdering his wife. For months before trial, I had to ambush his friends and colleagues in parking lots all over town to personally hand them a subpoena duces tecum—a demand for documents. Those documents were the defendant's handwritten letters, composed behind bars, detailing how he planned to trick the system by acting crazy to get an insanity verdict. Cook first claimed that his wife's death was suicide and then argued that if he *had* committed murder, he'd been insane at the time. His friends and relatives begrudgingly handed over the letters that outlined his plan. I had the letters blown up at a local Kinko's to show them in enlarged detail to the jury. That cost money I didn't have at the time and I knew the D.A.'s office didn't have it in the budget, so I had no choice—I charged it!

FOR THE LOVE OF MONEY

In 1987, in the first major drug case I tried, I was up against Bob Fierer, ironically pronounced "fear." He was by far the slickest defense attorney in Atlanta. This wasn't a case where the accused was a street-corner hustler or a drifter nailed at a traffic stop with a joint in his ashtray. This case involved a huge chunk of pure, uncut cocaine worth millions on the street. I remember reading the file and driving by the luxury high-rise where the drugs had been discovered. I wanted to see what I could before the first calendar call on the case. The building was in Buckhead—one of the swankiest parts of Atlanta, home of multimillionaires, an area where old money is mixed with that of rich up-and-comers. The next morning, I got to court early. The defendant had managed to get out of jail on a huge bond before I was assigned the case. I naturally would have opposed bond, with such a large amount of uncut cocaine involved. What that indicated to me was that the defendant, Charles Ehrlich, also known as "Charlie Tuna," was no amateur but a major drug distributor in the city.

That morning in court, though, it was the lawyer himself who bowled me over.

For the first time in my practice of law, I was acutely aware that I was the underdog. Robert Fierer was wearing a suit that had to have cost $4,000. His shoes were polished Italian leather, his cuff links had diamonds in them. Even his hair was perfect—I found out later he got it highlighted every three weeks like clockwork (while I was still using bleach from the drugstore). I even noticed his nails, which were, of course, perfectly buffed. His briefcase had that dull glow of expensive leather. My files were organized in a plastic mail carrier's box with handles on either side that I'd found in the hall of the courthouse. That's when it hit me like a ton of bricks—I was outgunned.

I was a novice prosecutor, and at the time I didn't know a thing about organized crime. Ehrlich was clearly a player of some sort in a drug cartel, serving as the distribution hub in that part of Atlanta. Amazingly, his bust came about by accident. Ehrlich had received a FedExed brick of pure, uncut, white cocaine in the lobby of his apartment building. When it was delivered, the doorman signed for the package on behalf of the tenant. As I worked with that doorman (who, I quickly learned, was not, let me say, afraid of a cocktail) during one of our many interviews, he explained how he discovered the contents of the package. He told me that ordinarily he never looked in people's packages, because he could lose his job over such a violation. On the night Ehrlich's box was dropped off, the edge of the package was already torn open, and the doorman could clearly see inside. The brick was obvious, so he called the cops. When the police searched "Charlie Tuna's" apartment, things got even worse. They discovered that the place was wired, so he'd know if someone got in. Cops found a silencer in the closet. Who needs a silencer? That did it. This was a bad guy, and he had to be stopped from poisoning the streets of the city.

I knew this constituted a warrantless search when there'd been plenty of time to get one, but those rules are for the cops conducting a search (the opening of the package), not private individuals like neighbors or doormen who spot your friendly messenger service dropping off cocaine. With Fierer as the defense, I knew he would have a fleet of assistants poring over the law as it applied to these facts, so I had to get ready. I researched for days in order to prepare for what was sure to be a down-and-dirty court battle. On that first day, I felt ready and armed to the hilt with law and testimony for the suppression hearing. According to my research, this was the bottom line: Sorry, Charlie, but the Constitution doesn't protect you from the doorman.

For the first day of the trial, I wore my lucky black trial dress and shoes (recently resoled) and got to court early to set up all my legal documents. I sat behind the state's table, closest to the jury box, with the beat cop on the case seated beside me. We had been through a lot together working the case. His part was done—it was now up to me to win the legal battle. Right before court was gaveled into session, Fierer, who stood six foot three, strode into the courtroom looking like a quarterback about to toss the winning touchdown. Instead of going to counsel table, he went straight up to the bench, where, as if by cue, the judge came out from his chambers, black robes flowing, hand extended to shake Fierer's. They both broke into broad smiles and chatted like old friends. My heart sank. *Were* they friends? Had Fierer dumped lots of money in the judge's last campaign for the bench? I didn't know what to think. Without looking at them, I strained to hear what they were saying but couldn't. I sat there stunned when I realized what favoritism could mean to my case.

The defense announced it wanted a bench trial—one without a jury. I fought the motion, which of course offended the judge, and was overruled. The sole decision in the case would be that of this judge. I couldn't do anything but argue my guts out. I knew to at least act as if I were used to arguing against lawyers of Fierer's caliber. Then it was time for witnesses. I put up the beat cop first to pave the way for the weaker witness, the doorman. From what I could tell, the doorman was stone-cold sober, and he testified looking straight up at the judge, like an angel singing—to me at least. At the end, I argued not just the law but the importance of the case. I spoke about how all the eyes of the community were on this courtroom, how so many people were counting on us to do the right thing. I had little hope when the judge went to chambers and left us to stew, waiting on the ruling. The Honorable Don Langham honored the bench and ruled for the state. The cocaine was in evidence. The case was over. My faith in the system, including judges, was bolstered.

Afterward Fierer refused to speak to me. He just gathered his files as if nothing had happened and stormed out of the courtroom. He didn't speak to me for a very long time after the trial, which was perfectly okay with me. Even when we'd meet in the courthouse elevator, just the two of us, we were like two wet cats in a barrel.

Here's an interesting postscript to the story: Ehrlich went to jail, and Fierer continued his high-flying, high-profile practice of law. We never crossed swords again. But years later, the feds launched a secret investigation of Fierer and his alleged practice of scamming clients out of hundreds of thousands of dollars. It boiled down to a carefully executed scheme in which Fierer and his associates, Conviction Consultants Inc., arranged for federal inmates to exchange fake information against other inmates in order to "cooperate" with the feds.

If it worked, the feds would reduce the snitches' jail time considerably in exchange for the phony information. Those behind bars who could afford to cough up about $25,000 a pop were then connected to outside informants who supplied information helpful to unwitting agents and prosecutors in other cases. Fierer's scheme erupted into a major scandal and threatened the legitimacy of multiple convictions based in part on informant testimony. The whole concept of rewarding inmates for their information became fair game for defense attorneys to then argue to judge and jury, jeopardizing hundreds of verdicts and investigations. Fierer went to the federal penitentiary and lost his law license. There is a moral here, I'm sure, but what I'll remember most is the untouchable defense lawyer who unwittingly taught me to believe that justice can and will happen if you fight hard enough. You have to have faith in the system. I have the vivid memory of Fierer entering the courthouse for his own sentencing at the federal courthouse, much the same way he strode into the courtroom that day, as if he had the world by the tail. Head held high, hair carefully blown back, with that million-dollar smile—that's how I remember Bob Fierer.

PROSECUTORS ON TRIAL

As a prosecutor, you definitely pay a price. You get paid slave wages and are then attacked as the bad guy at every turn. Your every move is publicly painted by the defense as nefarious and sneaky. After all, defense attorneys argue, you are responsible for and dedicated to putting innocent people behind bars. After fifteen years in the courtroom, I have come to the realization that very rarely is there an evil plan or a conspiracy hatched by the prosecution.

And you know why?

Because, frankly, when you're looking at a workload of about eight hundred to a thousand cases, you really don't have time to plot and plan to put innocent people behind bars. It's all you can do to prosecute the guilty ones! But that has never stopped the defense from painting a very twisted and dark picture of the prosecution.

During Scott Peterson's trial, I remember how on-air pundits continued their nightly attacks against prosecutors Rick Distaso, Dave Harris, and Birgit Fladager. They were portrayed as bumbling at best, unethical at worst. After I met them and watched them in court, I saw they were nothing of the sort, but instead were excellent, dedicated, and honorable.

Another prime example of personal attacks against prosecutors is what was leveled at Marcia Clark and Chris Darden during the O. J. Simpson trial. They were state employees pitted against a multimillion-dollar defense team of courtroom stars and master manipulators that included the consummate defense attorney Johnnie Cochran, evidence whiz Barry Scheck, Robert Shapiro, and world-renowned orator F. Lee Bailey. Realistically speaking, did Darden and Clark ever have a chance?

Despite some inevitable mistakes they made during the course of the trial—and there were some whoppers—I always supported them. I knew how it felt to give 200 percent, to do the right thing and end up with a kick in the teeth. But it wasn't always easy. Their biggest mistake, of course, was the infamous episode when Simpson was allowed by the state to try on a dried, bloody glove in open court. Darden allowed the one person in the world who would most want to harm the state's case—the defendant—to participate in an unrehearsed, unprepared, in-court demonstration in front of the jury with the critical piece of state's evidence. Darden handed it to him and allowed Simpson, in one defining moment, to blast the state's case to pieces. Of course the glove didn't fit—because Simpson wouldn't *let* it fit. What could Darden do then? Wrestle Simpson to the ground and force him to put on the glove? The whole thing was a disaster.

Another egregious error committed by the state in that case was not preparing for the bombshell that exploded during the cross-examination of Mark Fuhrman. The reality was that Fuhrman should have been prepared for what was to come, so he could own up to his past and say, "Yeah, I said it. Hate me, but I found the glove. I'm not the one who killed two people—he did" (pointing at Simpson of course). Because he apparently was not prepared for the devastating cross-examination, Fuhrman's past became the focal point of the trial—not the two dead bodies that were found lying in the front yard of Nicole Brown's home on a warm June evening in Brentwood, California.

Despite all that, I would always defend Christopher Darden and Marcia Clark every time I was on television talking about the trial, because I believed—and do believe—that they were doing the right thing. I believe firmly they had the right guy and that they were seeking justice with all their might. But their efforts were thwarted in that California courtroom. Not just by the defense but by Judge Lance Ito, who had fallen in love with the spotlight and lost control of the courtroom.

In the circus that was the Simpson trial, the private lives of Clark and Darden were laid bare. When reporters weren't writing articles speculating about whether they were lovers, they were posing and answering the burning questions of the day (often with little or no hard facts to back up their stories): Who were they dating? What happened in her divorce? And, probably the most moronic and hurtful of all questions: Why wasn't she spending more time with her children? I remember storming off a network radio interview because all they wanted to ask me about was Clark's hair. I found that incredible in light of the fact that she was trying a case based on the slaughter of two innocent people.

Whether you agreed or disagreed with her, Marcia Clark became symbolic of the state. If she wore short skirts, the state lost credibility. If her hair was made fun of, the state lost credibility. If you didn't like her makeup or thought she had bags under her eyes one day at trial, the state appeared "worn, haggard, defeated" before the jury. She couldn't win for losing. Was it fair? No. But that is the reality of being a prosecutor. You are held to a much different standard. Being a woman makes it even tougher. I learned early on that this was simply a fact of life. Whenever I would go out, I was always very careful about where I went and how I behaved. I was always very aware of the people I was with, because when you are standing in front of juries four or five times a month, with each panel made up of one hundred people from your community, you are identified with the state. You represent the state. You become the state. If a prosecutor's behavior is deemed unseemly by any number of sources—in or out of the courtroom—then the state loses credibility.

Sometimes the attacks against the prosecution veer into disturbingly dangerous territory. I was prosecuting at a time in my life so close to my fiancé's murder that in my grief I simply didn't care one way or the other about what happened to me. This may be better for a shrink to decide, but it could, when I look back on it, very well explain why many times I acted as if I were invincible. I thought I had already lived through the worst thing that could happen to me. I guess I thought, *What else could happen?* Despite being in some pretty scary situations, I don't remember ever being afraid.

I often got death threats on my answering machine. There were always plenty of hang-ups and obscene phone calls, but I shrugged them off as being from malcontents at the jail. One night, though, I'd had enough. I was working at my desk when I got a threatening call, and I finally answered back, "You know what? You're probably in a jail right now, but as soon as you can, grab a bus and come on over here. I'm waiting here with my investigator and his .357. We can't wait to see you!" Click. Of course, nothing ever happened.

Getting heckled on the way to my car after leaving the courthouse was pretty much a regular occurrence. There were lots of nights when I would have my hands full of files, my pocketbook, my briefcase, and be clipping along in my high heels while walking up the steps to the sixth floor of the parking deck. It would be eight o'clock at night, and I'd be on my way to go teach night school—on my way to yet another enclosed parking garage. Once in a while, it would dawn on me—*You know, I'm here all by myself in this big concrete structure*—but I'd just keep walking. Sometimes, I'd get to my car and find the windshield smashed in. I knew the number of "Dr. Glass" in Atlanta by heart, because they would come and fix your car right there. But it never got to me. When things like that happened, it just made me dig in even more.

THE PROSECUTOR WORE A SKIRT

It may not be politically correct to say, but being a female prosecutor comes with its own set of challenges. Sexism is alive and well in the courtroom. You'd think that having more women in the system would fix the problem, but I haven't found that to be true. I'm not sure why, but sometimes female judges are harder on female lawyers.

When I first came to the district attorney's office, there were very few female cops and lawyers—female judges were even harder to find. At the time, women were usually assigned to work juvenile cases, which are not jury trials and do not apply many of the standard rules of evidence. We were usually going after deadbeat dads, writing appeals, or acting as assistants to trial lawyers. Practically everybody involved in the actual trial of cases was a man—except the jury and, in many cases, the victim.

I've been called "little lady," "young lady," "lady lawyer," and other not-so-nice names, right in front of juries by defense lawyers, experts, and judges—pretty much by everybody but the jury. Every time it happened, I'd look that person right in the eye and act as if I hadn't heard it. I'd inevitably catch at least one woman on the jury with a look of disgust on her face, as if to say she couldn't believe that someone had said something that condescending. So what was meant to knock me off balance usually had just the opposite effect and offended at least a few jurors. I never said a word. I didn't have to. The women on the jury said it for me with their verdicts.

Sometimes the sexism was far more insidious. During a 1995 trial in which I was prosecuting a defendant on rape, sodomy, and murder charges, I was working late one night when I heard the sounds of someone outside my office. My first thought was, *Why is somebody still here this late?* An investigator for the defense had gotten into the building and delivered a motion under my door. He didn't know I was still in there working. I went over and picked it up and then sat down in tears— mortified. It was a motion filed to enjoin me from wearing skirts a specific number of inches above my knee or a blouse that was too low-cut. It also enjoined me from bending over in front of the jury facing either way.

I felt completely humiliated. All court documents are public. Anyone can find out anything about a case by going down to the courthouse and looking it up. I cried (behind closed doors, of course), because it was a public embarrassment to be accused of dressing inappropriately— and it was flat-out not true. I still have every one of my ten trial dresses that I wore over and over and over. Every one of them covered me from neck to wrist to knee. I was personally attacked on a groundless charge that was meant to deflect attention away from the trial.

This ended up becoming a major distraction, because feminist publications from all over the country sent reporters to Atlanta to cover the story. Scores of television journalists from as far as New York came to court wanting to interview me about the motion. At the same time I was seeking justice in a case where an unnamed woman was found raped, sodomized, and strangled to death by the defendant on trial, I was being forced to address questions about what I wore to court. Even without this unwanted sideshow, I had a very difficult case to prove. I never even knew the identity of the victim.

The motion, one of the many ways the defense attempted to derail the case, was scheduled to be argued in court. The trial was a murder case and based strictly on scientific evidence. There were no eyewitnesses and no confessions. It was being heard by the same judge who had presided over my very first jury trial nearly ten years before, an attempted shoplifting. He had seen me in court many, many times. The room was filled with reporters, fellow lawyers, and witnesses, all seated and listening intently. I kept my eyes trained on the judge. Miraculously, as if an angel had heard my prayer, the judge cut off the defense lawyer who had stood to deliver his oral argument. The motion was overruled. He was told in no uncertain terms: No discussion, no dramatics—now call your first witness. Many days later, the jury convicted on murder one.

While I remained focused on the victim, the defendant had something else in mind. Guards at the jail discovered during a routine search of his cell that he had created a file on me, complete with creepy poems and death threats. All the material was confiscated and handed over to the police. In my mind, the lawyer's behavior in this case was just a reflection of his client's. They were perfectly suited to one another. But the truth won out in the end. The defendant got life plus twenty plus twenty.

One of the reasons I am writing this book is to propose remedies for the existing problems in our justice system. Sexism is still an issue. It's the same way in the courtroom as it is in every other profession in this country: Women have to work twice as hard to be taken seriously and get the same job done as their male counterparts do. Lawyering is no different from any other profession in that way. There is one big difference in how it affects female lawyers, though. The prejudice against female lawyers has an impact on more than the individual—it affects her clients, her cases, and her causes. A case could be won or lost because of a sexual bias. Traditionally juries love judges, because they look up to them and respect them. Whether that bias originates with the judge or the defense, the jury picks up on it.

During my years as a prosecutor, it definitely wore thin when judges or defense attorneys behaved like jackasses. I'm convinced this sometimes occurred simply because I was a woman. You can laugh it off and pretend it's a joke only so many times. I always knew that there was the avenue of suing or making a complaint, but my eye was on the prize of the trial. The most important thing to me, regardless of the circumstances, was getting justice for the victim. I always felt that whatever complaints I had, they were nothing compared to what the victims and their families were going through. If the situation were different and I was the only person involved, I would have filed a complaint in a New York minute—but I never did.

The reality is that if a lawyer files a sexual-harassment complaint or a motion for the judge to recuse himself or against the other side, it could seriously harm the case. That attorney could be sacrificing the case in exchange for different treatment for herself. That's why you rarely see harassment complaints about judges or opposing counsel filed by attorneys, because it's basically cutting off your nose to spite your face. You'll likely see the same judge and lawyers on the next calendar call, and there's always the possibility that it will be taken out on your current case or your future cases. Thankfully, overt sexism among judges is rare. But sexism is a very difficult thing to combat in the courtroom. It's not fair, but it's the truth.

I always tried my best to stay focused on my goal and keep fighting in the courtroom. I'd like to be able to offer remedies to this situation, but, honestly, it's not that easy. It pains me to say this, because I don't by any means want to dissuade women from filing sexual-harassment claims in the workplace. I am talking strictly from my own perspective as a female prosecutor who worked in the courtroom during the eighties and nineties—long after the so-called sexual revolution. It is my ardent hope that as more and more women enter the field and we become more enlightened as a society, the need to address this issue will disappear.

A COURTROOM
REALITY CHECK

Everything about how a case is handled in the justice system is meant to ensure that the defendant gets a fair trial. It begins with striking the jury. In many jurisdictions, the state gets ten strikes (people they can dismiss for any reason) and the defense gets twenty. You never hear too much about the state trying to suppress the defense's evidence. Most often it's the defense trying to get search warrants and testimony thrown out of trial.

During trial, if the state makes a blunder, the case is reversed, but if the defense makes a mistake, the state has little recourse. A mistrial will hardly ever be granted because the prosecution has been harmed. If the state does something objectionable, the defense can also ask for a mistrial with prejudice, which means that not only is there a mistrial and the case ends but the state is not allowed to retry the case. This is possible only if the state's error is extreme—one example of this would be if evidence has been excluded pretrial but the state gets it in anyway. It's rare, but it can happen.

Mistrials almost always work in the defense's favor. The defense has gotten a chance to see the state's playbook during the first trial and can now go on a fishing expedition with the state's witnesses, who are locked into previous testimony for the retrial. All of this allows the defense to better tailor its case on the second go-round. The state has the burden, rightfully, to go first and give its best shot. Yet if there's a mistrial during the state's case, the jury never hears the defense's case.

Sometimes the defense doesn't make an opening statement at first but waits until the defense's case, after the state has rested. The reason for this strategy is a simple one: The attorneys want to tailor their defense to what the state puts up. Which to me means they don't know what their defense is going to be at the beginning of the trial—which also means to me that their guy is guilty. If you don't know what your defense is—"I was not at the scene of the bank robbery. I was at home watching *Murder, She Wrote*"—why do you have to wait to give your alibi, unless you're fabricating something? It's just common sense. Here's one example of how an entire defense can be tailored to fit the state's case. The state will put up its case—the jury (and the defense) will hear that the eyewitness has a cataract or wears bifocals or that the light fixture wasn't working in front of the bank the night of the robbery—and suddenly the defense will be saying, "He's not a credible eyewitness. You can't possibly convict on the word of this person."

Most legal proceedings are shrouded in mystery, which also feeds into the misconception that there are treacherous goings-on behind the scenes that compromise the fairness of the case. The so-called secret grand jury convened in the Michael Jackson case is a perfect example. All the hoopla made about this "secret" panel was due in large part to the enormous spin the defense employed in feeding the media hype that surrounded every aspect of the proceedings. All grand juries are secret, because witnesses—who may or may not be called at trial due to the rules of evidence—are not to feel any pressure one way or the other. There was nothing unusual about the way the Michael Jackson case was handled. The only necessary change was that the grand-jury meetings were frequently held in different locations so the press wouldn't be able to drive the grand jurors insane and hound them with interview requests. The funny thing is, this entire setup benefits—guess who?—the defendant. But you can be assured defense attorneys will never admit that.

The word "grand" in grand jury simply refers to the number of people on the jury, which ranges from nineteen up to forty-three, depending on the jurisdiction. A petit jury, or small jury, is seen at the ultimate trial and is composed of six to twelve people. Grand jurors are not secret moles working for the state—they are average citizens who are missing work while having to come in two or three times a week and who are most likely not entirely happy about being there. A grand jury is created through "blind selection"—the names of those people called have simply been taken out of the city's voter-registration or the tax logs. Jurors get there about eight-thirty in the morning and work until about four-thirty in the afternoon. At best they get coffee and doughnuts, and they work straight through to the end of the day listening to witness after witness after witness.

There are two types of grand juries—those that investigate and those that charge. In the JonBenet Ramsey investigation and in the matter of Chandra Levy, the grand jury investigated the cases, not necessarily ending with a formal charge. "Charging grand juries" meet regularly and listen to evidence the state has subpoenaed and then, after asking questions of witnesses and considering the evidence, vote to formally charge a target or "no bill," which means decline to charge. On its face, a "secret grand jury" sounds nefarious and conjures up images of the star chamber, but that's about as far from the truth as it could possibly be. The grand jury typically meets in secret to protect the reputations of those targets it considers.

BALANCING THE SCALES OF JUSTICE

Several things should be done in order to balance the scales of justice in the courtroom, starting with the rules of evidence. I mentioned earlier that the defense always maintains a higher profile during cases than the prosecution does, and this certainly applies to press conferences and contact with the media. Public statements on the evidence made by the defense during press conferences should be disallowed. The state can't comment on the evidence, so neither should the defense. Despite a gag order issued by the judge in the Laci Peterson case, Mark Geragos floated theories about the case from the very beginning by making allegations in open court and in filings. First we heard about the mysterious brown van, then it was a satanic cult, and later he introduced his theory involving murderous drug dealers. All of that is out there in the jury's mind. Various theories ended up in documents that are public record, which allows the press to take hold of these comments and run with them. That kind of backdoor lawyering should be stopped.

I also believe that so-called defense experts should be exposed for what they really are—hired guns. All defense experts are paid. The state's experts often are not paid—they are government employees at the local crime lab working for modest salaries. That's not the case with defense experts, and the fact should be made crystal clear to the jury.

Defense attorneys should also be prevented from causing unnecessary delays that tamper with the system. By asking for multiple changes of venue in the Peterson case, Geragos caused a major delay in the trial. His motivation was simple: He wanted to get the case tried in Los Angeles. All he wanted to do was to get closer to his own jurisdiction and to Hollywood. That's what it's all about for him, and I'm calling him on it. Thankfully, the judge didn't go for it. Robert "Baretta" Blake is another high-profile defendant who played for time. He faced trial for the murder of his wife, Bonny Lee Bakley. Blake fired several rounds of defense lawyers. Each firing delayed the trial from going forward—and the judge let him do it. I say if he's got the money to fire and hire repeatedly, so be it. But be ready for trial come calendar call. Allowing Blake to manipulate the system is unfair to the state, to the victim's family—and to other defendants who are not allowed the luxury of playing the system and who go to trial when scheduled.

There's a whole host of changes that could be made to the justice system that would affect every case—not just those that hijack the headlines. In most jurisdictions, the state has to hand over most, if not all, of its evidence to the defense ahead of time. The defense isn't under that exact burden. In some states, they have reciprocal discovery, but the penalties for not following this rule are not the same nationwide. As I've already said, if the state doesn't hand over evidence, it cannot be used at trial; if the defense doesn't hand something over, attorneys for the state may get an hour to digest it once they discover it before going forward. There's no real penalty—no bite—for the defense if it fails to disclose anything. That's a major problem. The same penalties need to be exacted on the defense, but here's the rub: On appeal, if there's a conviction, the defense can claim that it would have won if not for the ruling, and there could be a whole new trial. It's a no-win situation. If you allow it in, then you're not ready to cross-examine on the new evidence or new witness. If you don't allow it in, the defense will appeal it and get a new trial. The whole thing is very one-sided and stacked against the state.

I believe that polygraph tests should be admissible under the law, and that sword definitely cuts both ways. Then, as with every other test, the defense should have the right to cross-examine those results. As an example, in the Simpson case, the jury at the criminal trial heard all about the prosecution's DNA evidence, but on cross-examination the defense chipped away at it. This procedure should apply to polygraphs as well. Why hide it from the jury? In Simpson's civil trial, Judge Hiroshi Fujisaki gave special instructions dealing with the plaintiff's mention that Simpson had previously flunked a lie-detector test. The judge allowed the attorneys to question Simpson about the alleged polygraph. I firmly believe that the science behind polygraph tests is solid and can be controlled by court and evidentiary guidelines to make the tests even more reliable and, therefore, admissible at trial.

There are quite a lot of evidentiary tools that are not always allowed—cadaver dogs, drug dogs, accelerant dogs, to name a few. Some are not admissible in certain courts because certain judges don't think they're reliable. Two hundred years ago, nobody believed in fingerprints. It's time to reexamine the law in the area of scientific evidence. Although initially it may seem black and white, every piece of evidence can be attacked. That's why I believe there should be a broader view of evidence that may be allowed in the courtroom. Allow the evidence in and let a jury determine its weight and reliability after it has been tested by the fire of cross-examination. We have a jury system—let it work!

We must look carefully at the current interpretation of the Miranda rights. During the Kobe Bryant case, the defense tried to claim that when he talked to police in his hotel room and in the parking lot of the Colorado resort before being charged with rape, he'd actually been in custody and under arrest at the time. They contend that his comments were made before he was given his Miranda rights and that everything he said should be thrown out. This type of argument signals it's time to reexamine exactly what Miranda means.

Murder victims are often found to have made declarations such as "If anything ever happens to me, my husband will be the one responsible." I've tried many cases in which I discovered that the murder victim had made such claims. This has happened in several recent high-profile cases as well. Millionaire Robert Durst's late wife plainly said that if she were killed, it would be at the hands of her husband. Nine days before her death, Nicole Brown Simpson wrote that Simpson had threatened her by saying, "You hung up on me last night, you're gonna pay for this. . . ." She also wrote at length in her journal about Simpson's abusive behavior. Prosecutors wanted to use Nicole's writings as evidence, but Judge Ito ruled them "inadmissible hearsay." His ruling was not uncommon, because this type of evidence is often deemed hearsay and is disallowed, since it can't be cross-examined. It certainly should have to undergo testing for veracity but I don't think these types of claims should be dismissed out of hand because the victims are no longer there to defend themselves.

Very often when you have a dead victim and the defendant is caught red-handed, the accused will claim that it was an act of self-defense even when the victim was unarmed. Whenever the issue of self-defense is raised, it is one of the only times a victim's reputation gets to come into evidence ("I thought she was about to pull a gun on me, because she's been violent toward me before"). I think it's inappropriate to put victims on trial when they can no longer speak for themselves. During Durst's trial, he claimed that the seventy-year-old man he killed was trying to kill him when they struggled with the gun and it went off accidentally. There was no evidence to support this scenario.

Reform extends past the guilty verdict. I am firmly opposed to appeals bonds, which allow a criminal defendant to walk free even after a jury conviction for the price of the bond. Simply put, after a jury has rendered a verdict of guilty, in most cases it's time for the defendant to go to jail. After the first Jayson Williams trial, that didn't happen. Williams walked free, post-conviction. Unless the defense can plainly state that a valid error was made at trial that will likely result in a reversal or the granting of a new trial, the jury verdict must rule—not a judge's whim.

CHAPTER SEVEN

BLAME THE VICTIM

DURING AN APPEARANCE ON *LARRY KING LIVE* in February 2003, I got into a verbal sparring match with the defense attorney for Gary Ridgway, the notorious "Green River Killer." In the early 1980s, one of the longest serial-murder investigations in U.S. history began. For two decades, police sought to capture a serial killer who terrorized the Seattle area of Washington State. The first victims were discovered in 1982 near the Green River, thus giving the killer his name. In 2001, investigators finally arrested Ridgway. As part of an outrageous plea to avoid the death penalty, the murderer pled guilty to killing forty-eight women. He is currently serving life without parole in Walla Walla, Washington.

I am firmly convinced that a life sentence is not a severe enough penalty for a man who bragged that murder was his talent and pled guilty to the brutal sex-torture murders of so many women. Authorities are convinced Ridgway is responsible for even more vicious killings. That night on *Larry King Live*, I argued that if forty-eight murders of young girls and women don't equal one death penalty, what does? The comment was made that the victims (some were as young as fifteen years old) were found in areas known to be frequented by prostitutes. In describing some of the victims, my opponent said, "Anybody that says a fifteen-year-old can't be a hooker just doesn't know much about hookers these days." When I fired back, "[Are you] suggesting that because [someone] was a hooker, she's less of a victim?" he denied it. I was so angry my chest actually began to hurt right there on the *King* set. Several of the victims were murdered and thrown away like trash along the side of Washington State's Green River. They weren't disposable. All were victims.

Families of the victims felt frustrated and deceived. They were led to believe Ridgway would receive the death penalty, but capital punishment was plea-bargained away. Ridgway had actually forgotten many of his victims and had a "hard time keeping them straight." He never learned their names and wrote them off as thrill kills. His contempt for women seeped out of a statement he made at plea bargain. Among his chilling words: "I picked prostitutes as my victims because I hate most prostitutes and I did not want to pay them for sex. I also picked prostitutes as victims because they were easy to pick up without being noticed. I knew they would not be reported missing right away and might never be reported missing. I picked prostitutes because I thought I could kill as many of them as I wanted without getting caught."

Ridgway is a serial killer and a psychopath. I will never understand why his lawyers would attack the victims on national television. Why would they use a victim's alleged lifestyle as some sort of justification for murder or rape? Because they can. I learned that answer in court many years ago. Attacks by the defense, as vicious and unreasonable as they may be, are usually aimed straight at the victim. When there is nowhere else to turn, no one else to blame, the tried-and-true defense tactic is to blame the victim.

When the defense has no alibi, when prosecutors present eyewitnesses or DNA, when the defense is trapped and there's nowhere to go, what can they do? Point the finger in the other direction—at the victim. It's an old strategy that has become standard operating procedure in courtrooms across the country. There's a reason this chapter is the longest one in the book—the list of cases where this deplorable strategy is employed by the defense just keeps growing.

THE KOBE BRYANT CASE: THE NEXT GENERATION BLAME-THE-VICTIM DEFENSE

The Kobe Bryant case has brought back into the forefront a legal issue that has existed for decades: the treatment of a rape victim in the courtroom. Think about it for a moment. Say there's a bank robbery in your town. When the teller who was robbed at gunpoint takes the stand, can you imagine the defense attorney asking, "Isn't it true you had several one-night stands in college?" Or how about, "Isn't it true you've been on birth control pills for some time now?" The state's attorney would scream bloody murder, and the defense attorney would be—rightly—thrown out on his ear. Not so with sexual-assault cases. And therein lies the problem.

Statistically, sexual assault and domestic violence are the two most underreported crimes on the books. All too often, the tables are turned and the victim is put on trial. It's not unusual for a rape victim to be questioned about everything—from whether she drinks alcohol, goes to bars, or has frequented "bad areas." Even her appearance comes into question. What possible difference does it make if a woman wears short skirts? I find this type of behavior exhibited by defense attorneys appalling. Rape-shield laws were created to protect against these unconscionable actions and to encourage victims to come forward, while protecting them from having their reputations ruined. These laws disallow from evidence a victim's unrelated sexual past or anything touching on it. That includes evidence showing that a victim has lived with boyfriends, uses birth control, had abortions. Rape-shield laws also aim at preventing direct questions posed to the victim about her unrelated sexual history. The important thing to remember is that the victim isn't the one on trial.

One of the things I believe that this country has learned from the Kobe Bryant case is that these laws don't always work. Inevitably, there are always ways around laws protecting victims. Whether Bryant was guilty or not guilty, the alleged victim in this case was repeatedly attacked by his defense team and others out to exploit the sensational tabloid aspects of this case—and that is wrong.

The alleged victim in this case went through hell. She received thousands of angry, menacing, or obscene e-mails and messages. An Iowa man pled guilty to leaving death threats on her answering machine. Another man broke into her home. Yet another man, a Swiss national, faced charges of offering to kill the woman for $3 million to "help out" the Bryant defense team. It's ironic to me that it's so much easier for some people to blame her for flirting with a married man or being in the wrong place—basically reinforcing the theory that rape victims "ask for it" and that somehow they deserve the treatment they get. I'm not quite sure why, but it's more comfortable for many people to believe that the alleged victim in this case is a "gold digger" than to believe that a then-nineteen-year-old girl was raped by an NBA superstar. How can we expect victims to speak out if we cannot protect them from another, more insidious form of attack?

THE NAME GAME

Stories about the alleged victim were planted like bombs and exploded almost daily during the Kobe Bryant case. Some accounts claimed that the young woman was bragging about her encounter with Bryant, while others focused on stories of multiple sex partners in the days surrounding the alleged incident. Most of the allegations were based on the loaded questions put on the record by Bryant's defense attorney, Pamela Mackey. She asked highly objectionable questions in front of the full press pool, knowing they would repeat them as fact in their stories. Her strategy worked.

The Kobe Bryant case was over before a jury was even struck. Perceptions of the alleged victim were publicized there in Colorado and all over the country. Thanks to satellite dishes tacked on to towers, homes, and huts, the "news" was spread around the world.

Mackey started out by calling the victim by name in an open courtroom packed with reporters—six times during the preliminary hearing alone. The judge repeatedly admonished the lawyer, to no avail. She knew who the real judge was: the jury pool reading all the news accounts of what went on in the courtroom that day. Judge Frederick Gannett's admonitions were like water off a duck's back. At the same hearing, in direct violation of the state's rape-shield law, Mackey then alluded to the alleged victim's sexual history. It was too late. The horse was out of the gate.

While the defense blurted out the alleged victim's name over and over in court within earshot of reporters, Bryant's defense team insisted they were concerned about bad publicity. Sure they were, but only as it applied to their client. As for the press, the judge issued warnings in a three-page "decorum" order to lawyers and the media, promising reporters they wouldn't get a seat in court if they publicized the name or photographs of the accuser.

There is no law disallowing the media from publishing a rape victim's name. Up until this point, there has simply been an unwritten agreement among outlets not to do so, since rape is so underreported largely because of the vicious treatment victims get in the courtroom. In the Bryant case, we saw the long-standing traditions of self-governing thrown out the window.

Practically all U.S. news organizations, including the Associated Press, have policies against releasing identities of rape victims and did not release the name in the Bryant case. While Judge Gannett ordered lawyers and investigators to keep her identity secret, the press is a different matter. Similar rulings have been ruled unconstitutional, in that the name of the chief witness in a case is by its nature public, not secret.

There's no way to enact a law requiring the media to withhold the name of a rape victim because it would infringe on the First Amendment to the Constitution. However, the alleged victim in the Bryant trial does have the right to seek civil action in that she is not a public figure, and during the case certain media divulged facts that put her in a bad light. A lawsuit on her part against outlets that printed her photo with damaging stories about her would not surprise me.

A RUTHLESS PLAN
OF ATTACK

The blame-the-victim defense in rape cases has grown bolder with every passing year. In the past, the first line of defense was the traditional claim that there has been no sex whatsoever between the accused and the victim. Very often, the perp claims he's never even met the rape victim. Once a rape is medically or scientifically proven, the defense then moves to the next stage, which is "Yes, we had sex, but it was consensual." Along with the consent defense, often thrown into the defense pot for good measure is something like "She's a tramp, she's a hooker, she sleeps around, or she came on to me." Yet another version of blame-the-victim is "She wanted money," or "She wanted powder cocaine" and now, "She wanted crack."

In the Kobe Bryant rape case, we saw a tangle of traditional blame-the-victim defenses used. It started with "She's a star seeker," went to "She wanted her fifteen minutes of fame," then on to the usual fall-back—"She's promiscuous." This is one of the first times I've seen the inference that "she's too ambitious" used as the subtext for the defense, although there was a hint of that in the infamous Central Park jogger case in 1989. Long story short, the Bryant case launched an attack on the alleged victim's lifestyle and sexual history, real or imagined, like no other in recent memory.

More than one woman was targeted for vicious attacks during the Bryant case. Katie Lovell was misidentified as the accuser early in the case. Lovell and the alleged victim went to the same high school and had a number of physical similarities. A photo of Lovell, who'd been a member of the school's dance squad, was posted on the Internet naming her as Bryant's accuser along with her name, phone number, and other personal information. More than a dozen Web sites followed suit. Her home was swamped with reporters, Bryant supporters, photographers, and hangers-on. Lovell had to hire an attorney to get her name and photograph removed from the sites. After a brief taste of what the actual complainant lived though, Lovell summed up the experience during an appearance on ABC's *Good Morning America* by saying, "It has hurt me as a person."

Because of the nightmare she had to live through, Lovell demanded that Colorado lawmakers tighten the rules on identifying sexual-assault victims. In a room crowded with politicians, Lovell said Bryant's real accuser, who by that time had already been identified on a radio broadcast and in a supermarket tabloid, had received death threats. "I can only imagine what she is actually going through. It will make people think twice about coming forward . . . ," Lovell said to a legislative committee.

This new generation of attacking the victim in rape cases flies in the face of rape-shield laws, which are designed to protect against such tactics. Why? Because rape cases are supposed to be tried on the facts at hand, not the victim's alleged sexual history. You'd be astounded at the tactics I've seen used. I've heard defense attorneys ask everything from, "What were you wearing that night?" to "How many drinks did you have?" to "Isn't it true you take the birth-control pill?" Besides being offensive and ridiculous, these questions are legally irrelevant.

In the Bryant case, information would have been permissible during trial only if it was "offered for the purpose of showing that the act or acts charged were or were not committed by the defendant." Preliminary hearings, though, are not specifically mentioned in Colorado's rape-shield law, as opposed to the actual trial. That is how Mackey's actions at the preliminary hearing snuck through a legal loophole. In theory, there was no jury seated to be "tainted" against the alleged victim by the illegal evidence. The reality is, however, that the whole world, including the jury pool, heard not only the alleged victim's full name, but numerous defense allegations that would likely never be allowed at trial—just as Mackey intended.

RICH MAN'S JUSTICE

On September 1, 2004, there was a shocking turn of events in the case of *State v. Kobe Bryant*. The alleged victim in the case refused to go forward. Reports surfaced that there was a civil settlement in the works, rumored to be in the millions. Prosecutor Mark Hurlbert seemed to have tears in his eyes when he announced that the state of Colorado was dropping charges against the NBA star. People all over the country booed and hissed and said, "I told you so." For once, I had nothing to say.

I was stunned. I have championed rape victims' rights for so long. I vividly remember being present when the Georgia Senate Judiciary Panel passed the Georgia Rape Shield Law, which protects rape victims from having their names dragged through the mud and being painted as tramps—or worse. Whether this particular girl was a runaround or a tramp or a party girl was no one's business. What I cared about was whether she had been raped. Her blood on the front tail of Bryant's shirt along with vaginal lacerations and a bruise on her jaw said it all to me. I believed her. And then, bit by bit, it trickled out. Her sexual history, her medical history, her alleged suicide attempts—you name it. But those didn't erase the blood and the bruise. I could never turn away from that.

After watching the defense attorney, Pamela Mackey, in court and hearing what the judge was letting her get away with, I accepted that a conviction would likely never happen. I repeatedly predicted either a hung jury or an outright acquittal. I never predicted that the case would simply be dropped.

That ain't justice.

I don't blame the young woman. Her whole life was turned upside down. Despite the outrageous personal attacks she endured, I always thought in the end the case would go to trial and that a jury of twelve would make a decision. It didn't happen. After the last round of highly personal information about her, garnered through a series of closed-door hearings, was released on the Internet, I shouldn't have been surprised it ended the way it did, but I still was.

The only one ripped off was Lady Justice. A common ploy to raise the price of a civil settlement is to wait until the last minute—until you are literally on the courthouse steps set to strike the jury. I believe that's just what happened here. At the eleventh hour, when trial was so near, the jury was waiting to be struck, when the price was as high as it would ever be—at that crucial hour—the case was dropped. Bryant released a public statement in which he stated that he believed their encounter to be consensual but now recognized that the alleged victim thought that the sex was not consensual. It read, in part, "I now understand how she feels that she did not consent to this encounter." Hello! That's what rape *is*—nonconsensual sex. It is logical to reason that Kobe's defense would never have allowed the statement unless a settlement had been locked in at the highest price. Even though, as of this writing, both sides have denied there's a financial settlement in the offing, I'll wager a multimillion-dollar deal will go down. Count on it.

Was she wrong? Yes. Do I blame her? No. I haven't been in her shoes. Who I do blame, however, is the trial judge who took the case after the preliminary hearing. Judge Terry Ruckriegle allowed one devastating leak after the next and never got to the source of multiple leaks. I also blame the prosecutor. If I believed in my heart that a rape had occurred, then that case should have been taken to trial, win or lose. I'd have called the alleged victim to the stand and then made my case. I would never, never let the courthouse be a high-class brokerage firm for an NBA star and an alleged victim, a middleman who brokered "justice" for money.

THE AFTERMATH OF
STATE V. KOBE BRYANT

In the next two minutes, someone will be sexually assaulted in America. Six minutes from now, another woman will be raped. Each hour, thirty women are sexually assaulted, ten of them raped, in this great country of ours. After watching the Kobe Bryant saga, how many of those women will come forward?

The way the Bryant accuser was treated was a disgrace, regardless of what one may think of Bryant's guilt or innocence. Every alleged victim is due a certain degree of respect. Guilt is for the jury to decide. She was ridiculed, forced by threats to leave her own home, tracked like a hunted animal, and betrayed by "friends."

The defense team made sure the alleged victim's reputation was poisoned long before opening statements were ever to be given, and nothing was done by the judge to remedy that. Now, believe it or not, a rape-crisis counselor is actually under federal investigation for allegedly trying to sell the girl's private file. The judge in this case even disallowed the prosecution from referring to Bryant's accuser as a "victim." I guess vaginal bleeding and a bruise to the jaw weren't enough for Judge Ruckriegle.

I predict my colleagues on the other side of the fence and I will argue about this case forever. There is, though, one thing that even they will silently agree to: After the Bryant case, would they come forward and report the crime if they were raped? No way. Think about it. Would you?

A SMALL VICTORY

The goings-on in the Bryant proceedings triggered a change in Colorado state law in 2004. It's a small step in the right direction—but there's a lot more that has to be done to protect rape victims and prevent attacks on them in court.

In April 2004, Colorado governor Bill Owens signed Senate Bill 46 into law with the support of the Colorado District Attorneys' Council. It gives alleged victims of sexual assault a better chance of maintaining anonymity as their cases make their way through the courts, by offering them the option of being identified in records and open court by a pseudonym, like Jane Doe.

As of this writing, another bill in the legislative pipeline is Senate Bill 217, which would require all motions filed relating to rape-shield issues to be sealed, to ensure the allegations presented to a judge don't become public until a decision is made on their admissibility. The bill would also affect Colorado's current rape-shield law, ordering that evidence about a victim's or witness's sexual history must be presumed irrelevant unless it can be shown to bear directly on the facts of the case. Had this bill been passed into law prior to Bryant's case, many of the defense's claims about the alleged victim would never have been made public—at least until trial.

THE "PREPPY MURDER" CASE: TAKING THE "BLAME" DEFENSE MAINSTREAM

Long before the Kobe Bryant rape case put the alleged victim on trial, there was the "Preppy Murder" case. Jennifer Levin, a pretty teenager who lived in SoHo in New York City, was killed in Central Park in August 1986. Her partially nude body was found early one morning by a cyclist. She was lying on her back with her legs spread. Her neck bore wounds indicating she was strangled to death. Levin also had bruises and bite marks suggesting she'd tried to fight back against her attacker.

The morning police were called to the scene, a crowd had gathered and stood at a nearby wall. One witness, real estate broker Susan Bird, noticed a young man with "a nice face" among the onlookers. The next time Bird saw the man, it was when his photograph appeared in the papers in connection with the case. That man was Robert Chambers.

Nineteen-year-old Chambers was dubbed the "Preppy Killer" because of his deceptively clean-cut looks and Upper East Side address. Once Chambers was charged with murder, his defense attorney, Jack Litman, based his defense on the hateful strategy that pitted the "party girl" Levin, who got what she asked for, against a handsome preppy who was simply defending himself from her sexual demands. It worked. The jury was deadlocked on the murder charge. Chambers pled guilty to manslaughter. He got fifteen years.

Chambers walked free from New York's Auburn Prison on February 14, 2003. He was scheduled for an even earlier release, but a long series of violations and infractions behind bars added several years to his release date. The Associated Press reported that between July 1988 and June 1997, Chambers was docked seventy-five months of good time due to multiple violations of prison rules. Now that he is free, Chambers isn't even under parole supervision. In the eyes of the law, he has paid his debt in full for the brutal choking of Jennifer Levin. As predicted by prosecutors, Robert Chambers was back in trouble with the law in no time following his release for the death of Jennifer Levin. On November 24, 2004, Chambers was arraigned on two misdemeanors— drug possession and driving with a suspended license. Chambers, naturally, claimed he had nothing to do with the crime and that he was once again a victim of circumstances.

Chambers's release is not the only disturbing aspect of the trial.

The long-term legacy of the so-called Preppy Murder is that it was the first highly publicized case where the victim was crucified to save the killer. The treatment of Levin by Chambers's defense team, as well as by the media, was disgraceful. That's the only word for it. Levin's murder "entertained" New York City like no other. The reports of the killing in Central Park mesmerized the public with stories of "rough sex" and allegations of a promiscuous lifestyle among the city's wealthy and pampered teens. The public frenzy was fueled by tabloids that ran headlines like JEN'S SEX DIARY, SEX PLAY GOT ROUGH, KINKY SEX, EARLY DEATH, and HOW JENNY COURTED DEATH. For two years, those headlines, and others like them, seeped into the jury pool.

The headlines somehow made these sleazy versions of Levin's death official. All the nasty innuendo by the defense was given the stamp of believability simply because the papers reported it. Day in and day out, it was reported that Jennifer had caused her own murder. The seed was planted that a young girl who drinks in a bar with a man late at night and leaves with him deserves whatever she gets.

By the time the trial began, defense attorney Litman's venomous attack on Levin was going full speed, and the blame-the-victim defense was firmly established. Levin was trashed before the jury and in the media and portrayed as a drunken, promiscuous brat. Six-foot-four-inch Chambers claimed Levin, at five foot three inches and 120 pounds, attacked him and roughed him up during sexual play outdoors in the chilly air behind Manhattan's Metropolitan Museum of Art. He stated in a confession to police that he'd choked her to death in self-defense. The media devoured the story.

During the trial, Chambers was routinely described as "handsome," "promising," and headed for an exciting future, except for that pesky speed bump of a murder trial. Even the media's labeling of the case as the "Preppy Murder" was misleading. The dark side of Chambers's personality, which included extensive drug abuse and a criminal history of burglary and theft, never came out at trial. Chambers was not a preppy. He'd been thrown out of college. His entire scholastic record was one of failure and disappointment. After his poor performance in prep school, his mother somehow got him into Boston University, but there again his own behavior got him into trouble. Even before his second semester kicked off, Chambers was asked to leave the college over an issue with a stolen credit card. Alcohol and drugs eventually landed Chambers at the Hazelden Clinic in Minnesota.

There were many stomach-churning moments during the trial, but one stands out in my memory to this day. A home video shot by a friend that wound up on a tabloid television program showed a downright scary Chambers smirking and ripping the head off a female doll, then turning to the camera, flashing a big smile, and saying, "Oops! I think I killed it."

Chambers has never shown remorse publicly. At one of his parole hearings he said, "I guess I could also give you the party line and say I have learned my lesson, I will never do this again, but that's not how I feel at the moment." That says it all. Chambers is free, and Jennifer is dead and buried, leaving behind her devastated family and a tattered reputation. Her mother still grieves. As we've seen in the Bryant case, the Preppy Murder's legacy of the blame-the-victim defense is alive and well and living in America's courts.

THE CENTRAL PARK JOGGER

In her 2003 autobiography, *I Am the Central Park Jogger*, Trisha Meili wrote, "Shortly after 9 P.M. on April 19, 1989, a young woman, out for her run in New York's Central Park, was bludgeoned, raped, sodomized, and beaten so savagely that doctors despaired for her life and a horrified nation cried out in pain and outrage." New York City, and the world, reeled in shock as facts emerged surrounding the brutal gang rape of a woman who'd been left for dead and became known for years only as "the Central Park Jogger."

The 1989 trial made it clear that many of those in power were not interested in pursuing the prevention of violence against women. The victim's reputation was beyond reproach. She was a successful investment banker. She's wasn't a drug addict, she was an executive who worked long hours every day. She was monogamous with one boyfriend. She was a fitness fanatic who worked out by running religiously. None of that mattered—she was still to blame.

There are over two hundred rapes a day in this country—a fact that was rarely discussed in the press during the weeks and months following Meili's attack and then at trial. These women are victims. Instead of recognizing Meili as part of that group, the defense in the case sent a chilling message to independent women everywhere by casting blame on the investment banker herself. "What was she doing in the park?" they asked. "Didn't she know that a woman shouldn't be on the street after dark? Didn't she in some way 'ask for it'?" Other attacks labeled her a workaholic, an anorexic, and a control freak who thought she owned the park. I found this absolutely outrageous. When the traditional attacks on rape victims didn't work in this case, the defense dug deep to find a whole new way to crucify a rape victim. None of their slurs were true.

In retrospect, there are some important lessons to learn from this case about the deeply unjust nature of the attacks that were aimed at the jogger. We learned that when the standard slanders on a rape victim do not apply, we must not lower our guard. The blame-the-victim strategy is always there, ready to take on any form. For instance, there were a myriad of "should-have"s used to blame the victim in the jogger case. The jogger *should have* known that Central Park is dangerous. She *should have* known that thugs hang out there. She *should have* gone running with a friend. She *should have* been home tucked away behind a locked apartment door. But she wasn't. And we are not. We've all innocently taken some chances that looked unsafe in retrospect. Just because she chose to live her life, the jogger suffered horrific and painful consequences.

Luckily, she survived. Fourteen years after being known only as "the Jogger," Trisha Meili emerged from the shadows and authored a bestseller about her experience. She survived not only a brutal attack in New York's Central Park, but a punishing one in the courtroom as well.

SPREADING THE BLAME

The blame-the-victim defense isn't limited to rape cases. Consider these other high-profile cases where the victim was attacked in the courtroom by defense attorneys gunning for a not-guilty verdict at any and all costs.

BONNY LEE BAKLEY

On the evening of May 4, 2001, the actor Robert Blake, who starred in the television series *Baretta* in the seventies and is best known for his role in the film *In Cold Blood*, went out to dinner with his wife, Bonny Lee Bakley. The couple went to one of Blake's favorite Italian restaurants, Vitello's, located in the Studio City section of Los Angeles. Blake parked on a back street about one and a half blocks away, instead of in front of the restaurant as usual. The actor says that after dinner he realized he'd left his gun inside the restaurant, a gun he claimed he carried because he feared that Bakley's life was in danger. Leaving her alone in his car in a darkened alley, he walked back to the restaurant. No one, including busboys, remembers Blake retrieving anything. Instead he came back into the restaurant, drank a glass of water and returned to his car, where he says he discovered Bakley shot to death after being away from her for just a few moments.

A neighbor who came to help Bakley noted that the passenger window was rolled down and there was no shattered glass. The car's interior was covered with blood. Bakley was still alive, making gurgling sounds and gasping for air. The neighbor, not Blake, tried to render aid to the dying woman.

When asked by the police to take a polygraph test that night, Blake refused. He claimed he was too distraught. Blake also reportedly said that he feared he would fail the test because, as in the O. J. Simpson case, he'd had dreams of killing her and thought that could skew the lie-detector results. He also reportedly stated he blamed himself for her death because he'd left her alone in the car and thought that could skew the test results as well.

Court TV reported that two stuntmen who had once worked as body doubles on *Baretta* testified that the actor had offered them money in exchange for help in killing his wife. Gary "Whiz Kid" McLarty testified in 2003 that Blake offered him $10,000 to "pop" his wife in a bizarre setup similar to her actual murder behind an Italian restaurant. Whoever pulled the trigger that night didn't travel far from the scene to dump the murder weapon—LAPD found the gun thrown into a nearby Dumpster.

With facts like those stacked against the defense, there's only one place to point the blame—at the victim. On the night of the murder, Blake's lawyer, Harland Braun, moved in pronto, racing Blake to a hospital to manage his "high blood pressure." The antivictim posturing began with Braun himself taking all questions and diverting the media toward several far-fetched theories. Braun immediately began to poison the potential jury pool by lambasting Bakley as a lowlife who conned lonely men with topless photos of herself and promises of sex. Braun went so far as to hypothesize that any one of Bakley's swindled customers could have murdered her.

He also openly attacked the marriage itself, describing it as "troubled." It was then reported that Blake had married Bakley only because she was pregnant with his child. In order to shift focus from the obvious and most likely suspect, his client, Braun threw out another possibility: that a dangerous neighborhood burglar might have killed Bakley.

Bonny Lee Bakley's character was assassinated before the trial even started. Her past and her every wrongdoing were twisted into accusations, publicized, and used as a defense tool. I wonder what makes her any more disposable than you or me? Is her life less valuable because of who she was? I hope not.

The search for justice in Bonny Lee Bakley's case suffered intensely because she wasn't a "good girl." Plus, there's another victim who suffered as a result of all the horrible press about Bakley—her daughter. Rose Lenore Sophia, born June 2, 2000, was an infant at the time of her mother's murder. Someday she'll read the articles, hear the reports, and learn what was said about her mother. In their zeal to blame the victim, the defense has even managed to destroy a little girl's most precious memories.

NICOLE BROWN SIMPSON

Even now, more than ten years after the brutal slayings of Nicole Brown Simpson and Ron Goldman, O. J. Simpson still blames his ex-wife for her own murder. The former NFL star long ago gave up searching for her "real killer." Simpson has said, "Sometimes I think that instead of putting off the move to Florida, I should have grabbed Nicole and the kids and changed our environment. I wonder how things would have turned out." He blames the "bad crowd" his wife kept company with after they divorced and says her death resulted from her own ill-advised connections, possibly involving drugs. "A month before she died, I had an argument with her about those people," he has said. "Something was out of control here." All of his unsubstantiated claims are just words.

But words do matter. Simpson's defense team asked Judge Ito to order the prosecution to use the phrase "domestic discord" rather than "domestic violence." The defense preferred euphemisms for wife beating instead of the harsh truth. Terms like "battered wife" and "stalker" were taboo as well, according to the defense.

Shortly before her death, Nicole Brown told her mother, Juditha, that she was deathly afraid of Simpson. "I go to the gas station, [Simpson] is there. I go to the Payless Shoe Store and he's there. I'm driving and he's behind me. . . . I'm scared." It wasn't the first time Nicole's own words of fear and hopelessness had chronicled her deep-seated fear of her ex-husband. Detailed descriptions of the physical abuse inflicted upon her by Simpson were recorded in her diary. Brown even called a battered-women's shelter five days before her murder. There were multiple complaints of domestic abuse made by Brown against O. J. Simpson to the police. Most of those reports never made it to the jury. The jury saw one photo of her face bruised and swollen, but the majority of alleged prior abuse didn't make it into evidence.

Instead of learning about the private hell Brown endured, the jury heard endless references to her alleged drug use, her dating history, her "questionable" friends and their flaws, and her penchant for partying. The defense even tried to blame Brown's and Goldman's deaths on a mysterious Colombian drug dealer. Only Simpson was completely blameless.

In an interview that aired on Fox in 2004, Simpson actually said he often feels "angry" at Nicole for falling in with the wrong crowd. Unbelievable. These many years later, it continues, coming full circle on the ten-year mark of her murder, the relentless blaming of Nicole Brown, the victim.

GRUMPY OLD MAN . . .
THE ROBERT DURST DEFENSE

In the 2003 murder case involving eccentric millionaire Robert Durst, his claim that the murder victim was grumpy and cantankerous resulted in an acquittal. Back in 2000, Robert Durst left New York under suspicion that he had killed his wife, twenty-nine-year-old medical student Kathie Durst. The sixty-year-old millionaire had been a hot topic in the city's newspapers ever since Kathie disappeared without a trace in 1982.

After relocating to Galveston, Texas, Durst disguised himself as a mute woman. Later that year, he was arrested and charged with murdering an elderly neighbor in their run-down apartment complex. Durst was acquitted of the murder charge in November 2003. The defendant closed his eyes and dropped his mouth open in disbelief as Judge Susan Criss read the panel's not-guilty verdict in open court. I was just as shocked as the defendant. The verdict was a sickening surprise to many, as Durst had admitted to dismembering seventy-one-year-old Morris Black and disposing of his body in Galveston Bay. The courtroom was packed with reporters from around the world, drawn to the Texas Gulf Coast community by the bizarre facts of the case and because of the celebrity associated with the Durst name. The Durst Organization owns skyscrapers and other real estate in New York worth billions. Defendant Durst had been passed over for control of the family business despite being Seymour Durst's oldest child.

Durst took the stand at trial under his attorney's direct exam and attacked the victim. Without the traditional ammunition of the victim's having a bad reputation or an extensive rap sheet, Durst was determined to disparage a lonely senior citizen living in a $300-a-month rental. He portrayed his elderly neighbor as angry, complaining, unreasonable, and hard to get along with. He claimed under oath that Black was a cranky and confrontational loner and said that it was Black who'd threatened him, with Durst's own gun, on September 28, 2001. But it was Black who wound up dead after being shot in the face with Durst's pistol.

During several days on the stand, Durst testified that he panicked after shooting Black because he was living under an assumed name and being investigated in his wife's disappearance. He assumed the police would never believe his story about Black's death. He testified that while under the influence of alcohol, he dismembered Black's body, dumped it in Galveston Bay, and cleaned up the scene. The victim's head was never recovered.

THE SAN FRANCISCO DOG-MAULING CASE

A beautiful, all-American lacrosse player was mauled to death by two hundred-plus-pound Presa Canario dogs on January 26, 2001. The victim, thirty-three-year-old Diane Whipple, was simply trying to get into her own apartment while juggling an armload of groceries. There had been numerous complaints and fears raised in the apartment building concerning the two aggressive and seemingly uncontrollable dogs. It all culminated in Whipple's being mauled to death. To make matters worse, the dogs were in the care of one of their owners at the time. The dog's owners, Marjorie Knoller and her husband, Robert Noel, both attorneys, went on trial for the outrageous death.

I met personally with Whipple's friends, and they told me they were horrified by the personal attacks made at trial and in the press against Diane. Knoller and Noel had promptly gone on the offense, claiming that the victim brought on the attack by putting herself in harm's way. In letters to San Francisco prosecutors, the couple boldly claimed Whipple brought the attack on herself by entering the hallway outside her apartment after Knoller had pushed her inside and gotten control of the attacking dog, Bane.

The attorneys also accused Whipple of using steroids or wearing a pheromone-based fragrance that drew the dogs to her, provoking aggressive behavior in them. She's mauled to death and they blame her perfume! "The presence of either of those substances would also explain Ms. Whipple's behavior at the time of the incident in leaving the confines and safety of her apartment and coming into the hall to confront the dog after Ms. Knoller had secured it," according to one letter signed by Noel, demanding that police preserve evidence of such substances.

One resident of the building called the allegations outrageous. "I'm absolutely speechless," said Derek Brown, who was living one floor below the attorneys at the time of the attack. "Every time they [the dogs] have crossed my path, they've gone berserk and lunged at me, trying to take a chunk out of me."

The five-week trial riveted the country, as prosecutors described the horrific attack in which Whipple was bitten all over her body, her throat ripped and her clothes torn off. The jury of seven men and five women saw graphic photos of the victim's ravaged body. There were deep wounds visible from her ankles to her face. Pictures of the blood-stained hallway where the attack occurred depicted the horror Whipple must have felt as she fought for her life. Despite all that, Noel continued his contentions in a separate nineteen-page letter to the district attorney. The defendant placed the blame for the death squarely on the victim. It began, he said, when the victim, standing outside her own door, stared at Bane. Knoller told Whipple, who was uninjured at that point, not to move. Knoller crawled out on her knees with the dog behind. But Whipple did not stay inside, Noel said. "Marjorie has no idea why Ms. Whipple, rather than remaining in her apartment and closing the door, came out into the hall and toward Marjorie and Bane," wrote Noel. The defendants went on to write with some levity, in another letter not to the district attorney, that Ms. Whipple was "acting very macho, when in fact she lives in fear of the dog."

So here we see an unarmed, innocent victim whose throat was literally torn out, attacked on the grounds that she must have been on steroids (she wasn't), worn a fragrance enticing to dogs (she didn't), and taken foolish chances (certainly not true). Needless to say, their creative blame-the-victim strategy, although it was imaginative, didn't work.

The owners of the two dogs that attacked and killed Whipple were found guilty of all charges against them, including involuntary manslaughter and having a mischievous animal that kills. Marjorie Knoller was also found guilty of second-degree murder. Her husband, Robert Noel, sixty, sat without emotion as the verdict was read. Although he was not at home at the time of the attack, the jury agreed with the prosecution's argument that he and his wife had willfully ignored multiple warnings about their two large Presa Canarios, Bane and Hera, knew they were a danger, and refused to act. Both dogs were destroyed.

SUFFER THE CHILDREN

There are no winners in child-molestation cases. Even when there is a guilty verdict, no one is truly victorious. A child is forever harmed. They will go on to school, they'll play on the playground, they'll make their beds and clean their rooms and go on with their "normal" lives. But they will never, ever be the same. There will forever be flashbacks, insecurities, and overwhelming feelings of helplessness. Some will have thoughts of suicide. Their pain will follow them into their own adulthood and their relationships. When I prosecuted these cases, all I could do was let the victims and their families leave the courthouse knowing that, win or lose, somebody had fought back.

Child-molestation cases are unique in the way they must be tried. In these cases, you'd expect that children would be spared the blame-the-victim defense. Sadly, this is not so. Defense attorneys just position their strategy differently. Typical attacks made include claims that the child is lying or the child has been coached. In custody or divorce cases, it's not uncommon to hear claims like, "This is about the mother—she wants money" or "The child is making it all up." "The child has learning problems and doesn't know what he or she is saying" is another. Those are just a few of the don't-blame-me strategies commonly used. They are manipulated to fit the facts of each case.

In a child-molestation case I tried in 1988, *State v. McCann*, the defendant, Antonio McCann, was good-looking, successful, and articulate. He approached the victim, an eleven-year-old boy who was learning-impaired, and befriended him. For a period of months, McCann traded anal sex with the child for rolls of quarters. He had found the victim in a video arcade and was using the child's love of video games to gain his trust. He disgusted me. I was fearful of the he's-making-it-up defense, because my victim, who stood maybe four feet tall, had a severe learning disability. It was incredibly difficult to unlock the truth, interpret the child's language, and tell his story to the jury. The rolls of quarters McCann gave to my little victim for use in the arcade were the greatest thing to him. The defense was right about one thing—the boy didn't understand what was happening. But I did, and so did the jury. McCann was found guilty of aggravated child molestation.

Sometimes local laws don't help prosecutors of child-molestation cases. In an effort to aid the defendant, the statute often equates children with "idiots." In other words, a child below a certain age must first be "qualified" under the law to testify. It is a simple matter of going through a series of questions with the child witness before beginning substantive testimony. Questions like "How old are you? Where do you go to school? What is the difference between telling the truth and telling a story? What happens if you tell a story? Is that a bad thing?" are frequently asked. The questions seem innocuous, but the reality is that it doesn't help to go through the "qualifying" questions with a witness in front of a jury. No other witness is treated in this manner. Straight out of the gate, the prosecutor has to bolster the witness's credibility before a word of testimony is uttered. This is a clear advantage to the defense in every case with a child victim.

In some jurisdictions, the "qualifying" groundwork for substantive testimony can apply to a child up to the ages of thirteen or fourteen. It is presumed that children may not know truth from fantasy. It represents one more hurdle for prosecutors to clear in order to have a victim testify. Simply put, at the outset these young victims can then be attacked on the grounds that they are not old enough to separate fantasy from the truth. In my experience, children are the least likely witnesses to tell a lie. They don't always have the talent of guile, the ability to lie with a straight face that unfortunately we adults achieve over the course of a lifetime.

The ages for prosecuting various attacks on children vary. In other words, in a single jurisdiction it's a crime to videotape a sexual act with someone under the age of eighteen, but it's statutory rape to have sex with someone under the age of fourteen. The laws vary, especially when it comes to sex crimes, making prosecution confusing. Luckily, in *State v. McCann*, the jury could see through it all.

CAN'T BLAME THE VICTIM? BLAME THE PARENTS!

When an innocent child victim manages to escape blame by the defense and media, the defense's hands are tied. Defense attorneys certainly can't blame the perpetrator, their client. Who else is left? The victim's parents! It's their fault! Lawyers conveniently channel their vitriol toward the parents when victims are so young and innocent that even the defense can't blame them with a straight face. These heartbreaking cases illustrate a despicable practice that's quickly becoming the gold standard in child-molestation defense.

DANIELLE VAN DAM

I was in California during the search for seven-year-old Danielle van Dam when I was walking past a little twelve-inch television set and noticed on the screen there were helicopters swarming around a group of trees near a roadside. The news crawl across the bottom of the screen said a girl's body had been found. I stood there with my hand to my throat, frozen to the spot! I knew it was the missing girl. It wasn't long before others joined me, silently watching the story unfold. Some people cried, others couldn't bear what they were about to hear and walked away. It was the missing girl, and she was dead.

She was identified by a plastic necklace and a single Mickey Mouse earring she'd been wearing the night she disappeared. When I heard police describe the body as that of a young girl about three to four feet tall, it struck me how helpless this tiny victim had been against her attacker.

I'd been watching the case since first hearing of the child's disappearance. As the weeks passed, statistics increasingly pointed toward the likelihood she was dead, but until that moment I saw the recovery scene on TV, inside I held a spark of hope that she was somehow still alive.

The little girl went missing from her two-story home in suburban San Diego on Saturday morning, February 1, 2002. Her father had put her to bed around 10:00 P.M. that Friday night, tucked her in, and said good night. The discovery of her remains came just one day after the van Dams' neighbor, David Westerfield, pled not guilty to charges of murder, kidnapping of a child under fourteen, and possession of child pornography. Van Dam's only contact with Westerfield was when she had sold Girl Scout cookies to him earlier that same year.

Shortly after Danielle was reported missing, Westerfield appeared at his dry cleaner's wearing no shoes or socks and carrying a comforter with hair on it from the van Dams' dog. Westerfield also gave his dry cleaner a jacket spotted with van Dam's blood. Her blood, hair, and fingerprints were found in Westerfield's recreational vehicle. Prosecutors believe that Westerfield abducted van Dam from her bedroom and took her to his house just two doors away, all while her father and two brothers were asleep down the hall. Her mother was out for the evening with coworkers.

With overwhelming evidence stacked against their client, what was the defense to do? At first, Westerfield's team tried to blame the victim. That's pretty hard to do with a seven-year-old girl, but they did try. They argued it was the youngster's own fault that her hair and clothing fibers turned up in Westerfield's home, bedsheets, and laundry by claiming the little girl had found her way into his bedroom while in the home on the occasion she was selling the Girl Scout cookies. They claimed her palm print ended up on the nightstand beside Westerfield's bed in his giant RV because she played where she shouldn't have. They reasoned that her disobedience in leaving her own yard and venturing into his vehicle was why her blood and hair were also found in the motor home, not because their client killed her there.

When that strategy fell flat, the defense lawyers turned their creative attention to Danielle's parents, Brenda and Damon van Dam. The parents were crucified. It started with Westerfield's claim that he had been hanging out with Brenda van Dam and her friends in a bar. Brenda denied dancing with Westerfield but did testify she and her husband had smoked pot the night Danielle went missing. Brenda also disclosed she and her husband had been "swingers," partner-swapping in the past. Defense attorney Steven Feldman intimated that blond hairs found in Westerfield's recreational vehicle could belong to Brenda, suggesting that Brenda had some kind of relationship with the defendant. The attacks on Brenda van Dam were outrageous.

Feldman argued it was the decadent lifestyle of the child's parents that set the stage for her murder, not by his client, Westerfield, but by a "predator" the couple had unwittingly befriended. Feldman's argument stirred the pot, and suddenly unsolicited "activists" began publicly demanding that Brenda and Damon van Dam, in addition to losing their daughter in the most heinous way, be charged with negligent child abuse resulting in death—a felony. Feldman argued that the van Dams' lifestyle "put their children at risk," opening their doors to unsavory characters. So after their little girl was brutally murdered, her parents faced losing their other two children.

Even more disturbing about the treatment the defense dealt out to Danielle's parents, somehow blaming them for her murder, was the fact that Westerfield's lawyers knew all along that he'd taken Danielle. Sources said prosecutors were on the verge of accepting the offer of Westerfield's defense team, life without parole, in exchange for his disclosing the location of Danielle's body. Just before the deal was struck, volunteers found the little girl's remains just east of El Cajon. When prosecutors no longer needed Westerfield's information, the deal collapsed. Of course, evidence of plea negotiations cannot be used as evidence in a trial, so the jury never knew Westerfield could easily have directed police straight to Danielle's remains and eased her parents' suffering.

Despite all this, defense attorney Steven Feldman knowingly dragged Danielle's parents through the mud. Westerfield killed their daughter, and then his lawyer destroyed their reputation.

After one of the most brutal and unjustified attacks on a victim's parents I have ever witnessed, David Westerfield was convicted and sentenced to death by a California jury. While on death row, he has written numerous letters, still blaming the parents. Westerfield now claims the van Dams framed him. Many may scoff at these unfounded claims, but remember, there is still an appeals process ahead. Westerfield is sitting on death row with nothing to lose, so count on him to continue the vicious attacks on the van Dam family.

Danielle's death foreshadowed dangerous and disturbing times to come. Danielle's kidnap and murder preceded a series of child-abduction cases, including Elizabeth Smart in Utah, Samantha Runnion in California, Cassandra Williamson in Missouri, Erica Pratt in Philadelphia, Carlie Brucia in Florida, and others. I predict that the same blame-the-victim defense will somehow make its way into these trials as well.

"TOO PERFECT" . . . THE ELIZABETH SMART DEFENSE

I remember the night my face got hot and my voice cracked when I analyzed on national television the likelihood that Elizabeth Smart was still alive. I was the only one on the legal panel who would state what the statistics foretold. I could hardly bring myself to say it, but it was true, whether I liked it or not. Statistics are what they are, and they indicated that Elizabeth was dead. Many of us held a secret belief, a hope that somehow she would come home, but the hope dwindled every day. Then . . . a miracle.

I remember getting the news that Elizabeth was alive. I immediately dropped to my knees and thanked God. Over the months since her kidnap, I had gotten to know Lois and Ed Smart and through them, Elizabeth as well. The nation rejoiced when Elizabeth Smart was finally found in March 2003 and was returned to her family after being snatched from a second-floor bedroom of her beautiful home in the middle of an upscale neighborhood. By the time the citizens of her hometown of Salt Lake City gathered to celebrate the news in the same park where a candlelight vigil had been held after she was kidnapped, rumors and accusations that once lived only in late-night chat rooms made themselves public. Somehow, it was the parents' fault—they were too involved in their church, too trusting, too perfect. Something was horribly "wrong" inside the Smart home.

No one seemed to accept that a zealot had taken this lovely girl as his child-bride, held her prisoner, mistreated and abused her, hiding her in plain sight for months. It happened. But even her return and the arrests of Brian Mitchell and his evil sidekick Wanda Barzee didn't stop the painful and illogical allegations. The public wasn't appeased to learn of Elizabeth's unbelievable pain and misfortune; there just had to be a "darker side" to it all, and so the Smarts suffered even more.

The finger-pointing focused on her parents, Ed and Lois Smart. The two had battled tirelessly for the safe return of Elizabeth, yet there seemed to be little pity for them. Why? The list of things they'd done to earn public scorn was a long one. They had employed the homeless to work on their home. Shortly before Mitchell came along, down-on-his-luck Richard Ricci was hired for odd jobs at the Smart home. It was not until after Ricci was fired by Ed Smart for stealing that his rap sheet—including burglary, aggravated robbery, and attempted murder—was discovered. Somehow, for hiring the homeless, it was openly concluded that the Smarts had violated their sacred trust to protect their children. How heartbreaking this must have been for parents who had lived through so much pain and turmoil for such a long time.

There was already speculation that Elizabeth's disappearance was an "inside job," that Elizabeth was really a rebellious runaway, and that somehow the whole thing was mixed up with the family's deep involvement with their Mormon church. By the time the dust settled, the family had been skewered, polygraphed, and ridiculed. But you know what? They never listened. They believed. Even when police told them they were wrong to continue hoping for their daughter's safe return, they fought and they brought their girl home. Alive.

I'll never understand why people were eager to heap blame on the Smarts. It's not as if those blaming the victims were defense attorneys with a "job" to do. There was nothing to gain by attacking Elizabeth or her family. Then it dawned on me. People wanted to blame the Smarts as a way of saying that this would never happen in *their* home. I really believe that was the misguided reasoning behind a lot of the mean-spirited talk about the Smarts. The thinking was, *I'd never bring someone I didn't know into my home. I'd never be at risk the way the Smart family was because I simply wouldn't be that naïve.* This self-serving thinking was so pervasive that it allowed the hard truth to be avoided: *We are all at risk.* It doesn't matter if it's the cable guy, the mailman, the yard guy, the door-to-door salesman, the woman with a broken-down car, the Avon lady, or the pizza deliveryman. The world gets in.

The world finds a way in whether you are rich or poor, white or black, college-educated or a day laborer. I had to learn this at a very young age. Things can happen to you. They happened to me. Blaming the victim may make you believe you're insulated, may make you sleep better at night, but the reasoning is simply not true. Sure, the finger-pointers may feel better, but they make the victims feel so much worse. And in the Elizabeth Smart case, it all turned out to be lies.

As for the Smart family, it's not over yet. There is still a trial to come. Initially Elizabeth's parents did not want their daughter to take the stand in the case against her alleged abductors, Wanda Barzee and Brian "Emmanuel" Mitchell. They did not want their daughter to have to live through her ordeal again. After seeing the debacle surrounding the alleged victim in the Kobe Bryant case, can you blame them? Elizabeth will be cross-examined, and the usual defense tactics will be employed. None of them will be believed, of course, but the damage to this beautiful girl on cross-exam, after all she has managed to survive, will last a lifetime. The choice? Let them walk free. I believe that Elizabeth Smart will take the stand and that after hearing her, a jury will convict. The truth will shine out like a light.

BEAT IT! (THE MICHAEL JACKSON DEFENSE STRATEGY)

As a result of Jackson's most recent child-molestation charges, the "blame-the-victim" machine is in high throttle. Press reports and Jackson sympathizers assert outright that the boy's mother and other relatives coached him into claiming molestation. They also claim the child's family is only out for money—a multimillion-dollar settlement, to be exact, similar to the one in Jackson's first known molestation scandal in the early nineties.

Instead of focusing on the seriousness of the actual child-molestation claims in Jackson's case, critics wonder out loud and in print why the mother allowed her child to spend so much time with a forty-year-old man, especially in light of past molestation claims against Jackson. Attacks on the parents started almost immediately after the charge was made public. Media outlets seemed thrilled to announce that the boy's family was also involved in a lawsuit alleging that they'd been mistreated by mall security guards. Reports of the couple's wrangling over a divorce, including the boy's father pleading no contest to domestic abuse and child cruelty, were gobbled up like tasty appetizers in anticipation of a sumptuous main course . . . the trial!

Here's the reality that Jackson supporters don't want the public to know about: Regarding the mall incident, J.C. Penney Co. paid $137,500 in 1999 to settle the suit. Court records show that the family claimed that security guards had manhandled the boy, his mother, and his brother after alleging the boy had left the store carrying clothes that hadn't been paid for. The mother also contended that she was fondled by one of the guards at the time of the 1998 confrontation.

As to the domestic claims, when the mother filed for divorce, a bitter fight was ignited, one that included criminal charges of abuse filed against the dad. The father's attorney, Russell Halpern, claimed that the mother lied about the abuse and had a "Svengali-like" power to make her children repeat her lies. The reality is that the boy's father pled no contest to a 2002 claim of child cruelty. The father also pled no contest to spousal abuse in 2001. So much for "coaching." Those are the facts.

While the boy and his family were taking the heat, no one seemed to be taking a hard look at Jackson himself. After all, *he* was the one accused of child molestation. Jackson's career stalled well before the current criminal case surfaced because of bizarre and highly publicied behavior, but in my book that's the least of his credibility problems. Prior bad acts, known legally as "similar transactions," are coming back to haunt him. The 1993 child-molestation scandal rebounded like a boomerang, finally hitting him in court. The sworn affidavit of his first accuser, with whom Jackson settled for millions in order to keep the claims quiet, swears that Jackson kissed him on the mouth, fondled him, and twisted his nipples in bed while the boy's mom was not around. Remember, this is the 1993 alleged victim under oath.

Even though he was never charged with a crime in that case, the King of Pop's credibility is in grave jeopardy, all by his own doing. Publicly denying his obvious and extensive plastic surgery, attributing a drastic change in skin tone to the pigment disorder vitiligo, publicly stating on national television he has sleepovers with boys, and blaming his troubles on racism and on some wacky conspiracy to get Michael Jackson, all turned many die-hard fans against him.

It is apparently a lot easier for people to dwell on the boy's family dysfunction as opposed to dealing with claims that a pop superstar molests little boys. Nevertheless, the family's issues are critical to the case. Jackson's defense insisted that the mother and child are not to be believed, fueling the credibility contest between a world-renowned superstar and a middle- to low-income little boy.

THE EVIDENCE MOUNTS

In the summer of 2004, stunning new developments in the Michael Jackson case landed like a bomb and bolstered the state's case against him. It seems that once again Jackson has escaped criminal prosecution by paying off another alleged child victim, to the tune of millions. According to the French news agency AFP, Jackson admitted to making multimillion-dollar settlements to avoid court in the past, not just in 1993. Jackson's statement was issued just hours before American media outlets were set to report new claims that the pop star had paid $2 million to another boy who accused him of inappropriate touching.

Jackson's statement read, "Years ago, I settled with certain individuals because I was concerned about my family and the media scrutiny that would have ensued if I fought the matter in court. . . . I have been a vulnerable target for those who want money."

Dateline NBC reported Jackson paid over $2 million to the son of a Neverland Ranch employee after the child said the star fondled him. The abuse allegedly went on for a period of time in 1990, when the child was twelve. It was widely reported the boy was the son of a maid at Neverland who quit working for Jackson once she learned of what had allegedly happened. It appears authorities discovered this 1990 case when they were investigating 1993 allegations involving a thirteen-year-old boy.

The second boy originally agreed to testify along with the thirteen-year-old in 1993, but backed out when the thirteen-year-old stopped cooperating and dropped out of the case. In 1994, Jackson's lawyers announced he had settled a civil lawsuit for an undisclosed sum of money, now known to be nearly $20 million.

Throughout the latest chapter of Jackson history—claims he molested a child cancer patient—Jackson's fans and supporters worldwide have demeaned the boy and his mother, showing up at every court appearance waving banners and ridiculing the boy, who miraculously seems to be beating deadly cancer. In light of a third boy coming forward, I wonder what they're writing on their posters tonight? "We're sorry" would be a good start.

R. KELLY

Sex allegations involving grown men and young boys are still perceived as more aberrant than assaults on young girls. Just look at the case of R. Kelly. The singer, whose hits include "I Believe I Can Fly," "Bump 'n' Grind," "Feelin' on Yo Booty," and "Your Body's Callin'," is known for his sexualized lyrics and playboy lifestyle. He once told MTV, "I walk into a club and I can come out with two or three women, and that's a problem for me."

That's the least of his problems. The Grammy Award winner has several charges leveled against him for having sex with underage girls. In February 2002, the *Chicago Sun-Times* gave Chicago police a videotape that authorities claim was made between 1998 and 1999, allegedly showing Kelly having sex with a fourteen-year-old girl. Kelly was charged with twenty-one counts of child pornography. He denies the charges.

When you don't know a horse, look at his track record. Kelly was the focus of four lawsuits accusing him of sex with underage girls. He tried to explain this away during an interview on BET, when he told interviewer Ed Gordon that he'd settled two of those suits only because his lawyers had told him to do so. There's also a dancer who says Kelly failed to mention that their sexual encounter was being taped. In August 1994, Kelly married the then-fifteen-year-old singer Aaliyah. Her age made the union illegal, and it was annulled. Kelly won't comment on his relationship with the late singer, he says, "out of respect for her parents."

How often do you hear the argument, "What do you want? A video of the crime?" Well, in the case of R. Kelly, there *is* a video. Enter the parents. The Illinois Department of Children and Family Services is reportedly investigating whether the parents of the girl knowingly allowed her to have sex with an adult. Look for the blame-the-parents defense somewhere in the defense attorney's summation when the case comes to trial.

With Michael Jackson, it is arguable that his lyrics generated a picture of wholesomeness. The public—and a jury, for that matter—may very well construe Jackson's credibility issues as more a personal hypocrisy. With R. Kelly and the sexual nature of his music, his criminal charges may be interpreted as much more realistic and more believable. But we cannot ignore the power of popularity. Director Roman Polanski pled guilty in 1979 to drugging a thirteen-year-old girl so he could have sex with her, then fleeing the country right before sentencing. When Polanski won an Oscar in 2003 for his film *The Pianist*, even in his absence he got a standing ovation. History does repeat itself. Kelly was nominated for an NAACP Image Award in January 2004. Incredible. As of this writing, R. Kelly still awaits a trial date for his child-porn case in Illinois.

STARVING THE CHILDREN— LEGALLY

While thousands of criminal cases involving child abuse come into court each year, some of the most tragic involve foster children. We have come to know these defenseless children through some of the most shocking headlines in recent memory. They live in horrific conditions and suffer at the hands of monsters who routinely go undetected by the system.

On October 10, 2003, before the bombshell dropped that foster children in the community were actually starving, Collingswood, New Jersey, police responded to a neighbor's late-night call that a "little kid" was eating out of an outdoor garbage can. The "little kid" weighed only forty-five pounds and stood just four feet tall. He was actually nineteen years old, stunted by years of abuse and malnourishment. Bruce Jackson, who lived with foster parents Vanessa and Raymond

Jackson, had three little brothers at home just like him—starving. Department of Youth and Family Services workers had been in the home on visits at least thirty-eight times since 1999 and seemingly didn't notice the children were starving. Many now doubt the DYFS visits ever took place.

It pains me to even write this: A 1994 entry in a caseworker's notes reveals that Bruce Jackson begged the caseworker just to take him to McDonald's, to Dunkin' Donuts—anywhere at all the boy could get something to eat. She refused. The "boy" was so starved he found a cookie in the car's glove compartment and ate it, then begged the social worker not to tell his foster mother. Caseworkers chose to believe the foster parents instead of the boys' doctors when it came to the truth about their health. The "mother," Vanessa Jackson, told caseworkers Bruce was so small because he had "bulimia and depression," writes Kevin Ryan of New Jersey's Office of the Child Advocate. Doctors disagreed.

Although the Jacksons received around $28,000 a year from the state for the children's care, Bruce and his little brothers, ages fourteen, ten, and nine, were kept locked out of the home's kitchen and lived off nothing but a diet of uncooked pancake batter, peanut butter, jelly, and cereal. The boys chewed on wallboard and insulation to live. A blistering report by the above-mentioned Office of the Child Advocate cited sloppy casework, an ignorance of the rules specifically passed to protect the innocent, and a shocking lack of internal communication as the unacceptable reasons the state's child-welfare agency had allowed four "intentionally malnourished" adopted children to live in near starvation for almost a decade.

The Jackson parents were actually praised for "doing an excellent job" and being "very consistent on doctor's appointments" in one 1997 foster-home evaluation. In reality, the four boys suffered painfully, both emotionally and physically, for years on end. Doctors' reports—that DYFS had full access to, had they bothered to read them—showed that in no uncertain terms. For example, one doctor, during a routine physical on one of the boys, wrote that he was "markedly underweight, undersized and presented with failure-to-thrive syndrome." At three years old, he weighed only twenty-one pounds. Shockingly, just one year later, the department approved his adoption by the Jacksons, with no concern or even mention of his disturbingly poor health. With full approval of DYFS, judges, and special law guardians assigned to the "family," the other boys' adoptions by the Jackson "parents" were a breeze. There was just one problem no one mentioned—the children were being systematically starved to death.

As of this writing, the Jacksons stand charged with child endangerment and assault. Bruce Jackson is still living in a hospital but doing well on a "normal diet," gaining thirty-seven pounds and growing six and a half inches in just three months. He and his brothers appear to be recovering. Each one of them weighed less than fifty pounds when removed from the Jackson home. Their adoptive parents, Vanessa Jackson, forty-eight, and Raymond Jackson, fifty, have been arrested and formally charged with four counts of aggravated assault and fourteen counts of child endangerment. Nine child-welfare employees were fired, including one caseworker who was supposed to be visiting the family regularly.

Ryan's report on the foster-adoptee program is a real-life horror story, if anyone cares enough to read it. It's all about bureaucratic dysfunction, detailing how the Jacksons became foster parents in 1991 and, since that time, DYFS did practically nothing to help the boys. The scariest part, aside from the fact of children starving under the noses of visiting social workers, is that the report suggests that 2,500 of 14,300 other "safety assessments" DYFS workers claimed they made were nothing more than reviews of notes taken during alleged visits months earlier. How many other children are starving, molested, and abused with the sanction of the government? This is a real problem, and our government, our laws, our system are not just allowing it but perpetuating it.

There are solutions. Ryan sets forth several that I back completely. The Department of State Human Services must require in-person safety assessments of all children adopted and/or fostered out by the state, as well as interview all members of the household during the in-person visits. No relying on months-old "notes." Another great idea is to coordinate medical care for these children by creating and funding medical offices there at DYFS offices. This will prevent kids from getting lost in the shuffle between physicians, caseworkers, and foster and adoptive parents. The right hand must observe the left hand when it comes to these precious children. Further, the state must require foster and adoptive parents to show proof that their child has at least an annual physical as a condition of getting state money. The federal government pays adoptive parents several hundred dollars a month. When did raising children turn into a moneymaking proposition?

In addition to the improvements listed above, and contrary to what many supporters of the current system contend, I firmly believe that child caseworkers who make bad decisions regarding our country's littlest victims must be prosecuted criminally. Show me you visited. File the paperwork. Show me that the children went to annual doctor visits, had their shots and weigh-ins as normal, and aren't covered with welts or bruised black and blue. Show me that there have been counseling visits. We are the richest country in the world, and the government already takes at least a third of what we bring home. This problem is too important to remedy with a simple reprimand or a firing where the individual goes on to another job, possibly to cause the pain and suffering of some other innocent child. No way. In my mind, it's off to jail for such people, with a guarantee they will never work with children again. Why are children suffering? If the state's child-care system can't handle the problem, maybe the criminal-justice system can.

CAN YOU HEAR ME NOW?

Another tragedy occurred in New Jersey within months of the Jackson debacle. A seven-year-old boy, Faheem Williams, was found dead, and his two brothers were found emaciated and locked in a basement filled with feces and rodents. Social workers had also supposedly paid multiple visits to that family, investigating allegations of abuse and neglect. Now the man suspected in the child's death, Wesley Murphy, will not be charged with murder, even though the autopsy showed that Faheem had died of blunt-force trauma and starvation.

Murphy's mother, Sherry Murphy, forty-one, was taking care of the boys for their mother, Melinda Williams, while she served time in jail on an assault charge. Police rescued Faheem's brothers after Murphy's boyfriend found them living in their own feces, vomit, and urine. He reportedly had lived in the house for two weeks without even knowing that the children were there. Police later found Faheem's body in the basement with his brothers, hidden in a plastic container. He had been dead for more than a month.

Wesley Murphy was charged with assault and child endangerment. Sherry Murphy, whom police found sleeping in a Newark apartment, was charged with child endangerment, but she has not been charged in Faheem's death. Reports have come to light that the boys' natural mother may have abused them as well. There is also suspicion that her boyfriend had molested one of the children. As if that's not enough, here's the rest of the story: New Jersey's Division of Youth and Family Services had received ten complaints over ten years about Williams's abuse of her children. An October 2001 report accused Williams of beating and burning them.

It was widely reported that three of the reports were substantiated, but the state agency closed the case in February 2002 because it could not find the children. That month, Williams was jailed for child endangerment. She entrusted the boys to Murphy, a go-go dancer. Police say Murphy has a crack problem but no criminal record. Ten complaints in ten years. Can they hear you now, Faheem?

FALLEN ANGEL

Lisa Steinberg was illegally adopted along with another child, a baby boy, by a New York lawyer, Joel Steinberg, and his enabler/lover, Hedda Nussbaum. This little girl had the smile of an angel. Now she *is* an angel. How these two ever got children in the first place, I don't know. Why the state of New York didn't seek the death penalty on these two child killers will also forever remain a mystery in my mind. Lisa's cold little body was found by police in November 1987. She was covered in welts, her body was black and blue, and she was lying on the floor of the family's Manhattan apartment. She died three days after she was brutally beaten in the apartment Steinberg shared with his lover. The little boy, tethered at the waist and lying in his own urine, naked, was found nearby. At least he lived.

The children were tormented, abused, beaten, and mistreated their entire lives. No one ever came to their aid: not the state, the neighbors, or the police. The government used Nussbaum's testimony to get a conviction on Steinberg. She claimed that because he beat her, too, she wasn't responsible for the death of Lisa, nor for the years of torment these two helpless children endured. In my mind, she is a modern-day Pontius Pilate. She just stood by and watched two innocents be mercilessly destroyed and did nothing. Check again, Hedda, there's blood on your hands. Lisa's blood.

As for Steinberg, he was released from jail in the summer of 2004. A long white stretch limo picked him up to usher him to freedom. In an interview with *New York* magazine, the convicted child killer says he's "a good father" who only pushed his six-year-old adopted daughter but did not hit her. Steinberg showed up on the streets of Manhattan, carefree in Times Square and at the USS *Intrepid*'s Sea-Air-Space Museum, ambling along without a care in the world. He was kicked out of the halfway house where he lived following his release from jail because administrators there were livid after Steinberg told *New York* magazine that he shouldn't be blamed for Lisa's death. Ever concerned only for himself, Steinberg complained about his time behind bars, "I went from a middle-aged millionaire to a penniless old bum!"

Not only should Steinberg and Nussbaum be facing the death penalty right now, social services in New York should be ridden out of town on a rail. Two children were handed over to a sadist like Steinberg and no heads rolled? An illegal adoption? What rules were bent so this child could be tortured and ultimately die a painful death? As in so many other child-abuse cases, a wall of silence protected the state, and no one listened.

A CALL TO ARMS

According to a report presented to the House Committee on Ways and Means by Representative George Miller of California, the story of suffering of state-protected children is an old one. These tragedies are symptomatic of a chronic failure of our nation's child-welfare systems to care for our children. There are more than 550,000 children in foster care nationally, taken by the state out of dangerous homes and supposedly placed in safe, nurturing environments where they will receive the services they desperately require. The reality is very different. And New Jersey is not alone. A recent Health and Human Services report assailed California's system of care for abused and neglected children. Michigan officials recently admitted that they had lost track of 302 abused or neglected children. An audit of Maryland's child-welfare system revealed that the state had lost track of some foster children for months, had failed to ensure proper health care, and, in at least one case, had entrusted a foster child to a known sex offender.

In Milwaukee, Wisconsin, 48 percent of families investigated for abuse had prior involvement with the child-welfare system; in the District of Columbia, 32 percent of such families had been previously reported to child-protective services; and in Florida, at least 37 children died of abuse or neglect over the past five years, despite having been the subjects of abuse or maltreatment complaints, says Miller. Of the estimated 1,500 children who die of abuse and neglect across our country annually, the sad plight of more than 40 percent was already known to the child-welfare agencies. This is incredible, shocking, but sadly true.

Over twenty-five years ago, an investigation into the failures of this country's child-welfare system was launched by Miller. For tens of thousands of children, foster care was a living horror where services were denied, placements were unsupervised, and legal rights routinely flouted. Simply put, it was no more and no less than "state-sponsored child abuse." The investigation brought about the Child Welfare and Adoption Assistance Act in 1980, requiring states to improve the level of services and accountability in their foster-care programs, and to promote adoptions for children who couldn't ever go home again. Yet twenty-three years later, nothing has really changed. Children are still not just abused, they are dying. Today's headlines are simply rewrites of the ones of two decades ago, all filled with stories of states' failures to protect foster children.

In just two years, thirty-two state child-welfare programs have been subjected to federal reviews, and every single one has failed to meet national standards. Miller, along with California Representative Pete Stark, is backing the Child Protective Services Improvement Act, whose aim is to improve outcomes for children in foster care, address substance-abuse problems, update eligibility standards, minimize multiple placements of children in foster care, and move quickly to either return them to their families or find permanent adoptive homes. The bill is designed to enhance caseworker retention by providing grants to enhance social-worker training, raise salaries, and reduce caseloads.

The federal government spends $5 billion annually to protect abused children, but the feds must raise serious questions about the adequacy of federal oversight of state child-welfare programs. There are those who propose changes in the child-welfare system that would diminish accountability and grant even greater latitude to the states in managing their federally financed foster-care systems. With thirty-two state agencies failing to meet even basic standards for foster children, it's crazy to blindly award states a block grant pinned on the groundless hope they'd run their programs any better than they do now. I join Miller in urging Congress to reform the system under the Child Protective Services Improvement Act. Who knows how many thousands of children it might save?

There is something else we can do to safeguard these helpless children: Add an independent third party to monitor the system that is supposed to do everything in its power to protect them. Our government is choking with bureaucracy. We have departments that monitor virtually every other aspect of our government, but no one monitoring child-welfare cases. An independent body with the investigative powers to oversee child-welfare caseworkers is essential if these heinous wrongs against children that have gone unnoticed and ignored are to be stopped. We can't afford not to do this in our fight to protect what is our most important resource—our children.

TURNING TRAGEDY INTO INSPIRATION

There are some victims who somehow manage to take the tragedy they and their families endure and transform some of their grief into the inspiration to help others. I have met many heroes during the course of my career who have selflessly worked to prevent others from suffering the same devastating fate that nearly ruined their lives. Since I have written so extensively about what's wrong with our system of justice and heaped a big helping of (justified!) criticism on those who I believe are trying to destroy it, I'd like to let the light in. Thankfully, there are those brave souls who refuse to be stopped by the evil in this world. Here's a look at just a few of the people I admire not only for surviving their grief, but for becoming role models in their quest to help other victims.

MARC KLAAS

In a previous chapter, I told you about Marc Klaas's work with victims'-rights advocate Andy Kahan in championing the Notoriety for Profit Law, designed to prevent killers from cashing in on their crimes. Klaas is a tireless voice for parents of missing and murdered children, whose activism has taken many forms.

When Klaas's daughter, Polly, first went missing, the police, as is customary, immediately suspected people closest to the victim, including Klaas and his family and friends. Unlike many suspects we have watched over the years, Klaas didn't shrink from suspicion. Instead he opened his home and vehicles voluntarily for the police to perform an exhaustive search and demanded that the police immediately subject him to a polygraph, which, of course, he passed. Klaas rightly deduced that any reluctance or protests on his part would be a waste of valuable time, time that police needed to find the real perpetrator. When dealing with a child's abduction, every minute counts.

Mark Klaas worked side by side with the police in their efforts to find Polly and bring her home alive. When that dream didn't come true, he worked to make sure other families could retain their hopes for the safe return of their missing children. The KlaasKids Foundation, established by Klaas in 1994, gives meaning to Polly's death and creates a legacy in which her name will help protect children for generations to come.

The KlaasKids Foundation acts as a clearinghouse of information related to the protection of children. It distills the best knowledge and information by forming and promoting partnerships with concerned citizens, the private sector, organizations, law enforcement, and legislators to take responsibility and to become part of the solution to fight crime. Klaas's mission is a simple yet very important one: to put an end to crimes against children. Take a hard look around, and you will see, as I have, that when there is an injustice, Marc Klaas is speaking out against it.

JOHN WALSH

For more than twenty years, John Walsh has been a tireless crusader for children's and victims' rights. Walsh's knowledge of law enforcement was gained firsthand through personal sorrow. His battle against crime started on July 27, 1981, when his six-year-old son, Adam, was kidnapped and murdered. Adam was taken at a Sears store in a Hollywood, Florida, mall. The child was left alone for only a scant few minutes to play a video game while his mother looked for a lamp. Without warning, he was gone forever.

Walsh and his wife, Revé, battled for the passage of the federal Missing Children's Act of 1982 and the federal Missing Children's Assistance Act of 1984. The statutes created the National Center for Missing and Exploited Children, which maintains a toll-free hotline number—(800) THE-LOST—to report a missing child or the sighting of one. The Walshes also founded the Adam Walsh Child Resource Center, a nonprofit organization dedicated to legislative reform, which later merged with the missing children's center.

Walsh went on to launch the highly respected television show *America's Most Wanted*. The show is dedicated to stopping crime and apprehending violent perpetrators. Walsh brings the nation together to fight against violent criminals every week and has been incredibly successful in bringing some of the country's most violent offenders to justice. Taking hundreds of thousands of calls, many of them anonymous, *America's Most Wanted* has caught so many criminals that the numbers are truly staggering. Since the series began airing in 1988, *America's Most Wanted* has helped apprehend more than eight hundred fugitives in the United States and elsewhere. As of September 2004, sixteen of them have been on the FBI's Ten Most Wanted list. Perhaps even more important, the program has helped rescue thirty-nine children abducted by strangers.

BRENDA VAN DAM

Brenda van Dam is another parent who turned her suffering into activism. I interviewed Brenda and her husband, Damon, for a special hour-long presentation on *Larry King Live*. Afterward, I met them and their two sons for dinner. Brenda van Dam's composure and her will to make something positive out of Danielle's death is something that inspired me. I walked out of the restaurant that night humbled.

After the devastating loss of her daughter, van Dam created the Danielle Legacy Foundation to promote awareness and support new laws aimed at helping protect this country's children. As of this writing, van Dam was advocating the passage of the Sexual Predator Punishment and Megan's Law Expansion Act, authored by State Senator Dennis Hollingsworth and Assemblyman Jay La Suer of California. The bill proposes extending Megan's Law (which states that a community must be notified if a convicted sex offender moves in) so that information on those offenders is made available on the Internet, on a Web site maintained by the Department of Justice. Van Dam believes that this is vital information that must be easily accessible to parents, and I agree. Not everyone is lucky enough to live in exclusive gated communities or penthouse suites, guarded by hired security, doormen, and alarm systems. Everyday people deserve to know if there is a registered sex offender living five doors down, and the Internet provides 24/7 information to all.

The bill also advocates increasing the penalties for child pornography and exploitation, eliminating good-behavior credit reductions for sexual predators doing time to ensure that they fully serve out their sentences, and lays out a plan for comprehensive sentencing reform. These are all excellent ways to help combat crimes committed against children.

Opponents of the law argue that it is a violation of the civil liberties and privacy rights of the offenders. Van Dam has worked with the Kid-Safe program to collect enough signatures to get the initiative on the ballot for the upcoming general election. She also posts photos of missing children and related victims'-rights information on her Web site, DanielleLegacy.org.

FRANCIS AND CAROLE CARRINGTON AND THE CAROLE SUND/CARRINGTON MEMORIAL REWARD FOUNDATION

Carole Sund, Juli Sund, and Silvina Pelosso suddenly went missing near Yosemite National Park in February 1999. The Sunds immediately mobilized in an effort to find the women. During the search for the women, Francis and Carole Carrington, Carole's parents, at the request of the FBI, posted rewards for both their safe return and information leading to the whereabouts of their rental car. The Carringtons believe that the reward fund and the media attention contributed to the car's being located, giving them the first break in their case.

Unfortunately, the story didn't have a happy ending. They learned of the violent deaths of their daughter Carole Sund, granddaughter Juli, and family friend Silvina Pelosso. That spring, Francis and Carole decided they would do what they could to help find missing people and solve unsolved homicides. The couple founded the Carole Sund/ Carrington Memorial Reward Foundation in memory of their lost loved ones, to help families who do not have the resources themselves to offer rewards in exchange for information that might help law enforcement bring home the ones they love. The Carringtons' theory that reward money does make a difference has proven to be true. The foundation has assisted in the apprehension of nineteen murder suspects and one child molester and helped to locate four missing persons. Additionally, the foundation is intent on raising public awareness on the issues of missing persons and violent crime in this country. It is its goal to bring loved ones back to their homes and to secure the arrest and conviction of the criminals responsible.

The Carringtons are known for their good works. From golf tournaments to fall festivals to candlelight vigils, the fund is raising reward money and awareness for a vital cause. Currently, rewards offered by the foundation have led law enforcement to suspects in five states, all of whom are in custody. As of this writing, the foundation has paid a total of $150,500 in rewards to citizens who did the right thing by coming forward and sharing information regarding these cases. I agree with the Sunds' position that we all have a responsibility to do our part to help make the world and our own community "a safer place," according to their spokesperson, Kim Petersen. The Carringtons are making a difference in what can sometimes be a cold world, especially for crime victims who don't have the money or resources to fight back.

SHARON ROCHA

I first met Sharon Rocha when I interviewed her for *Larry King Live*, before the judge issued the gag order in the Laci Peterson case. At that time, both families—the Petersons and the Rochas—were standing behind Scott Peterson. Later the truth behind Peterson's affair with Amber Frey, along with other evidence, came out, and things changed. I subsequently met privately with Sharon Rocha in Washington, D.C., when she was there fighting for passage of Laci and Conner's Law.

I remember it like it was yesterday. What sticks in my mind is not so much her face, what Sharon Rocha was wearing, or even what she ordered for lunch—although I remember it all very well. Mostly, I remember her pain. It was so intense, so palpable, that she could barely speak. But she was determined to see that Laci and Conner's Law became a federal statute.

Sharon Rocha and her family have endorsed the new law, which allows a violent crime against a pregnant woman to be treated as crimes against two separate people, allowing federal prosecutors to charge an individual who kills or injures an unborn child during the commission of a crime with a separate offense for the injury or death of the child. President Bush signed the bill into law on April 1, 2004. The statute does not override existing state laws but would instead apply to federal cases.

"As the family of Laci Peterson and her unborn son, Conner, this bill is very close to our hearts," wrote Laci Peterson's family in a letter to the bill's cosponsors, Representative Melissa Hart (R-Pennsylvania) and Senator Mike DeWine (R-Ohio). The letter went on to say, "We have considered various ways we could pay tribute to Laci and Conner. When we heard about this bill, we immediately thought of placing a request to have it named 'Laci and Conner's Law' in their memory. Knowing that perpetrators who murder pregnant women will pay the price not only for the loss of the mother, but the baby as well, will help bring justice for these victims and hopefully act as a deterrent to those considering heinous acts." It is signed by Sharon Rocha, Laci's mother; Ron Grantski, Laci's stepfather; her brother, Brent Rocha; her sister, Amy Rocha; and her father, Dennis Rocha.

That is the theory used by the prosecution seeking the death penalty for Scott Peterson. California law provides that if a third party intentionally harms a fetus, the act can be construed as taking a human life. To get the death penalty, there are certain aggravating circumstances that must be met, such as the murder of a law-enforcement officer; the murder of a symbol of our government, like an elected official or a judge; or mass murder. Scott Peterson was charged with killing two people, Laci and Conner, the aggravating circumstance supporting the state's seeking the California death penalty. By convicting Peterson on murder one in Laci's death as well as murder two in Conner's death, "aggravating circumstances" kicked in.

The bill had been introduced and failed over and over. Opposition from many camps repeatedly threatened its passage. Politicians couldn't do it, paid lobbyists couldn't pull it off, and Capitol Hill was at an impasse. Twice, in 1999 and 2001, the House of Representatives approved the legislation, but it never passed the Senate. It took Sharon Rocha—and a mother's love—to make it happen.

DOMINICK DUNNE

When I first moved to New York, far away from my home in Georgia, to cross swords with Johnnie Cochran on my first television show for Court TV, I didn't know a soul. I remember sitting in my office alone one day, looking at the East River, when the phone rang. On the other end was a voice I thought I knew. It was Dominick Dunne. He invited me to lunch. At the time, I didn't know how important and influential he was. He told me that he'd been a victim of crime. His only daughter, Dominique, who was just beginning a promising acting career after a star-making performance in the movie *Poltergeist*, had been murdered in 1982. Dominick Dunne was my first friend in New York, and he remains my friend today.

In 2004, I was honored with an award from AWRT, American Women in Radio and Television. In addition to being touched by receiving the award itself, I was extremely moved when the beautiful silver statuette was presented to me by my friend Dominick. I choked back tears as I thanked the women of the organization while he stood by my side. I remember that night so well, but I also remember that first time we had lunch and how eloquent he'd been when told me about his beautiful daughter in life.

Dunne belongs to perhaps the rarest of all classes: He's a Hollywood insider with a strong sense of conscience. After his career as a successful producer and director ended, my friend left Tinseltown branded, by his own admission, a failure. He knew he had to begin again but wasn't sure how.

A terrible tragedy changed the course of his life forever. When Dominique was strangled to death by her ex-boyfriend, John Sweeney, Dominick was enraged by the miscarriage of justice he witnessed at Sweeney's trial. My friend picked up a pen to vent his anger and frustration and has been an articulate, impassioned voice for victims everywhere ever since.

He has written about his ordeal in books and magazines. "The lies that are tolerated shocked me, as did the show-business aspect that has taken over the justice system," he wrote about the ordeal. "Anything can be said about the dead, and much was, but the killer's grave past offenses as a beater of women were kept from the jury. The testimony of another of his victims, who had been hospitalized as a result of his acts of violence, was inexplicably ruled inadmissible. John Sweeney received a sentence of six years, which was automatically reduced to three. He was released from prison after two and a half."

For more than two decades, my friend has committed himself to examining and revealing the flaws, the misconduct, and the blatant manipulation that taint our justice system. He has exposed wrongdoing in the Sweeney and O. J. Simpson trials, those of the Menendez brothers, and the investigation of Ethel Kennedy's nephew Michael Skakel for the 1975 murder of fifteen-year-old Martha Moxley. In fact, if it had not been for Dunne, the Martha Moxley case likely would have gone unsolved and unprosecuted.

With his talent, Dunne could do anything he wants. He is often a lone voice in the media wilderness. He is older now—his hair is silver, he ambles along slowly, and he peers at the world through thick glasses. But his voice and his pen are stronger than ever. These words were written for him: The pen *is* mightier than the sword. He speaks as a voice for victims who have no voice, he rails against injustice, and, thank goodness, millions of people listen.

THELMA SOARES

When I first saw Lori Hacking, I was struck by how radiant she looked. In the images that flashed across the television screen after her disappearance in the summer of 2004, her smile shone brightly; still photographs and videotapes depicted a lively and beautiful young mother-to-be. To others, it seemed she had the world by the tail: a loving husband headed to medical school, a happy home, and a baby on the way. Then she vanished, seemingly without a trace. On July 19, 2004, newly pregnant Lori Hacking was reported missing by her husband, Mark, a psychology student. In their hometown of Salt Lake City, Utah, volunteers swarmed the canyons, trails, paths, and acres of forest looking for where she might have been abducted or hurt while jogging. Her husband told police her car had been parked at the jogging trail. Almost immediately, questions surfaced, largely due to Mark Hacking's unusual behavior. Shortly after Lori was reported missing, he'd gone to a mattress store and purchased a brand-new mattress, strapped it to the top of his car, and took it home. He hadn't told the police about his shopping trip but instead offered that he'd been running along her jogging trail. When telltale bloodstains were allegedly found in the couple's apartment, Hacking checked himself in to a psychiatric ward and reportedly confessed to his brothers that he had murdered his wife, having shot her as she lay sleeping on the couple's bed, and then disposed of her body in a nearby Dumpster.

It wasn't long before it was discovered that Hacking had been living in a house of cards, built on an elaborate foundation of lies. The biggest lie of all: Hacking had not been accepted to medical school. In fact, he had never applied—nor even finished college. Lori went missing when his story began to unravel.

I interviewed Lori's mother, Mrs. Thelma Soares, that summer, when Lori's remains had not yet been located. Soares's emotional wounds were fresh and raw. The devastated mother repeatedly touched her fingers to her throat and her earrings. I was moved when I found out why. The pieces of jewelry she was wearing had belonged to Lori, and Soares told me she wears them to feel close to the daughter she loves and lost. Even in her grief, her courage and deep religious faith shone through.

During my conversation with Soares, I learned much about her relationship with Lori. When Soares began adoption proceedings in hopes of getting a long-hoped-for baby girl, she was told she was number five hundred on the list for adoption. Five hundred! But then, like a miracle, Soares found Lori. Her eyes filled with tears as she told me one story about Lori as a little girl. When she was around three years old, her long curly hair would tangle every time Soares tried to brush it out for her, no matter how much No More Tangles she poured on. Finally it was time for Lori's first haircut. When Soares went into the hair salon carrying little Lori, a man and his wife stood up quickly, walked over, and begged her not to cut the child's beautiful locks.

During our interview, Soares described Mark Hacking as a perfect son-in-law, who cooked surprise dinners for his wife, sold his own car to buy her a beautiful engagement ring, and asked Soares to move in with the couple when they bought a house. I interviewed Lori's brother, Paul Soares, as well, and he agreed—Mark never gave even a hint that anything was wrong. Thelma Soares even described term papers Hacking had her proofread for his "psychology" degree. One was about an orangutan mistreated as a baby, and the other was about art therapy. I was struck by the level of detail in Hacking's incredible web of lies. I wanted to ask Soares about the facts surrounding Lori's death and what she thought the appropriate punishment for her son-in-law would be, but her pain seemed so intense that I just couldn't bring up the issue of sentencing. She spoke of Lori in the present tense. I instinctively believed that the finality of a possible sentence, be it life behind bars or the death penalty, would have been too painful for her to discuss at that time, so I did not broach the subject.

Although she had wept openly throughout our entire interview, it was clear to me Soares had a strength of purpose. This grieving mother is channeling her pain into greater good. Thelma Soares has founded the Lori Kay Soares Hacking Memorial Fund. All monies donated to the fund go to the University of Utah to help women who have suffered financial hardship, abuse, and family difficulties. Lori had been an outstanding student at the university, having received the prestigious President's Award, a scholastic honor. How many lives—those of our sisters, daughters, mothers, friends—will be changed because of Thelma Soares's bravery and her desire in the face of overwhelming grief to turn evil into good? I know of one already: mine. She inspired me heart and soul.

STOPPING THE BLAME AND
TAKING RESPONSIBILITY

At the end of the day, it is the job of our justice system to protect all the parties involved. They have more of a responsibility in this than the media or any other party does. While advocates and concerned families must continue to speak out, the simple truth is that the courts are not doing enough to protect victims' rights. That must change.

After a criminal trial, a victim can pursue a civil lawsuit against the defendant, but the reality is that most defendants don't have any money anyway. Most times, victims are so torn up by the case that the thought of going through everything a second time in court is too much. But victims who have been slandered by the defense for being "promiscuous" or liking rough sex should have grounds for an oral-slander charge. Everything that's said in court is public record. If the defendant himself did not take the stand and utter those words, I would like to see the possibility of legal action against the attorney. It's all there in the court documents. I know it would be very difficult, but many victims would gain a degree of empowerment in having a court find in their favor on this matter. I am certainly in favor of slapping defense attorneys who raise these frivolous attacks on the victim or her reputation with ethical violations.

I also believe that restitution should be routinely ordered. If somebody breaks into your house and trashes it, or if you are harmed, the defendant should get a jail sentence plus victim restitution. The judgment on the defendant would make him pay the amount of money required for hospital costs, therapy, or whatever else is necessary for a victim's recovery. It would undoubtedly be extremely difficult to collect this money, but it's there on paper on the off chance a victim gets the guilty party to pay up.

I've said this before, but it's worth mentioning again: I advocate increasing the federal budget for victims' advocates and counselors at the courthouse. As a victim, you feel helpless because there's little that you can really do. All victims—regardless of the type of crime they're dealing with—need counseling, not necessarily to get over what happened but to deal with it. It's essential that someone be there to help them understand what has happened to them and learn how to move forward.

A counseling staff inside the courthouse as well as at the police stations and the local ERs could act as a social worker/advocate and be responsible for giving victims their rights under the law, apprising them of the status of the case, and researching if there's any money to be gotten out of the state's victim-compensation fund. Not all jurisdictions have them, and those that do don't offer much, but at least they recognize that there is a gaping hole in the system and are trying to fill it.

And finally, Congress must put politics aside and pass the Crime Victims' Rights Act (S.2329). As of this writing, it is being used as a pawn within Senate offices. The bill guarantees that victims be advised of upcoming hearings, court appearances, and the trial of the perpetrator in their case. Victims have a right to be heard. Their voices should matter. Is that too much to ask? I say no.

CHAPTER EIGHT

THE CELEBRITY FACTOR

ZSA ZSA'S HUSBAND SAID IT ALL. AFTER GABOR went on trial for slapping a traffic cop square in the face in 1989, her husband, Prince Frederic von Anhalt, actually uttered these words: "The rich and famous should be treated differently. They bring the money into Beverly Hills."

That kind of talk led to a little thing called the French Revolution back in 1789, and we here in America have never—at least officially—condoned a class system. Our government functions under the belief that all people are created equal and are treated equally under the law regardless of their bank accounts. Apparently the judge agreed, and Gabor landed in jail for three days.

One night on *Larry King Live*, just as the most recent Michael Jackson child-molestation case exploded, the debate was hot and heavy over the new charges. The legal dueling suddenly went horribly wrong, when the analysis of Jackson's child-molestation charges quickly turned to banter about how the charges would affect Jackson's latest CD release, *Number Ones*. I stayed quiet as long as I could, until I finally went on the attack, reminding the groupies that justice isn't based on fame, power, and privilege. Justice is blind as to race, creed, gender, wealth, or poverty.

No other suspect in a child-molestation case, especially with the specter of additional victims surfacing, would be handled with kid gloves like Jackson. The Jackson case highlights everything that's wrong with our justice system, one of the most grievous offenses on display: the blatant special treatment the defendant received because of his wealth and celebrity. We have seen the rules bent to accommodate Jackson in a manner unheard of for "regular" defendants. The celebrity factor was clearly at play when he pulled up at the time of his choosing for fingerprints and book-in in a shiny, chauffeured SUV. What other defendant gets to have his hair and makeup perfectly styled (freakish as it may be) for a mug shot? From showing up late for his first court appearance, then holding a "dance-off" on top of a Jeep outside, to violating gag orders, issuing press releases, and having fans the world over malign the alleged child victim, the celebrity factor is alive and well in this case. The most disturbing aspect of this display of sideshow justice is that it still has the power to skew the outcome of the law.

History has shown us that when it comes to celebrity, the sword cuts both ways. If he hadn't been a major silent-screen star back in the 1920s, actor Fatty Arbuckle might not have been prosecuted for the 1921 death of a young actress whom he allegedly crushed during sex. On the other hand, if he had not been a star, Arbuckle might never have been acquitted.

No discussion of celebrity defendants is complete without O. J. Simpson. In 1994, after the double murders of his ex-wife and her friend, there is no doubt that the actor and former football star got preferential treatment. It was clear to the world that both the police and the courts brushed off earlier domestic-violence charges against Simpson. Then, when two dead bodies were identified as Nicole Brown Simpson and Ron Goldman, Simpson was again handled with kid gloves. Police interviewed the former NFL star briefly, inconclusively, and gingerly. Even after he was charged with double homicide, police worked around his schedule, waiting for him to surrender when he could work it into his DayTimer. Result? The low-speed Bronco chase, threats of suicide, and a public spectacle that turned a double-murder investigation into home entertainment that's still the butt of jokes years later.

And the degree of celebrity trumps all the others on the docket at that moment. Kobe Bryant, Martha Stewart, Phil Spector, Robert Blake, Glen Campbell, Courtney Love, and Rush Limbaugh, all stars in their own right, must have danced up and down the halls with glee when the King of Pop, with legions of fans worldwide—some of whom believe he is a deity—caught a hardball: seven counts of child molestation. For a few short moments, all the others were trumped by Jackson's greater celebrity and were briefly kicked out of the twenty-four-hour news cycle.

Another thing that distinguishes celebrity cases is that while most people live, eat, and breathe largely unnoticed, everything a celebrity has said or done in the past will be dug up—most likely on video—and reinterpreted. Michael Jackson was in the position of explaining away a documentary in which he admits to sharing his bed with young boys. Years of documented bizarre behavior are extremely difficult to surmount. Regular people rarely have those particular worries. But as the saying goes, "Live by the sword, die by the sword." When it comes to celebrity, truer words were never spoken.

Once celebrity enters the courtroom and becomes a factor in the process, there is a radical sea change and unequal treatment under the law is the result. From demanding a higher standard of proof for celebrity convictions, outgunning local prosecutors with sheer manpower alone, receiving special treatment by police, and getting lenient sentences handed down by starstruck judges, celebrity casts a long shadow over Lady Justice. In all these and other instances, celebrity threatens to overpower justice.

BY INVITATION ONLY

Michael Jackson. Kobe Bryant. Robert Blake. Winona Ryder. Martha Stewart. This is the era of the celebrity trial. It is also the era of the secret trial. The barriers to an open courtroom are becoming stronger and stronger. What with the exclusion of cameras from the courtroom, sealed documents, gag orders, limited seating, endless "in camera" (behind closed doors) hearings, and secret jury selection, access to the truth is becoming a thing of the past. Do you think if you went on trial for shoplifting, that (a) the press would report on your clothing every single day, right down to the style of your headband? and (b) access to the courtroom would be denied? No way! But for celebrities, trials are now by invitation, and those not invited—the rest of us—can only wonder what's going on inside. In the process of turning a public trial into an engraved-invitation-only event, celebrity trials held in closed courtrooms, "star" defendants and their lawyers—with the judge's consent—are chipping away at the backbone of our system: the right to a public trial.

Consider these elements that have been kept secret in the recent spate of high-profile trials: the actual events of preliminary hearings, search warrants used by police to gain evidence, the actual legal briefs, text messages that are likely deemed evidence at trial, results of scientific tests also used at trial by one side or the other, witness lists normally deemed public information and generally listed on the back of the indictment. We're even kept from seeing the parties involved walk into the courthouse. There is a new privilege in the Celebrity Bill of Rights—the private trial. For celebrity-laden proceedings, the public is held at bay, kept behind the rope like it's a red-carpet event or a rock concert. The result is that the same public who is served up endless helpings of spoon-fed publicity about these "stars" is being excluded from the guts of the case (who wants the negative publicity?) and the heart of the judicial process.

The media screams to high heaven, of course, that their "rights" are being violated. I know they're right, but I'm less concerned about their losing a dollar made off tabloid headlines than I am about the disturbing trend developing around celebrity defendants. The star-studded trial has become an exclusive event, with us, the peasants, on the outside trying to look in on a system we built and paid for, many of us with our lives. It's we, the general public, the people who are locked outside our own courtrooms. We have been trumped by celebrity and will be allowed in by invitation only.

Don't believe me? Members of the jury, let's review the evidence.

MICHAEL JACKSON: BEAT IT!

Even in its beginning stages, the public was left out and lawyers on both sides were barred from talking about this case outside the courtroom. The judge rejected a request by media for live broadcast coverage, a request that included voluntary omission of the young accuser's name or face. Documents, including search warrants and their returns (records of what was found and taken during the search), were often sealed from the public. Many of the legal arguments have been held in camera, in the judge's chambers. Other than the lemonade and hot-dog party Jackson threw for his fans after his first court appearance, the public is the odd man out on the real evidence.

WINONA RYDER: CAREER, INTERRUPTED

This star, loved by millions, went to trial, right or wrong, on a simple shoplifting charge. Shoplifting cases are handled by the thousands every week in this country, so why were cameras, and hence public access, banned from seeing all but the very end of the trial? We were shut out of the bulk of Ryder's trial, left to basing our opinions about fairness in court on secondhand accounts. Various bits of evidence leaked, including a video of Ryder entering the department store with a very thin bag and leaving with a very fat one. The announcement of the guilty verdict, however, was covered live. The reason behind that remains a mystery. In a disturbing trend, courtrooms are either refusing camera access or parsing it into bits and pieces. In Ryder's case, what many thought should have been a simple plea blossomed into a full-blown trial, complete with defense allegations that members of Saks store security were all in on a conspiracy, a plot to get Winona. If store security is up to all that, I certainly want to know! Joking aside, this case represented something highly important. Unlike murder or sex-assault cases that deal with devastating emotions, sorrow, frequent humiliation, and personal angst, a shoplifting trial is run of the mill, handled by hundreds of prosecutors on a daily basis. In Ryder's case, even this simple process was hidden from the cameras and kept from the public. There was no real reason other than celebrity to ban the camera during the trial. There were no undercover cops, no sex-attack victims, no disturbing crime-scene photos— just a beautiful and gifted young woman on trial with a zany defense. Short and simple: In this case, star power trumped the rights of the public.

MARTHA STEWART: IT'S NOT A GOOD THING

To start with, the public was kicked out of jury selection during the domestic diva's trial. I don't just mean photos or live coverage or broadcasting names—the public was completely disallowed. Stewart's case was over a federal regulation and thus conducted in federal court, where cameras have long been banned. Ultimately a higher court, the Second U.S. Circuit Court of Appeals, overruled the trial judge in her decision to bar access, but in the end no cameras were allowed. It was ironic how the jury-selection process was so secretive, because the minute the verdict was in, some of the jurors ran straight to the cameras and talked until, thankfully, there was nothing left to say.

KOBE BRYANT: JUSTICE FOULS OUT

Although I agree with the general rule that sex-attack victims not be outed, in so many other aspects this trial was shrouded in secrecy. This wasn't out of concern for the young woman who accused Kobe Bryant of rape. It was all about protecting Bryant, the alleged rapist.

The case became an exclusive event before the trial date was ever set, when the trial judge issued a broad order disallowing cell phones and tape recorders inside the courthouse. Normally court watchers are simply asked to turn off their cells in court. This time, their usage was barred from the courthouse. You think a judge would bend over backward like that for the typical rape defendant? No way! Key hearings were kept secret, such as those that dealt with medical records, DNA, and other issues involving the accuser. Still other evidentiary matters were closed to the news media and the public. Surprisingly, a routine motion to suppress Kobe Bryant's statements to police—standard operating procedure by the defense—was also kept under wraps. What did he say? Why was it kept secret? There was no way for the public to know if justice was being served in the Kobe Bryant case—because we can't see in the dark.

ROBERT BLAKE: IN COLD BLOOD

The public's access to jury selection was short-circuited when it started a month earlier than originally announced. Jurors' identities were kept secret; they were identified only by number. Live coverage of testimony was disallowed. In my view, this is an incredibly important trial, in that it goes to the core of the matter of just how much we as a people punish victims for their lifestyles. I want to know. I want to see how Bonny Lee Bakley is treated in that courtroom. I want to know and see for myself whether a star can buy his way out of murder in an American courtroom.

ANDREA YATES: A MATTER OF LIFE AND DEATH

I was dismayed when the judge in Andrea Yates's 2002 trial disallowed live trial coverage. This case centered on two bedrock concerns of our justice system: the abuse of children and issues surrounding the insanity defense. At the heart of the case was what role an alleged mental illness played in the murders of an entire family of children—the true victims in the case. We were left no real answers. Instead the public heard a lot of secondhand speculation in a case that will set precedent from now on. Not only did the issues of helpless child victims and the insanity defense come into play, but this was a death-penalty case. Because of the potential that the most serious punishment existed here, I believe it was even more important that the public have access to the trial, to ensure that the proceedings were fair and to uncover any wrongdoing that might have taken place.

In an unusual turn of events that stunned child advocates and emboldened Yates's supporters, it was announced in December 2004 that the Texas appeals court had reversed her conviction based on a comment made by the state's expert, renowned psychiatrist Park Deitz. When asked on cross-examination by the defense if a *Law and Order* episode prior to the tragic drownings dealt with a mother accused of killing her children and pleading insanity, Deitz recalled such an episode on the stand. It was implied that Yates had seen the episode, murdered her children, and used the insanity defense as a ruse. Yates's conviction was reversed and a retrial is now necessary.

LISA MONTGOMERY

Then, just before the 2004 holidays, more violence toward children surfaced, and in a gruesome manner. An expectant mother, Bobbie Jo Stinnett, twenty-three, was found murdered in her Skidmore, Missouri, home. Her unborn baby girl had been cut from Stinnett's body and taken. Police promptly searched her computer and discovered e-mail messages leading them to Lisa Montgomery, thirty-six, of Melvern, Kansas. An anonymous tip from North Carolina bolstered the e-mails as well. Sworn affidavits reveal a web of deceit and premeditation on the part of Montgomery, who contacted Stinnett through a chat room, asking to take a look at some puppies that she had raised. The two met at Stinnett's home. Ironically, Montgomery's Internet computer name was "fisher for kids." Adding insult to injury, the suspect dressed the baby she had cut from her mother's womb in pale pink and proceeded to show it off around her hometown. The baby, Victoria Jo Stinnett, now reunited with her grieving dad, has a heavy burden to bear the rest of her life, a life destined to be lived without her mother.

SCOTT PETERSON:
THE NOT-SO-PERFECT HUSBAND

In the Peterson trial, the public's access to court was blocked at every turn. The judge banned cameras in the courtroom; witness lists and names of jurors were kept secret. And, as I mentioned in a previous chapter, city officials' failed moneymaking scheme to charge the media $51,000 for each tent pitched outside the Redwood City courthouse and $7,500 for each truck certainly had the potential to keep out those that couldn't ante up the larcenous fee. Gag orders were handed down so parties involved couldn't speak openly about the case. Multiple search warrants and their returns were kept confidential and sealed, and the same went for a myriad of legal arguments held behind closed doors. Why? There's no reasonable answer.

Why are high-profile defendants granted exclusive trials? Of course jurors must be protected. No one wants a tainted jury pool that has already formed an opinion, but there are alternatives to avoid that problem, other than excluding the public from key evidence and hearings, much less the trial itself. Making the trial exclusive is not the answer. And when the public forms an opinion, what bearing does that have on the verdict? None. All that matters is the true verdict. It is essential that the jury be fair and impartial, but keeping the rest of us in the dark does not serve a purpose toward fairness.

The rulings in these and other high-profile trials are chiseling away at the public's constitutional guarantee to observe the legal process. Leaks will continue regardless, and without full access they may likely be incorrect. The truth of what actually happens in court in many celebrity trials is simply not made available to the public. In fact, celebrity trials should be even *more* accessible, so the taxpaying citizens of this country can be reassured that the select and privileged few—our celebrities—are not bestowed special treatment because of their status. Celebrity seems to guarantee that trial is by invitation only.

THE HIGH-HURDLE
STANDARD OF PROOF

Possibly the biggest difference between celebrity cases and lower-profile cases is the incredibly high standard of proof that juries require before convicting a household name. There is no doubt about it: Jurors tend to favor a well-known person. I've considered the problem of two-tiered justice for a long time. There is one standard for us regular folks and another, lower standard for celebrities. I think I know why. It's really pretty simple: Jurors think they know the star. Whether it's the professional athlete, the television personality, the singer, the pop-culture icon—they've all been invited into our homes on many occasions. We've watched them over dinner, spent our Friday and Saturday nights with them, and even had our morning coffee together. It doesn't seem to matter that this is all happening over the airwaves. When someone is literally invited into our home on many occasions, even if it is on a small TV screen, we know that person—or at least we think we do.

I'm guilty of it myself. I find myself shocked at various charges. I nearly fell over when Rosie O'Donnell became embroiled in a lawsuit against the publisher of her now-defunct magazine—I wanted her to win. I'd always believed that Paula Poundstone was a loving and caring mother, and before she was charged with lewd acts against her foster children in 2001, I had laughed right along with the comedienne many a time. I cried with Winona Ryder during *Girl, Interrupted* because she was so poignant, sad, and brave all at the same time. It seemed impossible that this Academy Award–nominated actress could be involved in a scandalous shoplifting incident. I've sung out loud to "Galveston" and "Wichita Lineman" along with Glen Campbell as I whizzed down the interstate, and I had a hard time reconciling the singing cowboy to the disheveled man in the book-in photo when he was picked up for drunk driving. I'd be the worst juror! I know what it's like to hear bad things about stars you have really loved. You just don't want to believe any of it. It's normal, but that is not what Lady Justice demands. Jurors must be deprogrammed from what they held to be true and must be forced to look at facts they may not like. It results in an additional burden for the prosecution—a burden it may not be able to surmount with only the simple truth.

Then there are those jurors who think they are somehow befriending the celebrity after the trial by rendering a not-guilty verdict. It's as if they think they'll be invited over to the mansion after the trial. Hello—that is not happening! Then there are the other jurors, the ones who are chasing a free trip to New York City and appearances on the *Today* show or *Good Morning America*. Are the odds of their getting the trip, the dinner, and the Broadway show greater if there's an acquittal—not a conviction?

There is, no question, a higher burden of proof on the state when trying a celebrity. Here are a couple of cases to prove my point.

SEAN "P. DIDDY" COMBS

Known as "Puff Daddy" at the time, Combs was charged in 1999 with criminal possession of a firearm after a shoot-out at a packed Manhattan nightclub. Several people suffered injuries as a result of the shooting. At the time of the incident, police said the shots were fired by nineteen-year-old Jamal Barrow, a rapper known as "Shyne" who was a Combs protégé. Combs and his then-girlfriend, Jennifer Lopez, fled the club after the incident with two other men in Combs's Lincoln Navigator. When officers stopped the car after it ran a red light, they found a pistol on the front seat—but no one in the car would claim ownership.

All were arrested for possession of a weapon and possession of stolen property. After several hours of questioning, Lopez was let go and no charges were filed against her.

As Combs headed to trial, his spokesman said that the rapper and his girlfriend were "victims of circumstance." But this was not the first time that year Combs had had a brush with the law. Months before the nightclub incident, the music man–turned–clothing designer was accused of beating an executive while arguing about a music video. That time Combs pled guilty to a harassment charge and was ordered to undergo counseling.

Faced with fifteen years in jail if convicted on four counts of weapons possession and one count of bribing a witness, Combs tapped Johnnie Cochran and Ben Brafman to represent him. The two-month trial was filled with theatrical moments. Every day presented enough photo ops to keep the city's tabloids in headlines. The defendant turned up in his best suits, with his mother and a host of celebrity supporters in tow. In court, Combs took the stand in his own defense, vehemently denying all charges. The day the verdict was announced, he spread snapshots of his two young sons in front of him on the defense table as the jury came back into the courtroom. When the forewoman (who had to wipe away tears from her eyes) announced the not-guilty verdict, Combs fell into Cochran's arms. Outside, he told reporters, "I feel blessed." He immediately cleaned up his act, began doing charity events, changed his name to P. Diddy, and thanked his lucky stars—and his defense lawyers!

WOODY HARRELSON

Even after watching a video of Harrelson proudly planting marijuana seeds, a Beattyville, Kentucky, jury acquitted the big-screen star for possession of marijuana in August 2000. Prosecutors thought they had a lock on the case, with several state's witnesses taking the stand, not to mention that video. Instead of facing twelve months behind bars and a $500 fine, Harrelson spent most of the day signing hundreds of autographs.

Harrelson has starred in films like *Natural Born Killers* and *The*

People vs. Larry Flynt. He is best known by millions of television viewers, very likely including the twelve jurors, for his role as the lovably clueless bartender in the eighties hit television series *Cheers.* I wonder if twelve of those autographs he signed were for jurors at his trial?

WARREN MOON

In 1996, after a full thirty minutes of deliberating, a starstruck jury acquitted Minnesota Vikings quarterback Warren Moon of viciously assaulting his wife, Felicia, in 1995 at the couple's mansion. Their terrified seven-year-old son ran to the phone and called police to save his mother. When they arrived, Felicia Moon had obvious and visible injuries. She told police that her quarterback husband had beaten her. Prosecutors used a new Texas law to force Felicia to testify against her husband, even though by the time of trial she no longer wanted to. That Texas jury set a heck of an example for the little boy—the seven-year-old son who was brave enough to stand up to an NFL quarterback. Final score: Celebrity Factor: 7, Justice: 0.

JAYSON WILLIAMS

As he lay dying from a shotgun blast to the chest, Gus Christofi carried an item on his person that only a few veteran courthouse watchers in the trial of NBA star Jayson Williams may remember, but in my mind it said it all. Inside the limo driver's pocket was a camera. Poor Gus Christofi, just like the jurors, was starstruck. The guy didn't want much—just to be close to a star he was working for that night. As he drove Williams from place to place, as Williams drank more and more and made fun of his driver for the night over and over in front of his buddies, the evening spiraled to its deadly conclusion. All Christofi wanted was to maybe snap a few pictures with the famous NBA great who'd hired him. Two years later, Williams was acquitted of the top count by a starstruck jury. Christofi's sister ran from the courtroom crying. The rest of Christofi's family had little to say. Perhaps that's because they received $2.75 million as a result of a civil suit they'd filed against Williams before the criminal trial had even empaneled a jury.

What did the Jayson Williams trial teach me? I learned a lesson when Williams bought his own version of a high-priced Dream Team, paid off Gus Christofi's family, and cried on cue on ABC's *20/20* when Barbara Walters asked him questions. I learned that no matter the facts, no matter the law, no matter the pain and suffering of the victims, if the celebrity factor is in the courtroom, get ready for the fight of your life.

From videotapes of the crime to cuts and bruises on the victim, evidence too often plays second fiddle to the celebrity factor. The increased standard of proof is real, not just perceived, and it plays out in case after case and trial after trial. The answer? I believe that additional jury instructions at the back end of the trial from the judge to the jury are absolutely essential, advising them that all defendants are equal under the law and should be considered so during jury deliberations. In addition, more carefully orchestrated jury selection to weed out the starstruck must be implemented. The lawyers in celebrity trials must choose twelve jurors more interested in justice than in dinner with a star.

OUTGUNNING THE STATE

The *New York Post* got it right with the two-inch headline MONEY TALKS on the heels of a 2001 scandal among the rich and famous in the Hamptons of Long Island when the über-wealthy Lizzie Grubman posted bail for running down a group of innocent bystanders outside a trendy nightclub for the East Coast elite. New York City's hottest young public-relations woman backed her Mercedes SUV into a crowd outside the club after arguing with a bouncer over a parking spot and reportedly calling him "white trash." Sixteen people were injured, and Grubman was charged with assault and leaving the scene of an accident.

The poor little rich girl managed to play possum until she could no longer successfully be tested for intoxication. By the time she was located at a friend's house two hours after the assaults, her lawyer had arrived and advised her not to speak with police. She was later released on just $25,000 bail. At her 2002 trial, she of course got a lenient sentence: in and out of a dormitory-style facility in a few months. Her latest project: starring in a reality show focusing on her glamorous life among Manhattan's rich and famous.

O. J. Simpson's Dream Team started a trend in contemporary celebrity trials. How many lawyers does it really take to defend one person? Simpson aside, there is definitely a tendency to hire "teams" of lawyers to outman the prosecution when there's a celebrity defendant. In Robert Blake's case, before the trial even started he'd already been through three fleets of lawyers, including Tom Mesereau, now representing Michael Jackson, as well as Harland Braun, a high-powered and high-ticket criminal lawyer. He went through fleets of lawyers in order to assemble his own Dream Team. Meanwhile, the judge continued to grant delays for the defense so Blake could find just the right lawyer. In other words, one who will do whatever Blake wants.

The prime example of assembling a defense "team" would be Michael Jackson. Jackson paid through the nose to retain two of the highest-profile criminal lawyers in the country—Ben Brafman, of Sean Combs's acquittal fame, and Mark Geragos. Then, in an erratic move following the formal grand-jury indictment, Jackson fired two of the most sought-after celebrity lawyers around and hired another, Mesereau.

It is well known that in the Kobe Bryant case, the defense team papered the district attorney's office with countless motions that were spit out of the word processor as quickly as they could be dreamed up. Many of them were pointless, but it took multiple man-hours for the state to respond. There's no question that money plays a major role in high-profile cases. Celebrities can afford to hire a battery of attorneys and investigators to prolong trials. As the prosecutor's workload mounts, the defense sits by, happily racking up their billable hours. Trials that normally require three or four days in court mushroom into months or even worse.

With celebrity comes wealth, and wealth buys more bodies at the defense table: investigators, experts, and consultants as well as other key players like videographers, publicists, and Web-site specialists. Celebrities get the edge in the courtroom not only because of their fame but also because of money—pure and simple. These are just a few examples to make the point that, while everyone should hire the best defense attorney he or she can, clearly, in the aforementioned cases, the goal was to overpower the prosecution. Guess what? It worked.

LIMO VERSUS PADDY WAGON (IT'S ALL IN HOW YOU GET THERE)

The headiest combination ever forged is fame and fortune. If you have them both, you can apparently get anything and get away with everything. When it comes to interrogating, arresting, booking, and getting court dates for celebrities, what police really need is a social secretary, what with all the scheduling conflicts, special requests, and hair and makeup requirements that come into play.

When most offenders are suspected of a crime, they are located by cop or canine, thrown down on the ground, handcuffed and hauled to jail for book-in, and fingerprinted. Once in custody, defendants are kept in a holding cell until they make bond (on less serious crimes) or wait for a bond hearing, which occurs within seventy-two hours. In contrast, think about what happened when Michael Jackson was "arrested" for multiple counts of alleged child molestation. Jackson's lawyers negotiated a time convenient for the star to be chauffeured to the police station of Jackson's choice at the time and date of his choice. He literally got curbside service book-in. He was escorted into the station by his then-lawyer Mark Geragos, allowed to use the bathroom in private, then booked. His mug shot is complete with hair and makeup artfully applied (not my style, but hey, I'm not the King of Pop). Nobody else gets that!

And consider this: Celebrities accused of a whole range of offenses, from murder to rape to child molestation, manage to walk free on bail when the average person could never post and be released if faced with the same charges. Stars even get to leave the country after being charged with a crime. *You* want to scoot down to the Caribbean with a child-molestation charge hanging over your head? Fat chance! But Jackson made it to London after *his* arrest.

Privileged punks have also gotten bond when the average guy would not have. Andrew Luster, the heir to the Max Factor cosmetics fortune, was charged in 2003 on eighty-six counts for drugging, raping, and sodomizing women while they were unconscious. Despite being a clear ongoing threat to the community and having the resources to flee the country, he made bond. But then—uh-oh—he somehow managed to leave the country and ended up in Mexico. As a no-show in court, he was tried "in absentia"—in his absence—after he took off. In February 2003, Luster was sentenced to 124 years in state prison and ordered to pay $1 million in restitution. Duane Chapman, an innovative bounty hunter nicknamed "The Dog," tracked Luster down and turned him over to the authorities. Finally, he's back in the United States and in jail, where he belongs.

But it's not just about celebs getting bond or preferential consideration at bond time. At many court appearances, special arrangements are made for the celebrity. Security is often brought in so no one will "bother" the star. The court appearance is planned with precision timing. The celebrity is in and out of court with little or no muss or fuss. Here's a reality check: Criminal calendars normally last for hours at a time. Hence, the orchestration for celebrities to be ushered in and out of the courthouse at their convenience is quite an ordeal. If this is to become standard operating procedure, the courts really are going to need to hire event planners.

Fame and fortune are at play when there are no consequences for what many judges would call contempt of court. Routinely, I had defendants who did not show up on time for calendar call, and by the end of the calendar. Every single one was placed in bond forfeiture. In other words, they lose the bond they posted and are faced with waiting in jail until their trial date.

Some celebrity defendants don't even have to show up to court, by agreement with the judge. Kobe Bryant did not have to appear at every court hearing regarding his case. I assure you that other rape defendants across the country must be in court for each and every hearing, motion, or arraignment calendar, or their bonds will be forfeited and they can consider the matter behind bars until trial time. Not so for the stars.

Aside from preferential treatment at book-in or calendar dates, there is the matter of delay in charging. Stars seem to be able to drag out the inevitable until it better suits their schedules. The most blatant example of this in recent memory has been Robert Blake. His wife, Bonny Lee Bakley, was fatally shot on May 4, 2001, a block from the L.A. restaurant where the two had just eaten dinner. Blake's alibi was widely considered to be completely incredible. When police arrived on the scene, Blake had gunpowder residue on his hands and had made no attempt to save his wife as she lay in his car dying. Their relationship was in great turmoil at the time of her death, and allegedly Blake had tried to hire others to kill Bonny in the past. For well over a year, no one was charged. Had it been you or me, we would have been hustled off to jail in little or no time. To top it all off, Blake didn't cool his heels in jail waiting for trial, but was out on bond. The last time I saw him, he was outside the courthouse giving an impromptu performance, singing "Over the Rainbow" while strumming a guitar in front of a television camera. In October 2004, my friend Dominick Dunne reported that Blake was deep into trial prep, getting custom-made pinstripe suits to wear in front of the jury!

Likewise, in February 2003, legendary record producer Phil Spector brought home actress Lana Clarkson after the two met one evening at the House of Blues in Los Angeles, where Clarkson worked as a hostess. The next morning, Spector's chauffeur reported to police that he'd heard gunshots coming from Spector's house. Inside, Clarkson was found shot to death. It took nearly a year for Spector even to be charged. He immediately pled not guilty and was freed on bail. The list of celebs who enjoy a long delay before charges are ever filed is incredible. It's almost as if police are afraid to charge them—or maybe they're just starstruck, too.

JAIL VS. "TREATMENT"

Not only does the system drag its feet in interviewing celebrity suspects, give them special treatment at arrest and book-in, and bend over backward to accommodate them for court appearances, the hand-holding continues even after the trial. Celebrities have the unique good fortune of getting "treatment" when the rest of us would be sentenced to jail. And even when they *are* sentenced to jail, there's no guarantee it will really happen or that they will be treated equally under the law. Here's my evidence:

Diana Ross was arrested on December 30, 2002, after driving the wrong way on a Tucson, Arizona, street. Her speech was slurred, she reeked of alcohol, and she couldn't write out the alphabet. Ross was arrested for driving under the influence. The singer pleaded no contest to DUI. The court in Tucson, where the drunk driving occurred, agreed to allow Ross to serve her sentence in Greenwich, Connecticut, where she lives. But during her "jail time," she left on several occasions, had takeout ordered in, and did her nails in the prison's conference room.

Want more? In January 2004, singer James Brown was arrested and charged with criminal domestic violence for allegedly shoving his wife, Tomi Rae Brown, to the ground and threatening her with a chair. Police reported that the woman had suffered scratches and bruises to her arms and hip during the altercation and was taken to a hospital in Augusta, Georgia, for treatment. He pleaded no contest and served no jail time. His punishment: He forfeited his $1,087 bond. This wasn't the singer's first brush with the law. In 1988, Brown was charged with assaulting his then-wife, Adrienne, but the charges were dropped when she refused to testify against him. He also has settled several lawsuits filed against him that alleged sexual harassment. No matter. Despite protests, in December 2003 the powers that be at the John F. Kennedy Center for the Performing Arts voted to give Brown a lifetime-achievement award at the center's annual gala.

While Brown's recent plea wipes it off the court docket, the scary mug shot of the "hardest-working man in show business" with "hurricane hair" and wearing a scuzzy bathrobe lives on in infamy.

Actor Gary Busey, star of *The Buddy Holly Story*, was charged with misdemeanor spousal battery in December 2001 after his wife, Tiani, called the police to their Malibu home. He got no jail time. In November 2003, television producer Ryan Haddon, wife of actor Christian Slater, was arrested in Las Vegas on a charge of misdemeanor battery domestic violence. Haddon reportedly threw a glass at Slater, cutting him on the head. Slater was taken to the hospital, where he received twenty stitches. Haddon was taken to the Clark County jail, where she was held for a twenty-four-hour mandatory detention period before being released. Don't think that's special treatment? Hit somebody on the head with a glass and see if *you* don't end up with some serious jail time.

In March 2000, disgraced Olympic figure skater Tonya Harding pled not guilty to charges that she hit her boyfriend, Darren Silver, in the face with a hubcap and her fists. Harding could have faced a year in prison and a $5,000 fine. She told officers that she hit Silver in an effort to protect herself, but police say that's not what the evidence showed. The end result: three days in jail and ten days of community service on a work crew.

Richard Hatch, the million-dollar winner of the first installment of the TV reality hit *Survivor*, was found guilty in September 2001 of domestic assault. Hatch was sentenced to just one year's probation for allegedly shoving his ex-boyfriend, Glenn Boyanowski, down a full flight of stairs at Hatch's Rhode Island home. Straight probation wasn't good enough—Hatch wanted to appeal. In February 2002, a judge overturned his conviction.

Another judge dismissed twelve of the fourteen charges against Philadelphia 76ers basketball player Allen Iverson during the first day of his trial in July 2002. Iverson pled not guilty to all charges that stemmed from his allegedly breaking into his cousin's apartment with a loaded gun and making threatening statements while searching for his wife after a domestic dispute. CNN reported that after fighting with his wife, Iverson threw her out of their house while she had little or nothing on. A municipal-court judge decided that Iverson probably did not have a gun during the incident and dropped charges.

In March 2001, basketball star Jason Kidd, then of the Phoenix Suns, was not prosecuted on domestic-violence assault charges. He had been arrested in January during a domestic dispute with his wife, Joumana. He got "counseling" for at least six months and a $200 fine. The National Basketball Association declined to discipline the point guard.

In June 1997, spousal-abuse charges against *M*A*S*H* star Harry Morgan made one year earlier were dropped after he completed six months of "counseling." Morgan had been charged with abusing his wife after she'd suffered injuries to her eye, foot, and arm.

Need I go on? Just trust me, if you or I had behaved anywhere near the way this rogues' gallery of celebrities did, we would be on work duty in the jailhouse laundry room right now. What do they have that we don't? Celebrity.

FAME'S DOUBLE-EDGED SWORD

It isn't always a free ride for celebrities. Sometimes—although it's rare—fame can be a toss-up. The flip side to the coddling of a celebrity defendant is the fact that the public expects police to do something about the accused and wants to see the system shift into gear and act. For reasons that aren't exactly philanthropic, the media stay on such stories 24/7. Most times, celebrity *is* a plus when it comes to a jury—but it all depends on that particular celebrity's persona. In the case of Martha Stewart, a self-made American billionaire who clawed her way to the top of the corporate world by founding the homewares company branded with her name, the interest in and coverage of her case and subsequent trial were relentless. From the length of her hair to the price of her pocketbook, Stewart was attacked every day in the press. It always amazed me that Kobe Bryant could show up wearing $50,000 worth of bling and nobody said a word, but Martha Stewart showed up at court with an Hermès handbag and it made headlines the next day. The woman couldn't win for losing. The consensus that she was arrogant and above it all carried over into the jury room. Juror Chappell Hartridge couldn't wait to express his glee over the guilty verdict and likened it to a "blow for the little guy."

The perfectionistic image Stewart had built up over the years, be it true or false, worked against her with the jury and in the media. Her case is the only one in recent history where I can recall celebrity's working against someone.

From the get-go, Martha Stewart's supporters screamed loudly that prosecutors had unfairly targeted her because of her position and success. Others argued she had only herself to blame for trying to cover up the original ImClone stock sale, arguing that Stewart was her own worst enemy. I have seen serial killers, child molesters, and bank robbers convicted, but the afternoon this verdict came in, March 5, 2004, will stick in my mind forever. The unadulterated joy that was expressed by scores of onlookers and trial watchers over the news that Stewart had been brought down was unlike anything I had ever seen.

I remember the day vividly, because I was covering the story live. Reporters were positioned inside and outside the courtroom to relay the news, as cameras are not allowed in federal trials. The courthouse doors swung wide open, and throngs of people came pouring down the steps waving sweaters and shirts in the air. They had expressions of such glee, such happiness, I just assumed that it was a not-guilty verdict. But then I found out the truth—the sweaters being waved around were signals to television crews that Stewart had been convicted. What

I never understood was the gleeful expressions. Convictions, even rightful ones, are usually not joyous events. They can often elicit a sense of relief or vindication at justice's having been done, but joy? It simply didn't make sense to me.

Any suggestion that Martha Stewart had received special treatment because of her fame and celebrity status disappeared for me after I interviewed Susan McDougal, the Whitewater "witness" who refused to talk and ended up behind bars for nearly two full years because of it. We spoke one night on *Larry King Live*. Take a listen:

GRACE: *Susan, we've all seen* Martha Stewart Living *on television. Whether we've attempted her projects or not, we've seen it. We've seen Turkey Hill. We've seen the beautiful surroundings she has created for herself. What is one day like in the women's federal penitentiary? What is a day in the life for Martha Stewart?*

MCDOUGAL: *Well, every visitor she has—if it is her daughter, her minister, every single visitor—she will be taken to a secluded area and strip-searched. She will be asked to bend over and to show her vaginal area, her anal area. It depends on the guard how very rough that search gets or how nice it can be. And some of the guards are very cruel. And I think that was one of the most shocking things. I used to say, "Look, I've had three visits. I don't need any more today." That is a very cruel thing for a woman to go through.*

When you get to visiting, for instance, they won't let you leave any time you want. For women, there aren't enough guards, and so you might need to go to the bathroom. Say that you are having your period. You might sit there and have blood all

over the seat, all over your clothes, and no one to
take you back to your cell. It is a very humiliating,
daily humiliation that you're not used to.

I saw a seventy-year-old lovely woman, hair
up in a silver bun, from Florida, who had been
convicted with her husband on some charge—I've
forgotten what it was—beaten with a phone
because she had dared to speak, you know,
unkindly to someone who had gotten in front of her
in a line, beaten unconscious in a secluded area of
a federal prison. And I really think—more than
anything, I want to say I don't think that Martha
Stewart's going to learn tennis, because every room
you walk into in a federal institution is a fearful
place. You don't know who's there . . .

We went to break. I thought of the few times I'd caught Martha
Stewart's show, her cooking or decorating or gardening, seen one of her
books, or spotted a recipe, and I tried to reconcile that image with what
McDougal had just described on national television.

I also interviewed a handful of federal prosecutors that same night
on the likelihood that Stewart would ever serve the full twenty years
behind bars—the maximum sentence possible under the law. We all
agreed. There was no way this would happen. Everyone predicted she'd
receive a light sentence.

Then came the afternoon of Stewart's sentencing, July 16, 2004.
Sure enough, Judge Miriam Cedarbaum ended up ordering the lightest
possible sentence the law allows: five months at a dormitory-style
women's correctional institution, followed by five months' house arrest.
Cedarbaum tacked on two years' probation and a $30,000 fine, the min-
imum the judge could impose under federal sentencing guidelines.

Afterward, Stewart gave a defiant speech outside the courtroom in
which she vowed to fight both the verdict and the sentence, and then, to

the surprise of stunned onlookers and ever the pitchmeister, she took the opportunity right there on the courthouse steps to plug her business—home goods and magazine both! Result? Within minutes, Martha Stewart Omnimedia stock skyrocketed 37 percent. Facing jail time, Martha Stewart was unbowed. In her first postconviction interview, she invoked the name of South Africa's hero, Nelson Mandela, who was held in prison for twenty-seven years before being freed and assuming leadership of the African National Congress. Stewart was careful not to compare herself to Mandela, but she made the point that good people—she included herself—sometimes end up behind bars. Not surprisingly, Stewart's comments just added to the frenzy surrounding her sentencing.

Later that night, I got to do live interviews with members of her new appellate team. I grilled Walter Dellinger and David Chesnoff on everything from whether Stewart was a celebrity target to her hawking her wares from the courthouse steps to the effect of outspoken juror Chappell Hartridge, possible issues on appeal, and whether she should have reported to her sentencing with her toothbrush and gone straight to Danbury and gotten it over with (as I advocated) instead of wrestling with the sentence on appeal for years to come, essentially holding her life and business in limbo.

The attorneys revealed little regarding appealable issues, except for hinting at an inappropriate charge in count number nine of Stewart's indictment, which charged her with manipulating her own stock by publicly proclaiming her innocence. The trial judge, Judge Miriam Cedarbaum, ultimately tossed the count, but the jury had already heard plenty about it. In the mind of the defense, that could constitute reversible error. The Chappell Hartridge issue loomed as an appellate possibility as well. Then, of course, there was a formal perjury charge against the government's ink expert. He told the jury that inked notations to sell Martha's stock were made separately, a key indicator that Stewart made a trade order based on insider knowledge well after the stocks were purchased. My prediction? They'll take the kitchen-sink approach on appeal. Instead of homing in on a few isolated but hard-hitting appellate issues, the defense will throw in everything including the kitchen sink and hope for the best. As to Martha Stewart's appeal, I feel strongly there will be no reversal, in that the evidence on appeal is always construed most favorably to the state.

A MAKEOVER FOR MARTHA

In September 2004, Stewart surprised many court watchers when she asked Judge Cedarbaum to make room for her behind bars and find an empty bed. During the press conference when she made the surprise announcement, Stewart seemed to speak directly to her shareholders, stating she was innocent but wanted to "move on." The down-but-definitely-not-out domestic diva made it clear she wanted to check into the Danbury Federal Correctional Institution in Connecticut, the closest possible prison to the home of Stewart's ninety-year-old mother, as soon as possible. Danbury, however, with its dormlike atmosphere, was already overcrowded.

Stewart went on to say she could no longer bear the "prolonged suffering" and stated, "I will miss all of my pets, my two beloved, fun-loving dogs, my seven lively cats, my canaries, my horses, and even my chickens." She mentioned "love" in relation to one entity in her address to the public—her love of her business, her brainchild, her creation. Stewart also revealed the uncertainty, regret, and sense of foreboding that all criminal defendants suffer. Her lawyers will, of course, continue their appeal. It was a stunning U-turn for the hardworking businesswoman, who transformed a one-woman business into a vast media empire. More important, it was also a clever strategic move.

In September 2004, Stewart was ordered to report to the federal prison in Alderson, West Virginia, to begin serving her five-month sentence. The feds ignored Inmate 55170-054's request to serve time at facilities in either Danbury, Connecticut, or Coleman, Florida, for a variety of reasons. Anonymous sources said Danbury was ruled out because it was "too accessible" to the media. The Florida prison wasn't an option because it was overcrowded due to an influx of prisoners who had been relocated after the state's devastating series of hurricanes. According to an Associated Press report, the decision to send Stewart to Alderson was made to squelch any rumors of preferential treatment.

I firmly believe Stewart's decision to go straight to jail ASAP was to preserve the thing she "loves"—Martha Stewart Living Omnimedia. The uncertainty of the sentence, the jail term, and her reemergence into society were taking a huge toll on the value of the stock. Upon her announcement, MSLO stock surged upward more than 12 percent.

Instead of living under a cloud, Stewart smartly decided she should bite the bullet. I agree with her decision. By the time you're reading this, she will have served her prison sentence and begun her additional five months of house arrest. I say, Martha, write a book and be done with it. Start over. The world loves a comeback kid and if anybody can pull it off, it's Stewart. *New York* magazine reported in October 2004 that Stewart, never one to be idle, was mulling over offers estimated to be worth upwards of $5 million from publishers. And of course, the domestic diva will be the new star of *The Apprentice*.

While it's true that the Stewart case is just one of a number of criminal indictments handed down against corporate executives in recent history, the small dollars at stake in Stewart's trial compared to the millions and millions in other trials make it stand out. Why Stewart? Why not others like her? And why did Stewart's case get the fast track to trial and sentencing? The reality is that her case, simply because of who she is, sent a powerful message that white-collar crime will be prosecuted. But will it? Or will prosecutors rest easier because they've now bagged their trophy defendant? I'm sure thousands of other corporate fat cats across the country are secretly laughing at Stewart, all the while devising methods in order to escape prosecution themselves.

Reverberations from the Stewart trial go on. In 2004, a sixty-four-year-old woman who was upset with the prosecutor's treatment of the homemaking icon, was convicted of jury tampering in Shasta County,

California. The unabashed Martha fan was accused of trying to influence a juror in an unrelated murder case thousands of miles away from the Manhattan courtroom where Stewart was tried and convicted. During a quick break during the trial, Alice Thomas reportedly told a woman wearing a juror's badge, "Just remember, the district attorney lies," according to California deputy district attorney Josh Lowery. Ms. Thomas just happened to be in the courthouse that day on a completely unrelated matter when she ran into the juror on the elevator. After being charged with jury tampering, Thomas found herself on trial and revealed on cross-examination that she was upset with Stewart's prosecution.

The felony charge carries a maximum of three years behind bars. Whether the sixty-four-year-old jury tamperer actually does time remains to be seen. This unusual case is hard evidence that Martha has some serious die-hard fans and that sentiments about her prosecution—both pro and con—run deep. And P.S.—don't worry about the juror who was "tampered with" on the elevator. The case was thrown out by the judge (because of lack of evidence) before the jury heard a word!

CHAPTER NINE

THE DEATH-PENALTY BATTLE

I'VE HEARD THE DEATH PENALTY DEBATED SO many times, in court and out, that when the argument starts up on air, I brace myself. The death penalty is not a "debate." It's a very real issue: the single most important determination a jury will ever make. Life or death. Both victims' and defendants' families know the gut-wrenching, heartbreaking, life-changing meaning of the words "penalty phase." Without that firsthand knowledge, legal pundits, law professors, and politicians don't know what it feels like to go through the experience.

During my years as a prosecutor, I had to go to the morgue and see autopsies of innocent victims. The crime-scene photos of murder victims I've seen are too numerous to count. People can say whatever they want about the death penalty, but unless they've walked a mile in the shoes of a victim or a victim's loved one, they don't know what they're talking about.

But I do.

One morning in 1979, I said, "I love you!" and waved good-bye to my fiancé. There was a chill in the early-morning air even though it was summertime in Georgia. I waved until he was nearly out of sight, because I've always heard that watching until someone is out of sight is bad luck. I ducked inside the kitchen just before his car disappeared around the curve in the road. His arm was waving outside the window, above the car. I never saw him alive again, except in the sporadic dreams I've had over the years.

I learned of Keith's murder during a phone call with his sister. I could hardly put the phone back on the hook, my hands were like butterflies flying around inside the phone booth . . . not following orders from my brain. Everything after that is a blur. I barely remember the events of the days and nights that followed, including the funeral and even the trial. There are, though, a few things that stand out in my mind. Before trial, the prosecutor on the case came to see me. I remember he was chewing tobacco. I was so young at the time, and he seemed so old—he was probably the age I am right now. He asked me matter-of-factly, "You want me to get the death penalty?"

I had never considered such a thing. I had never known such a possibility. All I knew was that Keith was dead. Nothing, no grief-counseling, no verdict, no death sentence could ever change that. In my youth, I answered, "No." Since that day, I've had twenty years to think about it.

I was wrong.

WHO DECIDES?

In this country, we have chosen to retain the death penalty as the ultimate punishment and deterrent. The battle has been raging for as long as I can remember regarding whether that decision is right or wrong. Who—just who, may I ask—should be the intellectual and moral arbiter of the will of the people? Television pundits? Law professors who have never tried a case, been on a crime scene, or sat in the back pew during the funeral of a cop gunned down in the line of duty? Do we want politicians who have never held the hand of a crime victim or walked through a housing project where crime rules the day, deciding the issue? Should it be some "investigative journalist" who once wrote a story about the "injustices" of death row or, at the other end of the spectrum, who rants and reminisces about bringing back the electric chair to cast the deciding vote?

I say, "No!"

Those people should not be the decision makers. It is our job. The victims, their families, the defendant's family who stands behind them, the workers whose taxes foot the bill for justice, the schoolteachers who see the defendants growing up, the preachers who visit the inmates, the nurses who try to save crime victims in the ER, and the mothers whose hearts ache with grief are the people who should decide.

We, the people, as members of the jury, must decide in each and every case where the death penalty is at issue, and then we must be strong enough to carry it out or wise enough to stop it if it is not warranted. It is our duty and burden. It is our obligation to decide when, how, and why the death penalty is carried out, answering only to our own consciences. I trust and I believe in us. I have the faith that we, the people, can live up to what our Founding Fathers believed we could be: a nation founded under God and indivisible, with a justice system that is blind to race, religion, sex, and creed. Our system is based on the belief that a jury will return a verdict that speaks the truth and decide if the penalty should be life or death. It comes down to twelve people in a jury box. "They" are us . . . the ones who should decide.

We, the people, will make that decision and nobody, but nobody, will make it for us. Not the European Union, the United Nations, visiting dignitaries, pundits with an agenda, not crusaders or hard-liners or bleeding-heart liberals should have the power to make that call. We, the people—we, the jury—have that right and that power. We are society's conscience. We decide right from wrong in our courts. Nobody can—or should—take that right away from us.

RULE OF LAW,
NOT RULE OF MAN

When there is no justice in the court systems, people will take justice into their own hands. The people of the United States and their English forebears, the source of our common law, made provisions to avoid just that eventuality with the alternative of the death penalty. This is no longer the case in the United Kingdom, where, despite overwhelming public support, the last vestiges of the death penalty were wiped out in 1998. A 2001 report in *Time* magazine stated, "While European advocacy groups, political officials and the media are touting the [Timothy] McVeigh execution as an argument against the U.S. death penalty, there is no sign of a mass mobilization of public opinion. . . . In Britain support for the penalty remains around 60%." Yet politicians refuse to act.

Against that backdrop, both America and Great Britain confronted the death-penalty issue head-on when faced with similar crimes in 2002, crimes that were so horrible, so despicable, I could hardly bring myself to think through the details of the murders. Both cases involved the worst crime on the law books: child murder and possible sexual assault on the little victims before their deaths.

When I heard about the facts of the case that took place here in America—including the existence of a tiny palm print beside the defendant's bed, the little girl's blood on his jacket, her blond hair in the sink at his home and her blood on his carpet—I got chest pains. I'm talking, of course, about the kidnap and murder of seven-year-old Danielle van Dam at the hands of David Westerfield. The sight of his jacket physically repelled me when it was held up before the jury with her blood on it. I cried when the jury saw the little Mickey Mouse earring used to identify her remains. A California jury found him guilty. If the jury had *not* returned a guilty verdict as well as the death penalty, I fear the courthouse would have been overrun by citizens fueled with righteous anger. God help me, but between righteousness and peace, I chose righteousness.

Thousands of miles across the ocean, the people of Great Britain were horrified over the disappearance of two ten-year-old girls. Holly Wells and Jessica Chapman, school chums from Soham, a small community in the English countryside, went for a walk together and never came home. Their disappearance launched one of the largest manhunts in the country's history. The search made the news every night, and with every passing day the sense of foreboding that hung over the case grew and grew. Thirteen days after Holly and Jessica vanished, the worst fear of every parent was realized. The burned remains of the two little girls were discovered in a ditch in the neighboring county of Suffolk, just eight miles from their homes. Ian Huntley, a twenty-eight-year-old school caretaker, was charged with their murders, and his girlfriend, Maxine Carr, was suspected of complicity.

In both cases, here and abroad, the public wanted the death penalty imposed for the crimes. During the trials, citizens of both countries who were seeking justice had to take on not only the defense but also the "intellectuals" who seem to know better than everyone else what is right and wrong. Westerfield was found guilty and today sits on death row. Huntley was also found guilty at his trial in 2003. Upon pronouncing sentence, the judge there said, "There are few worse crimes than your murder of those two young girls." When asked what should become of his daughter's killer, Jessica's father, Leslie Chapman, replied, "The next time I'd like to see him was how we last saw our daughter—and that was in a coffin." I believe that the laws of a country should reflect the will of its people. Thanks to the elected officials in Great Britain, the girls' families had no hope of seeing justice in the murders of Holly Wells and Jessica Chapman.

It's clear that Great Britain is bullied by the European Union, of which it is a part and which collectively denounce the death penalty, declaring it to be unacceptable for EU members. All too often, death-penalty opponents point at the United States and claim that no modern civilized nation endorses the enforcement of the death penalty. In the minds of these naysayers, it is more "civilized" to tolerate, feed, clothe, and house a child molester who killed without mercy and allowed the child's family to beg, cry, and suffer on national TV while watching from the comfort of his sofa at home.

Here, not everyone's silence can be taken as support. In California, politicians and judges have been far too politically correct and too worried about their own skins to actually come out and state that they oppose Westerfield's sentence to death by lethal injection. That would never do . . . they may not get reelected. Instead they employ much more insidious methods of opposition. Silently, protractedly, and under the guise of "justice," politicos endorse a decades-long appeals process that all but guarantees that when Westerfield does finally die, it will likely be of old age, with an AARP card clutched to his chest.

But at least American juries have the choice, in a majority of states, to impose the death penalty for a crime so heinous that it warrants the ultimate punishment. If we really care about preserving that right, we should inspect the records of politicians and, more important, judges, and then vote accordingly. Our friend and ally, Great Britain, is so emasculated by the EU that the country's politicians cower in the face of opposition by their own people. Thankfully, that is not the case here.

Still, we are sometimes left with the failure to implement the will of the jury—and when the rule of man takes over the rule of law, the threat of vigilantism looms. Militia movements like the Freemen, Christian Patriots, Branch Davidians, and vigilantes like the subway shooter Bernhard Goetz are just a few examples of what can happen when individuals take the law into their own hands.

Because Wisconsin does not have the death penalty, Jeffrey Dahmer, the Milwaukee serial killer who murdered sixteen young men and boys and committed unspeakable acts of cannibalism, dismemberment, and necrophilia, was sent to prison for his crimes. The notorious murderer was sentenced to fifteen consecutive life terms in 1992; another one was added to his sentence the following year for his first murder when it was discovered that it had occurred in 1978. A life sentence for butchering sixteen people? Is that justice? Even Dahmer's fellow inmates were outraged by his gruesome acts. No tears were shed when another prisoner killed him in November 1994.

Weak-willed politicians and judges have managed to hide behind a long and painful appeals process in death-penalty cases to achieve their own ends in a manner I argue is neither the will of the people nor democratic by any stretch of the imagination. If you ask them why, they're sure to pontificate over their reasons. What's important to remember here is that just because they recite their reasons over and over and over, it does not make them true—or valid. They sing the second verse same as the first. Tune in to any cable-television program, wait a few hours, and you will hear the same tired song: The death penalty is capricious, and the innocent may well be executed; it does not deter other crimes; nothing can possibly justify the state's taking a life; it simply isn't civilized. Opponents seem to equate support for a jury's choice to implement the death penalty in specific and heinous cases with incivility—as if we had somehow picked up the wrong salad forks or drunk from our soup bowls. Hello! It's not about etiquette, it's about whether our courts will seek and carry out justice as well as punishment. It's not about civility. There is nothing civil about murder or its consequences. Instead of living it, working it, dealing with the pros and cons of it, opponents mostly seem to enjoy whining about it.

Is their reasoning sound? Their arguments are repeated so often and with such a tone of moral self-righteousness that many listeners fall for them. They continue to sing the same tired chorus without ever truly examining the harsh realities of crime—murder, specifically—or the aggravating circumstances such as rape, child molestation, or cop killings that must accompany the murder in most jurisdictions before the death penalty is even considered. All of that must take place before the weighty burden of the jury's vote of yea or nay even kicks in. Wrestling with this decision, though difficult, is essential. It is not for the weak-kneed, but for those strong hearts that want the truth. Let's try the truth.

UNFOUNDED CLAIMS OF
WRONGFUL EXECUTION

I consider the most powerful weapon in the opposition's arsenal to be their argument that plays on people's fear of wrongful execution. This is a legitimate fear and must be confronted head-on without attacking the premise of the fear. I agree with the great libertarian John Stuart Mill in his analysis of the issue. He believed that the remote possibility that an innocent man could, in some contortion of the system, be wrongly convicted and executed is a risk that can never be entirely eliminated, and that such a miscarriage of justice would be in itself heinous. We as a nation, if we are truly dedicated to the cause of justice, must take any and all measures to avoid it.

Only a handful of wrongful capital convictions and penalties are known, and none has occurred since 1976, when capital punishment was reinstated in this country. Technological breakthroughs in DNA science have added another layer of protection for the accused. When we learn from the headlines that an inmate has been released from behind bars because of DNA analysis, in my mind the case for the death penalty grows stronger, in that injustice is even more unlikely and justice has been served well by the exoneration of the not guilty.

The examination of DNA evidence is just one aspect of the many precautions taken in death-penalty cases. Mill accurately reasoned that the mistake of wrongful conviction and execution can never be corrected; all compensation, all reparation for the wrong, is impossible. Wrongful convictions are grounds for abolition where the mode of criminal procedure is dangerous to the innocent or where the courts of justice are not trusted. This is probably the reason that the objection to irreparable punishment began so long ago and is greater in parts of the world outside America. There are countless court systems where criminal procedures are not nearly so favorable to the accused and do not offer the same protections against erroneous conviction that we revere in this country.

Believe me, if the U.S. justice system were so ineffective and unfair, I'd be the first to join in with the death-penalty protest. But that is simply not the case. Our justice system is the soundest in the world, with defects rare and rules of evidence that are typically all too favorable to the prisoner. In this country, the belief is firmly ensconced that it is better that ten guilty should escape than that one innocent person should suffer. Judges incessantly point out, and juries believe in, the barest possibility of an accused's innocence. While no human judgment is infallible, in our system the accused always has the benefit of the merest shadow of a doubt. Furthermore, when the death penalty is sought in sentencing phase, after a guilty verdict is handed down, juries are even more careful, more dedicated to their duty as adjudicators of fact, law, and punishment.

In June 2000, an article appeared in the *Wall Street Journal* written by law professor Paul Cassel in which he took a hard look at opponents of the death penalty in a Columbia University study that claimed the nation's capital-punishment system was collapsing due to wrongful convictions. The U.S. Supreme Court long ago instituted a system of super due process for death-penalty cases. The result of the long and tortuous appeals process is that capital sentences are more likely to be reversed than lesser sentences are, because of incredible caution. Publicized reports of a 68 percent "error rate" in capital cases is actually an amazing indicator of the bench's multiple safeguards for the imposition of the death penalty.

The so-called 68 percent error rate in the study had nothing to do with the "wrong man" defense, where an innocent person is convicted of murder. After reviewing twenty-three years of capital sentences, researchers have been unable to find a single case in which an innocent person was executed. The 68 percent error rate actually deals with any and all reversals of death-penalty cases for any reason at any stage in the process, be it a failure to read Miranda rights, not severing cases of codefendants, or any ground constituting legal error. And don't leave out the leagues of anti-death-penalty appellate judges who reversed sentences for their own political reasons, causing statistics to appear as actual miscarriages of justice.

Then there is the matter of confusing guilt with punishment. The "study" ignores the distinction between a determination of guilt of murder and a determination that the killer should get the death penalty. Reversals because of sentencing were lumped in with reversals on actual guilt—evidentiary grounds—i.e., did the suspect actually kill? The question of greatest concern was risking executing a person who'd neither killed the victim nor been a party to the killing. The report indicates that only 7 percent of cases remanded for retrial on guilt-innocence issues ultimately ended in acquittal. That's even including cases that are retried years later with missing witnesses and dimming memories.

Our system is so stacked in favor of the defendant that countless guilty people are deemed not guilty. Factor that into the 7 percent and find this conclusion: The incredibly low levels of acquittal on retrial bear out that the system works. The unvarnished truth is a far cry from the claim that we convict and execute the innocent. We don't.

THE DEATH PENALTY DOES
DETER CRIME

When an allegedly wrongful conviction has taken place, we hear about it eternally. My question is, why do we rarely hear the truth about perpetrators of violent crimes who are released and become repeat offenders? There are too many stories of murderers who, for whatever reason, get out of jail. The headlines have been full of tales of violent criminals who are released from prison and graduate to murder. The news is rife with horrific killings committed by repeat offenders. Here are two tragic examples:

Polly Klaas's killer, Richard Allen Davis, had spent years in and out of jail. Just a few months before he kidnapped that sweet little girl at knifepoint from her Petaluma, California, home in 1993, he had been released after serving just half of a sixteen-year sentence for kidnapping. Davis's crime against Klaas so horrified the nation that it became a driving force behind the passage of a California law that mandates a life jail term for defendants convicted of a third felony crime. Klaas's killer received the death penalty and remains on death row today.

On November 22, 2003, Dru Sjodin, a twenty-two-year-old college student, finished her shift at the Victoria's Secret store in the Columbia Mall in Grand Forks, North Dakota, and called her boyfriend, Chris Lang, on her cell phone. The conversation came to an abrupt end when Sjodin uttered a surprised cry and the line went dead. Three hours later, Lang got another call from the same cell phone, but all he heard was static on the line. It was subsequently determined that the call had originated from the vicinity of Fisher, Minnesota.

A registered Level 3 sex offender named Alfonso Rodriguez Jr. was arrested in connection with Sjodin's disappearance in December 2003. Earlier that year, the convicted rapist had been released from prison after serving a twenty-three-year sentence for an attempted kidnapping and assault of a woman in 1980. At the time, Rodriguez should have been considered for civil commitment, but it never happened. If it had, Rodriguez would have been kept in custody indefinitely and Dru would be alive today.

Sjodin's body was discovered in a ravine near Crookston, Minnesota, in April 2004. KVLY-TV in Fargo, North Dakota, reported that her cell phone was found near her body and had remained on for nearly twenty-four hours after Sjodin was abducted. Authorities were unsuccessful in trying to track the signal. There is no death penalty in Minnesota, so the feds stepped in. In May 2004, a federal grand jury charged Rodriguez with kidnapping and murder. Since he is charged with crossing the state line with Sjodin before killing her, Rodriguez will be tried in federal court and faces the death penalty. His trial is set to begin March 6, 2006.

The repeat-offender crisis never seems to be adequately addressed.

What about those repeat offenders who have graduated to murder number two or worse? Believe it or not, according to an August 2002 report by John O'Sullivan in the *National Review*, at that time there were 820 people in U.S. prisons serving sentences for their second murder committed while behind bars, typically of a prison guard, sheriff, or another inmate. Obviously, had the death penalty been sought the first time around, 820 victims would be alive and with their families today. One wrongly accused versus 820 innocent victims. I know it's not about numbers, but repeat murderers make a powerful argument for the death penalty.

One of the most disturbing facts about many murder cases is that the perpetrator is often a repeat offender. The Manhattan Institute reported that the average prison term of murderers released in 1992 was only 5.9 years. While the victim is sentenced to death, murderers are released after just 6 years, free to prey on the innocent—and free to kill again.

Let's take a hard look at murder with a dose of common sense. "Murder" occurs when one human willfully kills another who has posed no physical threat to the killer. *Webster*'s defines "murder" with the term of "malice aforethought." This is not self-defense, not an accident or a mistake, and not due to diminished capacity. Murder is murder.

Those 820 murders I mentioned earlier, contrary to anti-death-penalty sermons, constitute a powerful argument for capital punishment. Simply put, dead men can commit no more murders. That argument alone is more than adequate justification for capital punishment. It is a deterrent, and maybe that's why we hear it so rarely.

John Stuart Mill said there is nothing that makes a more dramatic impression on the imagination than the finality and the severity of the death penalty. The loudest shriek from anti-death-penalty proponents is that "no evidence" supports the contention that the death penalty is a deterrent. Even if that were true, it is not decisive, because there remains the issue of punishment sufficient to fit a heinous crime.

A noted group of economists from Emory University—Paul Rubin, Hashem Dezhbakhsh, and Joanna Melhop Shepherd—released a study in January 2001 titled "Does Capital Punishment Have a Deterrent Effect?" Based on a statistical analysis of the recent data amassed since the reinstatement of the death penalty in the 1970s, they proved that the death penalty is an extremely significant deterrent of potential murder. They conclude that each execution deters other murders to the extent of saving between eight and twenty-eight innocent lives, averaging eighteen lives saved per execution.

The idea of punishment greatly affects the imagination. The restraining influence the death penalty holds over a person considering a capital offense is impossible to assess. In evaluating the alleged failure of punishment by death as a deterrent, who is qualified to be the judge? We know there are those who were not deterred and went on to commit horrific crimes, but who will ever know when the fear of the death penalty stopped someone in his tracks? Can we ever really know who was deterred from committing murder or how many lives have been saved simply because of the existence of the death penalty?

WE ARE A CIVILIZED SOCIETY

Opponents argue that the death penalty somehow makes us less civilized than the rest of the world. In America, we have more freedoms than any other country, nation, or people in the world. Where there is great freedom, there is great responsibility. We value justice and fair play in our courts, insisting that the punishment fit the crime. Unlike some societies, we do not chop off a hand that steals, we don't gouge out the eye that covets, stone the spouse that commits adultery. We do not cane the perpetrator or employ torture or deny prisoners food, shelter, or medical care. We try to do good and remain blind as to gender, race, creed, or color in meting out justice. This is also true for the imposition of the death penalty. We are neither barbaric nor draconian. The simple truth is, if you do the crime, you pay for it. If you commit the ultimate evil, murder, there is a chance you will face the ultimate punishment—the death penalty.

The Danes and the Norwegians abolished the death penalty before the First World War but restored it for a period of time after 1945 in order to mete out justice to the Nazis. Uncivilized? Absolutely not. It was the appropriate response to unspeakable evil. The Bahamas, Barbados, Belarus, Belize, China, Egypt, Guatemala, India, Indonesia, Jamaica, Japan, Jordan, South Korea, Malaysia, Morocco, the Philippines, St. Lucia, St. Vincent and the Grenadines, Singapore, Taiwan (Republic of China), and Thailand are some of the other countries around the world that agree with Americans that the death penalty is appropriate in the face of heinous crime. So where does that leave the broad assertion that capital punishment cannot exist in a civilized society? What do opponents of the death penalty think a civilized society is? "Civilization" has created the measured response of the death penalty specifically to avoid the less civilized alternative called vigilante justice—or mob rule, to put it more bluntly.

Is a civilized culture one that claims low crime rates? Is that civility? O'Sullivan wrote in *National Review* that in the fifties, America had the highest-ever level of social tranquility and its lowest crime rate ever. At that time, we also had the death-penalty alternative. As use of the death penalty was gradually minimized by outright formal statute and by judges' reluctance to impose it, crime and violence increased markedly. America reinstated the death penalty in the 1970s, and within two decades violent crime finally began to decrease again. I believe a truly civilized society hears the cries of crime victims instead of the protests of heartless killers. *That* is civilized. And for those of you who disagree: This is not about gentility. Go spread your butter with your teaspoon, drink your water from your teacup, and pray like hell that you or someone dear to you is not the victim of a repeat offender.

IT'S THE WILL OF THE PEOPLE... LET'S SUBVERT IT!

Why do anti-death-penalty advocates insist that the majority of Americans are wrong and they are right? Why are these entitled few allowed to subvert the will of the many—in direct contradiction to the U.S. Supreme Court? America supports the imposition of the death penalty in egregious cases. The death penalty is authorized by thirty-eight states, the federal government, and the U.S. military. Those jurisdictions without the death penalty include twelve states (Alaska, Hawaii, Iowa, Maine, Massachusetts, Michigan, Minnesota, North Dakota, Rhode Island, Vermont, West Virginia, and Wisconsin) and the District of Columbia.

Support for the death penalty is high despite the concern of most Americans over the possibility that innocent people have been put to death in the past five years (although most consider this a rare occurrence). According to a nationwide poll conducted by the Gallup Organization in May 2004, the latest numbers show a continued high level of public support for the death penalty for those convicted of murder. Americans say that the death penalty is not imposed enough rather than imposed too often.

The poll found 71 percent of Americans in favor of and 26 percent opposed to the "death penalty for a person convicted of murder." While Gallup has been asking the death-penalty question since the 1930s, support has been above 70 percent over the last two years, after having been in the mid- to high 60 percent range in 2000–2001. The current number is the highest support level Gallup has obtained on this measure since May 1995, when 77 percent supported the death penalty. The highest support level was 80 percent in 1994, and the lowest was 38 percent in 1965.

In the last couple of years, there has been a growing belief that the death penalty is applied fairly in this country, despite news reports that some individuals were incorrectly given death sentences. Fifty-five percent of Americans now say that the death penalty is applied fairly, while 39 percent disagree. In 2000, 51 percent said it was applied fairly and 41 percent said it was not. That year, Illinois instituted a death-penalty moratorium, and the death penalty in Texas under then-governor George W. Bush was a major issue in the 2000 presidential campaign. The numbers were unaffected.

LIVING LARGE BEHIND BARS

Do convicted murderers repent? Are they remorseful? Do they exhibit a concern for their innocent victims? Let's examine the evidence.

Stardust Johnson was shocked when she logged on and inadvertently spotted a photograph of her husband's killer on the Internet, pleading for female pen pals to end his boredom on death row. Johnson's husband, Roy, a music professor at the University of Arizona, was kidnapped, robbed, and beaten to death after a concert in Tucson in February 1995. Beau Greene was convicted of the murder and sentenced to death. Johnson learned the hard way that while her husband was dead and buried, his killer was free to advertise for female companionship. The pen-pal site stated that it was "pleased" to present Greene and shows off a picture of the condemned killer cuddling a cat.

Ferreting out Internet mail generated from the Web and separating it from regular mail would necessitate more investigators, but with all the money federal, state, and local authorities lift from our wallets, I think they can afford it. The dating game shouldn't be allowed on death row. I was shocked to learn that multiple Web sites, created by everyone from human-rights groups and ministers to moneymakers, actively try to find "pen pals" for inmates. I won't give them the free publicity by listing their names here, but trust me when I tell you there's more than a handful of them out there. The sites solicit letters from those outside prison walls to fill the "lonely" hours of inmates on death row. Some are looking for women. Others solicit donations to their defense funds and ask people to send them stamps. Some insist they only want to hear from the outside world. Many inmates even have set up Web sites devoted to publicizing their cases and maintaining their innocence.

It's not surprising to learn that there have been several cases of inmates scamming people on the outside to support them. Individuals have gotten sucked into pen-pal relationships with inmates and have actually ended up mortgaging their homes and maxing out their credit cards as a result. There have been cases where women have sent inmates sexually explicit audio tapes and photographs and wound up depositing thousands of dollars of their own, hard-earned money into inmate bank accounts and defense funds. Here are just a few examples of killers looking for a little TLC through the personals:

Triple killer Michael E. Correll is a death-row Casanova and a self-described lover of "animals and nature" who actively tries to convince women he meets on the Internet to finance his legal defense. Robert Moorman, who killed his mother and chopped up her body, has said he wished women would write him to discuss poetry and *Star Trek*. Kenneth Laird, who strangled a woman with rope he tightened around her neck with a screwdriver, says he's trapped in a "lonely and scary place" and wants women of any age to write him.

In his personal ad posted on the Canadian Coalition Against the Death Penalty's (CCADP) Web site, Correll claimed he was wrongly convicted of murder. He said he was seeking "sincere and caring hearts" who wish "to bring the light of day" into his life. Correll has placed several ads on the Internet to garner support for his case. He even provided a Fabio-like picture of himself, showing off his muscular body and long hair.

Correll is not alone. There are many others like him. Clinton Spencer was sentenced to death after being found guilty of kidnapping a woman, sexually assaulting and stabbing her to death, then finally setting her body on fire. The victim was kidnapped from a Tempe, Arizona, convenience store in 1989. At the time of the murder, Spencer was on probation for felony child abuse. Arizona Department of Corrections records show Spencer to be a violent inmate, with fifty-two disciplinary actions filed against him between 1991 and 1998. He has been found guilty of seventeen major and nineteen minor violations of prison rules. Major violation charges against Spencer include verbal threatening, disobeying orders, narcotics possession, possession of a manufactured weapon, threatening physical assault, physical assault, threatening with harm, lying to an officer, and a pending charge of rioting. Spencer described online the "loneliness" of death row and said he hoped to find a friend who can understand and listen to him. He urged readers to write him at a "secret place" where "nobody could evade [*sic*]."

Death-row inmate Danny Jones turned to the Internet to "meet new friends and share their thoughts, ideas and dreams." In his online personal, he wrote that he enjoys reading novels and poetry and makes his own floral designs and greeting cards. Jones was convicted of killing three people, including a seventy-four-year-old grandmother and a seven-year-old child. Jones used a baseball bat to kill his friend Robert Weaver. He then went inside Weaver's house, attacking and killing the victim's elderly grandmother. Finally Jones chased down Weaver's seven-year-old daughter and hauled her from under a bed, where she'd been hiding during his murder spree. He strangled her. Jones then stole a gun collection from the home. ADC records show that during his time on death row, Jones has been found guilty of two minor and one major violation. His last infraction occurred in 1996, a major violation for drug possession and manufacturing.

Edward Bennett has been on death row since a jury sentenced him to die in 1988 for the shooting death of a Las Vegas convenience-store clerk. Bennett's ad soliciting pen pals states, "My life has gone afoul enough that my heart melts when I see someone else's troubles. . . . The only compensation I've ever found is to love people and so I'd like to love you. What do you like? Where does it hurt the most? I would like to be there for you." That may be true for Bennett's online "friends," but not for his victim or his grieving family left behind.

A FINAL WORD

I have finally accepted that I will never know why a human chooses to rob another of his life, but I do have the common sense to know that some people will never be rehabilitated. Some people are simply so evil, so uncaring, that they will forever pose a threat to innocent individuals like the victims I listed above. I have learned that there is no such thing as locking killers up and throwing away the key. Just think about Charles Manson and his "disciples." They were sentenced to death following the Manson-family murders in 1969, and then, in a political twist, the death penalty was banned in California in 1972. Manson's sentence was commuted to life. Eventually he ran out of appeals, but each time he has come up for parole, it has wisely been denied. Even though the death penalty was reinstated in that jurisdiction in 1978, Manson and his followers continue to live on California tax dollars and conduct business on Web sites that encourage a cultlike following. Who knows what an ever-changing parole board may decide in the future? One thing about the Grim Reaper—he doesn't grant parole. The fact that these murderers are not only living large behind bars but tormenting victims online is wrong. These crimes call out for the death penalty.

I rest my case.

THE REVOLVING DOOR
AKA OUR PAROLE SYSTEM

There is a theory that keeping criminals off the streets is the best way to reduce crime. It makes perfect sense, except for one tiny detail: Most criminals, even the hard-boiled ones, are sent away for a relatively short period of time. Fleeting time behind bars doesn't rehabilitate inmates; too many reemerge into society even more dangerous. Theoretically, parole is the ability to get out of jail under state supervision much earlier than the sentence from the judge dictates. For instance, a trial judge can sentence a child molester to thirty years behind bars and have that conviction and corresponding sentence affirmed on appeal. But—and it's a powerful but—the parole board in that jurisdiction will release the defendant whenever it sees fit, or when the bed space is needed, be it after ten years, five, or three. Too often, these decisions result in more kidnappings, rapes, and murders.

The case of Dru Sjodin's disappearance and murder is a particularly disturbing example of how a violent criminal falls through the cracks. The criminal complaint against her alleged assailant, Alfonso Rodriguez Jr., said that the crime was "especially heinous, cruel and depraved," and involved "torture and serious physical abuse." Detectives confirm that they found traces of Sjodin's DNA in blood collected from Rodriguez's car. They also found a knife in the trunk that matched a sheath found near Sjodin's car at the Grand Forks mall where she disappeared in November 2003.

A convicted rapist, Rodriguez has a long history of involvement with illegal drugs, dating back to his youth. He has admitted to problems with alcohol, marijuana, hashish, and LSD. His record also includes being charged and tried in 1979 for sexually assaulting a woman he abducted from the parking lot of a department store at knifepoint. Rodriguez allegedly raped her twice before releasing her. But the Minnesota jury returned a not-guilty verdict. A guilty verdict in a separate attempted kidnapping case, again with a female victim, that same year put him in prison for twenty-three years, and he was then freed.

As I detailed earlier in the chapter, at the time of Rodriguez's release he was eligible for civil commitment, continued time behind bars, but it never happened. Rodriguez fell through the cracks, and now Sjodin is dead. Federal authorities took the case away from Minnesota, a non-death-penalty jurisdiction, as the case crossed state lines and involved the federal crime of kidnapping. Whether the feds will seek the death penalty remains to be seen, but in any event Rodriguez is a perfect example of why the parole system is not working. Sources state that within two hours of the announcement of Dru's disappearance, Rodriguez's mother was concerned that her son was involved. How could he have been released? A known and highly dangerous registered sex offender? Rodriguez had been designated a Level 3 sex offender, or one who showed the highest likelihood of committing more sex crimes—it was no secret. And his alleged pattern with Dru is similar to the modus operandi of his other rapes and kidnapping. Incredible. Rodriguez should have remained locked behind prison bars, but he wasn't—and Dru Sjodin paid for that mistake with her life. Here's the kicker: Most parolees serve even less time than Rodriguez did—much less. This statistic is even more chilling when you consider that most crime, especially serious violent crime, is committed by repeat offenders.

I'll never forget the heart-wrenching case of eleven-year-old Carlie Brucia, abducted by a repeat offender at a car wash while walking home from a friend's house on February 1, 2004. Her stepfather was actually on his way to pick her up when she was abducted. In the short while she was gone, she was kidnapped and then assaulted and ultimately murdered. The nation was horrified by a video of the little girl being led away by the arm by a middle-aged man in a mechanic's-type jumpsuit that played out on television news programs after her disappearance. When the name of Brucia's kidnapper was released, immediately, officials who pride themselves on being tough on crime, learned that their justice system had failed little Carlie. Like Rodriguez, Joseph P. Smith, Carlie's killer, was no stranger to a courtroom. His first brush with the law came back in 1993, when he was arrested for attacking a woman on a street in Sarasota, trying to drag her away with him in public, much as he did Carlie. He broke the woman's nose by beating her with a motorcycle helmet. He pled no contest to aggravated battery and served a mere sixty days in jail, iced with two years' probation.

Smith has been on probation continuously ever since. In 1997, he got just one year of probation for carrying a concealed weapon, a five-inch knife hidden in the waistband of his shorts. In 1999, he was arrested for heroin possession and got eighteen months' probation. Just one month later, he was arrested for prescription fraud, but the court agreed to drop the charges. One year later, Smith was arrested again for prescription fraud and sentenced to six months of house arrest followed by a year on probation. According to court records, his probation officer said that it was impossible to tell if a positive drug test had resulted from an illegal drug or a legitimate prescription of OxyContin for severe, chronic back pain. "Needs long term residential treatment . . . prison if necessary," the probation officer wrote in a report that's now a part of Smith's court file. The newest judge on Smith's case, Sarasota Circuit judge Harry Rapkin, said he's never seen that report or others on Smith's crimes throughout the years. In 2001, Smith was picked up for prescription fraud and finally did jail time, thirteen months on a sixteen-month sentence, and was released on New Year's Day, 2003.

Eight days later, deputies found Smith passed out in his car with drugs on the seat beside him. He could have gone to prison for five years, but it didn't happen. Smith was put on probation for three more years. It's astounding that for nearly a decade the man caught on video abducting Carlie and now facing trial for her assault and murder has been under the "supervision" of the Florida justice system. Despite his long rap sheet, he's never done more than fourteen months' jail time during a decade-long history of committing serious crime. Joe Brucia,

Carlie's father, asked Florida governor Jeb Bush to investigate why Smith had served practically no jail time despite more than a dozen arrests. I wonder how he'll explain it all to Carlie's family.

        These men are only two examples of repeat offenders who commit violent crimes—the actual numbers are staggering. America's incarceration rate remained constant from 1925 to 1973, with about 110 people behind bars for every 100,000 residents. But by 2000, the number had more than quadrupled, to 478. When local jails are included in the grand total, the United States locks up nearly 700 people per 100,000. Some 4.5 million Americans are on parole or probation, and another 3 million are ex-convicts who've served some amount on their original sentences and are now free. These convicts all wanted parole. The prison system wants more empty beds in order to accommodate the newest batch of violent offenders. Translation? Criminals are on the streets—free but not rehabilitated.

Christopher Uggen and Melissa Thompson, sociologists at the University of Minnesota, and Jeff Manza, a sociologist at Northwestern University near Chicago, have done rough calculations suggesting that some 13 million Americans—7 percent of the adult population and nearly 12 percent of men—have been found guilty of a serious crime. Believe it or not, the average prison sentence is still only twenty-eight months. That's not all: Parolees are released conditionally, usually for a time on parole during which they are ordered to follow minimal rules like staying off drugs, not committing additional crimes, and keeping a job. Today a typical parole officer is likely accountable for 50 percent more people on parole than the same officer would have been in the 1970s. Methods of supervision like drug and alcohol testing have taken the place of personal support and supervision. An ex-offender may have only a few short meetings with his parole officer each month. Conservatively speaking, by 1999, 58 percent of parolees were found to have violated parole. Those who break parole represent one third of all prison admissions, the fastest-growing category. Approximately two-thirds of released prisoners are rearrested within three years of release; 40 percent are already back in prison in that time. Keep in mind, those are just the ones who get caught.

A California study by the Little Hoover Commission, an independent state watchdog agency, showed that 67 percent of offenders sentenced to prison each year are parolees who have violated the terms of their release. The fact remains that crime is about three times as prevalent in America today as it was as recently as 1960.

AN IMPORTANT REMEDY: MANDATORY CIVIL COMMITMENT REVIEW

When most people hear about rapists, child molesters, and killers being found guilty and sent to prison, they rest easy, believing that such predators are locked away and no longer walk the streets. The public doesn't much consider their whereabouts or what has become of them. Most people naturally assume that because their crimes are serious, they'll never see the light of day again. Unfortunately, too often justice doesn't work that way. Too many of these predators are released from prison and continue to prey on innocent victims like Carlie and Dru.

I am a believer in the three-strikes laws that call for life behind bars for a third violent felony. But in addition to three-strikes laws, twenty states have found a new way to keep such predators from being released too soon back into society. It's called civil commitment and has been known as "sexual predator legislation." It allows the involuntary confinement of sex offenders by the mental-health system for an indefinite period of time after the inmate finishes the sentence handed down at trial or as the result of a guilty plea. The idea got a great deal of attention in the Dru Sjodin case after it was made known that authorities secured civil commitment for Rodriguez. The only problem is that civil commitment is selectively implemented, and many predators like Rodriguez are not chosen—for whatever reason. Mandatory review for further civil commitment would most assuredly seal up some of the cracks in the system.

THERE MUST BE ACCOUNTABILITY

In addition to the concept of privatization of the parole and probation departments across the country, there is another important issue that must be addressed: accountability for the structure. The first step in reforming corrections is to assess the crime-control performance of existing corrections agencies. Holding corrections officials accountable for recidivism among their probationers, parolees, and prison alumni is certainly justified. While it is clear that there are multiple factors as to why felons repeat-offend, it is logical that if the percentage of arrests for new crimes is markedly less in one parole or probation office than in others, then there is something to be learned from the success story. Most serious violent crime is committed by repeat offenders. Therefore, homing in on those offenders whose names we already know should be a given.

The case for accountability is grounded in the theory that recidivism is not insensitive to how corrections agencies do their business— there is an obvious connection between how a parolee does once free and how the parole officer handles the specific case. Second, given accountability for failure and incentive to perform even better, to bring in better numbers next quarter than this quarter, is a theory tried and true. Why should state government workers be exempt from the same incentives and repercussions as the rest of the world, commonly known as the private sector? They shouldn't. Simply put, I believe that the standard should be perform or look for a new job. Good work equals incentive. Is that so hard to understand?

AND A WORD TO
TRIAL JUDGES

And to those trial judges who are responsible for sentencing: Did you read that last paragraph about accountability? Believe it or not, it applies to you, too.

CHAPTER TEN

THIS IS REAL REALITY TELEVISION

MY FRIENDS AND COLLEAGUES CAN'T BELIEVE it when I tell them I don't watch "reality TV." I'm talking, of course, about the growing list of reality game shows that seem to have taken over network television's prime-time schedule. When I hear the words "reality television," I get a very different mental picture from the one you see on *Survivor,* where a group of attractive people run around a beach in bikinis, eat bugs, and scheme to have each other thrown off the island. I do have to admit, though, sometimes I'd rather eat a bowl of bugs than hear one more word from a scamming lawyer.

Reality TV, as we've come to know it, is actually contrived TV. I want the real thing—the unvarnished truth. To me, *real* reality television is all about cameras bringing court proceedings and trials into our living rooms, eyes and ears that cannot tell a lie in courtrooms for trials—to ensure we know the truth.

I'm convinced the Founding Fathers would insist on televised court proceedings. The journals of the Continental Congress state in black and white that the Founding Fathers were strong advocates of granting public access to courts of law. They even wanted courtrooms big enough to hold the entire community in which the trial was held, "before as many people as choose to attend." Of course, that day and age and "community" are gone forever. In their stead is a different community that encompasses the entire world.

SECONDHAND JUSTICE

My favorite movie is *To Kill a Mockingbird,* the classic trial film set just after the Great Depression. Based on the Pulitzer Prize–winning novel by Harper Lee, the 1962 movie tells the story of Atticus Finch (played by Gregory Peck), a defense lawyer who courageously takes on the defense of a black man falsely accused of raping a white woman in a small southern town. One of the greatest scenes in the film occurs at the trial's climax. Atticus looks up to see the balcony of the courtroom packed with people waiting to hear the verdict in the case. The camera then cuts to outside the courthouse, where people stand waiting for word of the verdict. They have been forced to stand outside the courtroom, on the outskirts of justice. To disallow cameras in the courtroom is like making every citizen stand outside to hear justice secondhand.

Generations ago, courtrooms across this country were packed with friends and neighbors, court watchers all. That's why many courtrooms are so cavernous—so that everyone could see justice in action and there would be no "secret proceedings." The best disinfectant is sunshine, and when it comes to thwarting attacks against justice, an open court is the best cleanser. Trials have always been the subject of intense scrutiny and gossip. There's never been a time when legal cases weren't part of the conversation at the local diner, around the supper table, or on the front porch. These days, a lot of those conversations take place over the airwaves.

THE NEIGHBORHOOD
CERTAINLY HAS CHANGED

Today a single case can affect millions of people. That definitely was the case with the Watergate hearings, former president Bill Clinton's impeachment proceedings, and the September 11 Commission hearings. The little ballot dispute after the 2000 presidential elections brought the business of the greatest country in the world to a standstill. It was a case wherein judges from appellate courts all the way up to the U.S. Supreme Court repeatedly voted along straight party lines. The public wanted and deserved to see the hearing of then-governor George W. Bush's appeal of the Florida Supreme Court's decision to allow the manual-recount totals added into Florida's presidential vote.

That dispute started in a courtroom and touched the life of every American. While it is physically impossible to carry out our Founding Fathers' wishes that everyone get a seat in the courtroom, those bright minds created that idea as a framework on which this country stands. It is critical that every citizen have access to what is happening in our courts as the events unfold. Today, the camera is our eyes and ears in American courts of law.

Moreover, we are the people—"the people" specifically discussed in the Constitution. It is our trial. We created the government and the court system—and we foot the bill. We have a right to see and to know what is going on in the people's courts. If a camera happens to expose the wrongs of our system—that's all the more reason we need it there.

I believe that people want to know that the system works. People want to know that the jury is struck, that the judge is on the bench and knows the law, that fairness prevails, that no one is above or beneath the law, and that truth will triumph. The numbers bear this out. An estimated 150 million Americans watched the verdict in the Simpson case—millions more than witnessed the 1969 moonwalk. When the reality show *Survivor* hit big, TV critics swore that it would forever transform the country's viewing habits. The truth is, reality television had already found a home on cable a long time before, when Court TV debuted in 1991 and began televising trials. Today it's seen in 83 million homes.

IT'S NOT A MADE-FOR-TV MOVIE

Court TV gives viewers the unvarnished truth with its fly-on-the-wall view of trials. The network has offered gavel-to-gavel coverage of some of the highest-profile cases that have made headlines since the early nineties, including the trials of William Kennedy Smith, Jeffrey Dahmer, Jack Kevorkian, Rodney King, Lorena Bobbitt, Tonya Harding, the Menendez brothers, Jayson Williams, Rae Carruth, Rabbi Fred Neulander, and David Westerfield.

Other less publicized but equally significant trials that have also been televised on the network include the case in 2001 at which Chante Mallard was tried for running over Gregory Biggs, a homeless man in Fort Worth, Texas. After unsuccessfully trying to remove Biggs's mangled body from her windshield, she drove home with the man still dangling from her car. She let him die a slow death in her garage overnight and the next day had two men dump Biggs's body in a nearby park. A jury needed only an hour to convict Mallard of murder. She got fifty years for the murder and another ten for tampering with evidence. At the time of sentencing, Mallard's lawyer said, "If this case would have been moved somewhere else where there weren't cameras in the courtroom, there would have been a different result." Prosecutor Richard Alpert told reporters that the jury had returned "a just verdict."

Watching the trial every day, I was amazed at the lack of compassion Mallard displayed for the man she killed. Those impressions were only heightened when I watched the victim's son, Brandon Biggs, on the stand. This young man said he had always yearned for a relationship with his father and had now lost any chance of having one. The contrast between someone who cared so little about this person and another who was hurt so deeply by his death is something I'll never forget. A readback of testimony would never have shown me that. Only the camera let me see what was really happening. No wonder the defense attorney didn't want the world to watch.

I vividly remember watching the trial of Brandon Wilson in 1998. Wilson had murdered a sweet little nine-year-old boy, Matthew Checci, minutes after the child entered a restroom at a beach in Oceanside, California. The weekend before the trial, I had waited for my own little nephew to come out of the men's room at a mall. I nearly became ill when I watched the Checci trial as it started days later. I knew why people watched the Wilson trial. The stories told in court are things that could happen to your son, daughter, mother, father, spouse—or to you. We watch, and we wait to make sure that justice wins out.

The camera told the heartbreaking story of Checci's death—which Wilson gleefully reenacted for the police. Wilson took the stand against the wishes of his attorney, Curt Owen, and told jurors he felt no remorse for killing Checci and would murder him again "in a second." Although the Wisconsin drifter pled guilty to murder with a special circumstance of lying in wait, California law also allowed him to plead not guilty by reason of insanity. Justice did prevail. The jury decided that Wilson should face the death penalty. He is currently appealing the verdict.

THE BLOOM IS OFF THE ROBE

Federal courts and the U.S. Supreme Court ban camera access to their courtrooms. Why?

Remember when I mentioned the request for the public to hear arguments before the U.S. Supreme Court in the matter of the hand-tallied Florida ballots in the 2000 presidential election?

Also remember that the Court said no. That decision barring citizens the ability to see those proceedings was a grave mistake. Here's a clue as to why the Court was so adamant that the public not be privy to its functions: Justice David Souter told a House of Representatives subcommittee in 1996 that camera coverage of the Supreme Court would occur only over his dead body. That is who is making the rules that determine how you and I will live. Think about it.

Though the Supreme Court's duty is to interpret the Constitution and serve the people, barring us from the Court does not serve the interests of said people. By not letting us see proceedings that resulted in the Court's vote split straight down party lines over the 2000 election, I charge they ruled in their own interests, not the country's. Highbrow claims are often made to reason why the lens is barred from courtrooms. Some argue that lawyers will grandstand. Here's a news flash: Lawyers grandstand no matter what—camera or no camera. The ones that ham it up would ham it up if only the court's calendar clerk were present, and she's probably reading the local newspaper under her desk.

Maybe the Court could learn from the House of Representatives, which opened its doors to camera coverage in 1977. The Senate followed in 1986. In a November 2000 article for *National Policy Analysis,* Amy Ridenour reported certain elected officials lost weight, bought hairpieces, and started wearing makeup on camera, but reasoned no one could "seriously" argue "that the country is worse off because of C-SPAN." I agree. No one in his right mind could perceive the network as a security threat. Like Congress, the Court is doing the people's business, and the people have the right to see that.

Some opponents claim that cameras could cause concern for child witnesses and victims. Point well taken. I advocate that their desires must be strongly weighed by the court, along with those of the other trial participants. In most cases, the only trial participants who aren't in court as a matter of their own doing are victims and certain witnesses. Lawyers, clerks, judges, and bailiffs are all paid to be there. Defendants likely committed a voluntary criminal or wrongful act resulting in their "attendance." But this is not an issue for the U.S. Supreme Court.

There are never witnesses before that court. Only lawyers appear at that level, in order to argue violations of law in lower courts.

Others argue that the camera could reduce the public's respect for the Court. Well, that argument's not half wrong. After the Supremes' decision to bar the people from the election proceedings and then split their vote directly down political party lines, I'm not so sure they deserve the profound respect I always had for them. Since the beginning of my legal career, I revered them. The U.S. Supreme Court's handling of this matter forever changed my deep awe of the Court and what it stands for. I'm not referring to the actual election or its outcome. That's politics. I'm talking about the law of the land, by which we live and are governed. I'm directly referring to the Court, their predictable voting pattern down party lines and their decision to shut America out of their courtroom.

HOW DID WE GET HERE?

There is a long history regarding open courts and allowing cameras to bring those proceedings to the people. Truth be told, Charles Lindbergh unwittingly pioneered a new age for America's courts after the disappearance and death of his baby, Charles Augustus Jr. The twenty-month-old infant was stolen from his crib at the Lindberghs' New Jersey home one night in March 1932. A homemade ladder and a ransom note were found at the scene. Lindbergh delivered the money on April 2 with hopes that baby Charlie would come home unharmed. He did not. On May 12, the tot was found dead, his body buried in a shallow grave near Trenton, New Jersey. Things quickly spun out of control. Lindbergh and his wife learned the shocking news that after their son was recovered, reporters had illegally entered the morgue and taken photos of the tiny body.

The FBI arrested a German-born carpenter, Bruno Richard Hauptmann, two years later in the Bronx, New York: Ransom money had been found in his garage. The press was relentless. When the trial began in

January 1935, it created an unprecedented media frenzy, one that chronicled the Lindberghs' every move. Three months after Charlie's body had been found, Lindbergh's wife, Anne, gave birth to a second son, Jon. The grieving father begged the press to leave the child alone. His pleas went unheeded. At one point during the six-week trial, the case was so sensationalized that a photographer forced the car carrying Jon and the baby's nurse off the road.

After a jury trial, Hauptmann was convicted and sentenced to death. On April 3, 1936, he died in the electric chair. The Lindberghs couldn't escape the media hounding, so they moved to Europe in hopes of regaining some of their privacy and to protect their then-three-year-old son.

Like the Simpson case much later, the Lindbergh case was called the "trial of the century" and it was reported that 700 newspapermen and 129 cameramen had made their way to the Flemington, New Jersey, courthouse. Cars, planes, telegraphs, and telephones were used to get reports to metropolitan New York and out for worldwide distribution. The little New Jersey town with one telegraph operator suddenly sprouted forty-five direct wires; a special teletype machine connected directly with London; a direct wire to Halifax, Nova Scotia; and quick service to Paris, Berlin, Buenos Aires, Shanghai, Melbourne, and other major cities around the world.

Prior to this case, there had never been a trial more ripe for media exploitation. There was also never a case before Lindbergh that determined the rule of behavior during trials. Judge Newton Baker wrote that the trial displayed "perhaps the most spectacular and depressing example of improper publicity and professional misconduct ever presented to the people of the United States in a criminal trial."

The *New York Times* reported that on January 3, 1935, "Constables on duty at the door admitted 275 spectators without passes to an already crowded courtroom. . . . Men and women sat on the window sills and jammed the small space between the bench and the wall." The *Mirror* wrote that on January 22 of that year, "The Bronx subway was never like the courthouse here." On January 28, it reported that "the fourth broken courtroom window was registered at 3:01 during a recess, so choked to capacity are the window sills." One witness, the novelist Edna Ferber, described the court as "a shambles. . . . Planned to accommodate perhaps a hundred, it was jammed with what seemed at least a thousand, seated, standing, leaning, perched on window sills, craning over balcony rails, peering through doorways." Newspaper headlines screamed out THE FLEMINGTON CROWD; IT'S A SIDESHOW, A JAMBOREE; IT'S A HOLIDAY, A FREAK SHOW. The judge ordered that no photos would be allowed during proceedings, so of course the press published in-court photographs steadily, from "Mrs. Lindbergh testifying" to "Colonel Charles A. Lindbergh on the Stand" and "Hauptmann Juror No. 11," with color commentary on each. Recording equipment was placed in the courtroom's balcony.

It all ended with an American Bar Association Report in January 1936 in which a special committee of ABA members was tasked to work with the press to create standards regarding publicity of criminal trials. Naturally, the lawyers and the newsmen disagreed violently on one point: the use of cameras in the courtroom. The ABA stated that "no use of cameras or photographic appliances [will] be permitted in the courtroom," and "with regard to the foregoing recommendation, the committee is unanimous in recommending that the use of cameras in the courtroom should be only with the knowledge and approval of the trial judge . . . and the consent of counsel for the accused in criminal cases and of counsel for both parties in civil cases should be secured. The newspaper representatives believe that the consent of the trial judge is full protection both to parties and to witnesses, and that no further requirement should be interposed."

The media responded that the American public "has, by constitutional guarantee, the right to the most complete information as to what is afoot in its courts," and that "provided the picture is made without disturbing the decorum of the court or otherwise obstructing the ends of justice, the publisher of a newspaper has the right . . . both to make the picture and to print it." Another outlet opined that this right "is part of the constitutional privilege of the press to print the news, and also part of the people's constitutional right to be informed by its free and full publication."

While arguing over implementation, both sides agreed that regulation of publicity and camera usage was necessary. A final ruling by the bar in 1936 stated, "Proceedings in court should be conducted with fitting dignity and decorum. The taking of photographs in the courtroom, during sessions of the court or recesses between sessions, and the broadcasting of court proceedings are calculated to detract from the essential dignity of the proceedings, degrade the court and create misconceptions with respect thereto in the mind of the public and should not be permitted." The press was furious, and the battle continues to rage.

Fast-forward to today: After many more legal skirmishes, forty-eight states now allow camera coverage in at least some court proceedings. Our courtrooms are again becoming the people's court envisioned by our Founding Fathers so long ago. Since we, the people, foot the bill for the judges, prosecutors, many defense attorneys, and court personnel—since they work for us and carry out their duties on our behalf—we have a right to see what's going on in our courtrooms.

If a circus is mounted outside the courthouse, then the camera is the cure, not the cause. Full trial coverage, not spin from jousting reporters and pundits, allows people to make up their own minds. With or without cameras, trials themselves will always generate great interest. Some argue that the presence of cameras causes grandstanding and longer proceedings, but the facts do not bear this out. The case of California's Hillside Strangler began in late 1981 and dragged on for nearly two years, while Charles Manson's took nine months. Neither courtroom had camera access.

While those forty-eight states vary in their rules, they are unified in allowing true access to the people through the lens. Some allow extensive coverage, such as Alaska, California, Florida, Georgia, Idaho, Michigan, North Carolina, and Wisconsin. Other states, like Alabama, Maryland, Nebraska, and Oklahoma, allow only appellate coverage or apply other restrictive rules. As of spring 2004, Court TV has televised nearly one thousand trials. Justice is marching forward, whether the U.S. Supreme Court notices or not.

GOING TOO FAR

But there are limits to where cameras should be allowed to go. In 2002, Judge Ted Poe of Harris County's 228th District Court in Texas agreed to allow an unmanned television camera to film jury deliberations in the death-penalty case of seventeen-year-old Cedric R. Harrison for the PBS show *Frontline*.

The defense agreed with the judge's decision, but prosecutors fought back on day one of individual jury selection. The state appeals court sided with prosecutors, stopped the trial, and ordered Poe to explain himself. The judge defended his decision by saying that the camera would be there for "educational purposes." The case was ultimately transferred to another judge, and the camera was banished from the proceedings.

In my mind, Poe single-handedly transformed the most serious decision a jury will ever make into a (thankfully thwarted) reality show. The desire to appear on a television series should not be added to the qualifications for jury service. As a matter of fact, the decision immediately altered the jury pool. Every juror who objected to being filmed was automatically thrown off jury duty. Do you blame them?

The law seemed squarely opposed to Poe's position. The Code of Criminal Procedure states that no person shall be permitted to be with a jury while it is deliberating, providing confidentiality as to jury deliberations. In my experience, despite those renegade jurors looking for their fifteen minutes of fame, the great majority of those who serve take their duty extremely seriously and must decide the case without the threat of being judged, shamed, or ridiculed by TV audiences plopped on their sofas eating chips. They must remain immune from public scrutiny. It's hard enough for twelve strangers to reach a verdict. If they had to worry about what their neighbors would think of them, their job would be impossible.

The Constitution guarantees a public trial, not public jury deliberations. Can you imagine the new line of appellate attack by defense attorneys far and wide? Creating the precedent of allowing a camera in the jury room also will create a trend among criminal-defense attorneys. The new trial demand could be something like, "I demand to have a camera in jury deliberations to record jury misconduct. I want to have a videotape." And then, on appeal, every facial tic, every nuance during deliberations will be a perceived ground for reversal. It will extend it to all civil and criminal cases.

I'm against this dangerous precedent. Again, the Constitution says we have a right to an open courtroom, not an open jury-deliberation room. Juries don't deliberate in public for good reason. If they had to, they wouldn't be able to be themselves and couldn't express their thoughts and feelings. Another serious issue that arises out of filming jurors is the threat of reprisal, either real or perceived. A camera in the jury room takes away a juror's anonymity. If you were on the jury trying a murder case and you believed strongly that the defendant was guilty but in the end he was acquitted, would you feel safe? What about a mob case where the mobster walks and finds out which jurors wanted a guilty verdict? This outrageously bad idea not only puts jurors in potential danger but also jeopardizes the fairness of the entire system.

Ironically, the term "in camera," meaning "in chambers," refers to closed-door proceedings. Such proceedings are appropriately kept away from the camera. Much of what is discussed in camera is about the admissibility of evidence and involves a myriad of issues, some of which may turn out to be inadmissible at trial. One example is the results of a search, later deemed inadmissible; another could be about the defendant's rapsheet. In camera matters are usually treated as such because discussing them in open court could forever damage the defendant, the victim, or a witness. The same reasoning that applies to in camera proceedings applies to jury deliberations and to the jurors themselves. None should be put *on* camera.

If jurors want to make themselves known after the trial, as they did in the Simpson, McVeigh, and Martha Stewart cases, where many of the jurors granted interviews, that's their business. If not, they should not be forced into the spotlight for doing their civic duty. Lawyers and judges have chosen to be in the courtroom. The same cannot be said about the victim or the jury. I believe they should be protected from having their images broadcast for the entire world to see.

We, the people, are granted two weapons with which to fight the government: jury service and our vote in public elections. These are the two powers the Constitution grants citizens to police their own government. Both are done in private so as to ensure total freedom of thought and honesty. Trial by jury is guaranteed three times in the Constitution. More than a million Americans serve on juries each year. To do so, they must overcome prejudices and differences in order to come together as a jury to render a true verdict. Juries are the souls and consciences of their communities. They have the power to correct the errors of government officials and are the bastion between three parties often at war—the defense, the judge, and the prosecutor. The jury is the heart, mind, and soul of the justice system. Jurors and their deliberations must be protected from the cameras at all costs.

THE CAMERA DOESN'T LIE

When it comes to seeking justice, television is one of the last forums where you can tell the truth. As I've explained in these many pages, you can't always do that in the courtroom anymore. Often the very rules of evidence and judge's rulings don't allow the whole truth to be told. The truth is caught by the lens without interpretation, spin, or elaboration. Excluding cameras from courtrooms keeps the workings of justice beyond the purview of the taxpaying citizen. Why should the truth be available only to those who can afford to go and sit in the courtroom? What about everybody else?

I don't want somebody else's version of what happened. I want to see for myself every nuance of the defense, the demeanor of the defendant, the level of charisma or lack thereof of the lawyers and the judge. I want to know when the jurors get bored and take a break or when they furiously begin writing notes. I want to watch when the defendant smiles or scribbles or maybe is forced by his own conscience to look away from the witness stand during testimony. I want to know that the justice system is doing its job every day—and I certainly want to know when it isn't.

Thanks to the cameras in the courtroom at Jayson Williams's trial, we knew more than the jury knew. We were privy to the idea that the shooting was more akin to a drunk-driving manslaughter than anything else, due to the former NBA star's high blood-alcohol levels after a long night of partying. We also knew that the death of Gus Christofi was far from Williams's first brush with violence or with guns.

Williams had spent the night partying with a group of Harlem Globetrotters. Some of them told police that he seemed drunk and was driving "fast, dangerous, and/or erratic." One player in particular, whose demeanor I watched very carefully on the stand, told cops he said "a silent prayer because he was afraid." New Jersey State Trooper Melvin Saunders II testified that Williams was slurring his words, that he stank of alcohol, and that he told the others in the house that night "not to say anything because [Williams] had a lawyer coming." Paramedic Matthew Wilson testified that while houseguests were dressed as if they'd been out for the evening—which they had been—Williams was wearing a T-shirt and sweatpants, indicating that he'd changed his clothes after the shooting. It was later revealed at trial that Williams had wiped down the gun that night, then taken Christofi's hand as he lay dying on the floor and placed his prints on the gun to set the scene as a suicide. Blood tests later put Williams's blood-alcohol level at between .18 and .22, which prosecutors consider "severe intoxication." The jury never knew that due to a ruling by the judge. But the camera knew—and because of that, so did we.

The jury definitely got the sanitized version of Jayson Williams's history, while the camera again told the truth. Williams won major rulings when Judge Edward M. Coleman refused to allow the jury to hear about his earlier incidents of violence involving guns, like the time he fired a gun repeatedly at a car parked at the Meadowlands Sports Complex. As I mentioned in a previous chapter, jurors were also kept from hearing from Dwayne Schintzius's account of the time Williams shot his own dog. There were additional alleged prior bad acts that were kept from the jury, but, unlike lawyers and judges, the camera can't lie, withhold, or obscure.

The issue of having cameras in the courtroom surfaced again in the Scott Peterson trial in 2004. I felt it was a huge injustice that cameras were disallowed, because their presence could have exposed all of the posturing throughout the trial by the defense. At the same time, I understood that Laci's family did not want her life and death exposed to the public in this way. Stanislaus County District Attorney James Brazelton presented the motion to ban cameras from the courtroom to the judge with a letter from Sharon Rocha, which said, in part, "The family of Laci Peterson [is] requesting that no cameras be allowed inside the courtroom. . . . Please don't let memories be destroyed by televising the ugliness of the trial." I understand how she feels, I really do. But cameras could easily have captured facts, both in court and on endless television programs and in chatrooms. All of that went undocumented, save for stories based on secondhand news. Those accounts were based on an individual's spin and interpretation, not the actual testimony heard unvarnished for our own interpretation.

Of course, there was no end to the leaks during the case. We heard about the possibility that Laci vomited in the kitchen, leaving DNA evidence that necessitated the kitchen floor's being remopped by Peterson. We were also told that Laci knew about Peterson's affair with Amber Frey and had made peace with it. We heard endless theories, from Satanic cult murders to sexual predators being responsible for Laci's and Conner's deaths, none borne out by the evidence. Why? Because we couldn't hear the truth—because there were no cameras in the courtroom. All we had was spin.

FACING JUSTICE

According to the FBI in 1996, there were more than 100,000 rapes
that year, which meant that one sex attack occurred every five minutes.
That figure was most likely deceptively low, as many rapes and other
forms of sexual attacks go unreported because the victims are too trau-
matized, afraid, or humiliated to openly reveal the attack. Rape victims
who do summon up the courage to come forward are generally and uni-
versally reluctant to have their names exposed, much less their faces—
and their humiliation—revealed on camera.

In 1996, I was lucky enough to meet four women who broke that
mold. They said no to nearly every stereotype imposed on rape victims
by society and the justice system. When I was assigned *State v. Anton
Jermaine Smith*, I encountered some of the most extraordinary women I
have ever met. Without any hesitation, they decided to allow cameras
in the courtroom—and reveal their identities—during their trial.

Atlanta had been terrorized for months by a man whose pattern was
to stalk a particular woman for days without her knowledge, to learn her
habits and living conditions, and then break into her home at night to
demean and rape her. He disguised his face with a pair of nude-colored
pantyhose. Writing about it now brings back the sickening feeling I got
when I first read the case file. I couldn't imagine what it would be like
to wake up in the dead of night with a knife-wielding stranger over my
bed, his features distorted by the stocking over his head. But that
changed when I took this case.

I had been to the women's homes, walked every inch of the crime
scenes with my investigator, and compared their statements to hone in
on the attacker's modus operandi. I worked late into the night preparing
legal briefs to ensure that the cases would be tried together and to foil,
with preemptive strikes, any antics the defense would pull in an effort
to threaten the introduction of my evidence. But there was one thing I
couldn't prepare for—the surprising strength of the victims.

The women met one another in the aftermath of the attacks. In 1995, Kay Cross, Andrea Goode, and Lavon Skyers were attacked by Anton Jermaine Smith when he broke in to their homes late at night. Skyers was able to fight Smith off and escape. Smith was arrested hours after breaking in to Skyers's home but was mistakenly released from jail when lower-court prosecutors failed to inform the judge of the rape charges he faced. The judge had been told only about the burglary case, and Smith was released on $10,000 bond (he put up $1,000 and walked free). Less than three weeks later, he was arrested for the rape of Lynda Denham.

Denham's attack could have been stopped with a simple clerical correction. The person who made the mistake faced no consequence for the costly error. I believe that in cases like this one, the responsible party should face an automatic review of his or her job performance, at which the victim is heard, and if found grossly negligent, possibly face criminal action. All hell broke loose when the mistake hit the press. When I got the case, I was summoned to the district attorney's office for a meeting. He impressed upon me the need to resolve the case, help the women, and calm the firestorm started by some clerk in some courthouse annex whom we would never pin down.

I left with my marching orders, preparing for a serial-rape case. What I never counted on was meeting four of the bravest crime victims I've ever known. As we sat huddled together outside the courtroom for pre-trial motions, the women began to talk about being made to feel that what had happened to them was their fault. They got angry and turned to me. I didn't know what to say. I had already told them that I had opposed a request for press in the courtroom, because I assumed they would not want their faces revealed.

One of the women burst into tears right there in the hall, her face all red. I'll never forget her words: "I didn't do anything wrong. This is a crime. I'm not going to be ashamed about what happened to me. I want the world to know. I didn't do anything wrong."

I called Court TV that very day, and when the trial started, a lone camera sat in the back of the room. In the televised proceedings of the

William Kennedy Smith rape trial, a blue dot had obscured Patricia Bowman's face. *State v. Anton Jermaine Smith* was the country's first gavel-to-gavel coverage of a serial-rape trial in which the victims' faces were actually shown on television.

I had no experience with televised trials, but moments after we started, I forgot about the camera because I was so deeply embroiled in the case. The defense fought tooth and nail, contending that the victims were mistaken about their identifications of Smith and challenging the accuracy of the scientific evidence. But their IDs of the defendant won out. One of the victims was forced to listen to the defendant read the Bible aloud, as he had done to her before and after the rape. She also had to perform a voice ID. That witness was so distraught after her testimony and the attack she underwent on cross-examination that she literally fell from the stand when she tried to get up from her seat. I caught her. She looked straight at the defendant.

Smith was found guilty on July 12, 1996. He was sentenced to three consecutive life terms. The ladies in the Smith prosecution taught me about courage under fire. I also learned something else: A camera in the courtroom doesn't lie. It cannot. Like the Smith jury, it will always render a verdict that speaks the truth.

TAKING A HARD LOOK

When it comes to allowing cameras in the courtroom, I advocate that each trial be reviewed on a case-by-case basis, with all participants given an opportunity to be heard on the matter. The weight given to the testimony of each participant, be it a victim, a defendant, or an attorney, must be judged in the context of the case itself. I firmly believe that the general rule must be, under our Founding Fathers' wishes, for a completely open court, to be closed only after great consideration and only with great cause.

CHAPTER ELEVEN

TO MY CRITICS

NOBODY EVER SAID IT WAS GOING TO BE EASY. The realization sank in a few months after my fiancé's death that my life was not going to be what I had mapped out. Wife, mother, English professor—it was not meant to be. Instead, as part of God's mysterious plan, I found a new and very different life.

I'm reminded of a true story about a woman in New York City who was battling breast cancer. She took up running as part of her recovery from the devastating illness. After months had passed, she decided to enter a 5k—a 3.1-mile race through Central Park. She got there about an hour and a half beforehand and was surprised to see hundreds of other women already warming up. She quickly joined in. At the start of the race, when the gun sounded and the runners took off, the woman thanked her lucky stars she'd gotten there early and was ready for the competition. About an hour into the race, she passed the five-mile sign, and immediately thought, *This is not the race I signed up for!* She continued running as best she could and I'm happy to report that she ran, not walked, across the finish line, her arms raised in victory. It was not the race she'd signed up for, but, by God, it was the race she was in.

I think of that story when I recall my courtroom battles. There were many, many times when I sat alone in the courtroom at the end of the day—by then it was evening, and it would be dark outside when I left the courthouse. I'd often think, *How did I get here?* It was not what I had planned, not what I had bargained for, not the race I'd signed up for. But, by God, it's the race I am in.

Many times on air, when a defense attorney runs out of legal or factual attacks, I become the target. That's okay. There's a wise old saying in the legal world that goes like this: "If you have the facts, argue the facts. If you have the law, argue the law. If you have neither, just argue!" When I get attacked personally on air, I'm torn between the usual feelings of anger or hurt and the realization that the other side's assault is based on their knowledge that they have neither the facts nor the law on their side. I really believe that.

During all the years I practiced law, I kept Keith's murder to myself. I did not want it to be part of some ridiculous defense argument that I was bent on revenge. It simply was not true. There is no satisfaction in putting the wrong perpetrator behind bars.

There have been times on *Larry King Live,* on *The John Walsh Show,* and other programs when Keith's murder is used against me. During one live show, I recall being accused of wearing his death "like a badge." That hurt. The truth is, my story doesn't change the law or facts in any of the cases I argue. A reporter once told me during an appearance on *The John Walsh Show* that I wasn't fit to analyze cases because I had opinions as a victim of violent crime. Somehow the reporter reasoned I wasn't fit to comment. I didn't know how to react in front of a huge studio audience. I chose, naturally, to fight back, and it turned into such a battle, the incident hit the papers the next day.

I am proud to have survived many blows, proud to be the voice of those who cannot speak for themselves, and proud to continue fighting the good fight as I see it. I have been confronted many times, on air and off, by "journalists" who accuse me of not being one of them. I am accused of having beliefs, opinions, and convictions. I plead guilty.

I've never once made a secret of the fact that I am not a journalist. I never pretended I was. I am what I am. I am first and foremost a survivor who lived through the court system, endured the pain, and made it my business to master the law and the rules of evidence to return to that system and do battle there. I love the law. I believe in our system. It causes me genuine pain to see Lady Justice, who is really all we have to protect us, mistreated, tricked, and degraded. I am an advocate for other victims. I have tried to use my knowledge of the law as my sword and shield and studied it in great detail, keeping it at the tip of my tongue and at the forefront of my mind at all times. The reason I am not and never could be a journalist is that I also keep that knowledge of the law deep in my heart, and when I need the shield, I raise it. When I need the sword, I draw it out.

Defense attorneys—but amazingly not Johnnie Cochran—have routinely attacked not only my point of view but also me. That's okay, though. It's nothing compared to being accused of using dirty tricks to win a trial or being held in contempt of court. Nothing can sober you up like the thought of being thrown into the county jail overnight while you should be working your case. I remember that while under siege on air. If I were to back away from an argument, I would be letting down not only Keith but all victims who go unheard.

I recall the night in April 2003 when Scott Peterson's father, Lee Peterson, called in to *Larry King Live* and lambasted me. He insisted I had a "personal vendetta" and was out to get his son. I was torn between really lacing into him with questions I knew he couldn't answer about his son and thinking of my own father and how he would fight to the finish to save me. The thoughts of my own father won out, and I held back. Lee Peterson was hurting, too, and I knew that. Of course, it was "great TV," as several producers said after the show. It wasn't TV. It was real. And it hurt. The next morning, it was replayed on talk shows throughout the day. I didn't watch.

When I watch the manipulation of evidence, the endless arguments, and the posturing in a court of law, I can't pretend I don't know what is the truth. Trials are not "stories." They are the pain, the suffering, the raw emotions of victims and defendants, of witnesses—and many shrink back, either too afraid or too apathetic to speak out. I don't see it as fodder for conversation. I see it as a battle of right versus wrong. I want the truth to win out.

Political correctness be damned. On-air or in-court "performances," legalese, arguments for argument's sake be damned. None of it matters. All that matters is the truth and it remains the same, no matter how attorneys twist it and turn it and repackage it. The truth doesn't change. "See no evil, hear no evil, and speak no evil" while hiding behind the presumption of innocence and political correctness is something I'm not willing to do. It's not okay, and if people are not willing to take a stand for others, then who will take a stand for them when the time comes?

It's hard to swallow, but the truth is not always told in court. Contrary to what some of my critics have said, I don't believe in "guilty until proven innocent." I firmly believe in "innocent until proven guilty." That's the standard I followed in every case I ever tried, and if *I* am ever judged, that is the standard I pray my jury holds sacred as well. But that is not the end of the judge's charge. An accused is presumed innocent "unless and until that presumption is overcome by evidence of guilt beyond a reasonable doubt." That is the law. If we choose to ignore the law, victims have no recourse, no hope.

On *Larry King Live*, I have been confronted several times by legal analysts and defense attorneys like Mark Geragos about the fact that I, along with the police, contended Richard Albert Ricci was a perfect suspect in the Elizabeth Smart abduction case. I stand by my statement. Wisely and correctly, before his death, he was never charged. I recall that at the beginning of the search for Elizabeth, a man named Michael Edmunds, a drifter, was spotted in the neighborhood by a milk-truck driver and all hell broke loose. Edmunds was the first suspect we knew of. The press and the cops chased that poor guy all over the country until they got him. I actually agreed with Geragos on air at the time regarding Edmunds as a suspect and said, "This doesn't make sense to me. Something doesn't fit." To all the critics who claim I think everybody's guilty: Put that in your pipe and smoke it.

Now back to Ricci. Consider this: He had worked at and been inside the Smart home, had a long and extensive history of criminal behavior, had actually stolen from the Smart home even after they'd given him money and employed him. His bizarre behavior and reports that he failed a polygraph test made him a prime suspect in Elizabeth's disappearance. Ricci was out of jail on parole for shooting a cop in the head at the time he stole from the Smarts. The stolen items were found in his trailer—a clear violation of his parole. I have no problem with his parole's being revoked and his landing back in jail. His long history of both criminal and bizarre behavior made him a suspect. All this time, he was out free on parole for shooting an officer in the head.

Conversely, I also stated several times on air after meeting his wife, Angela Ricci, that she seemed credible and believable. I felt she held the key to whether he was responsible. If he were ever formally charged, her testimony alone, her genuineness, would win the day without further evidence from the state. I sat with her. I looked her in the eyes. I listened to her and questioned her myself. She was for real. She, and she alone, gave me the feeling the truth had not been uncovered. I could not reconcile her story and demeanor with the mathematical equation of Ricci's being the perfect suspect. It didn't fit. Now I know them both to be true. The reality was that he *was* the perfect suspect and she *was* telling the truth.

I remember one of my favorite judges I ever practiced before was the Honorable Luther Alverson. The former barber turned out to be one of the greatest judges ever to take the bench. His jury instructions ring in my mind to this day. He would look solemnly at the jury and charge them that they, the jury, were the sole judge of the facts and the evidence as well as the credibility of the witnesses. It was their duty, as best they could, to reconcile the evidence so as to make all witnesses speak the truth, imparting perjury to no one. In other words, sometimes the facts don't jibe, don't reconcile. The truth can be complicated and confusing, but there is a way to make all witnesses, all people concerned, speak the truth. Angela Ricci spoke the truth. I also spoke the truth and will not back down or pretend it didn't happen. Although Ricci made a perfect suspect, he didn't do the deed.

I believe in looking at all the facts as they truly exist, without blinders or rose-colored glasses, without a sugarcoating to make them easier going down. I don't mean the facts after they've been airbrushed and cleaned up and powdered and perfumed before being admitted in evidence at trial. I'm talking about the truth before it's twisted and contorted and argued away. I mean the truth, the whole truth. I look at those facts and make a deduction. That's not illegal. Some of the evidence might be ruled inadmissible, but that doesn't mean it doesn't exist and I can't form an educated and calculated opinion based on that evidence. The defense doesn't want to hear that. Maybe they want to believe that if something isn't admitted into court, they can pretend that it doesn't exist. But it does.

Evidence exists even when the jury doesn't get to hear it. Evidence exists that Scott Peterson did not want to have a child. He was hiding things from the police and then-girlfriend Amber Frey. He changed his story about where he was Christmas Eve afternoon. Many people know that these things happened. People know Nicole Brown was battered, and they know about the Bronco "chase." The jury didn't hear that— but it is true.

Ever since I looked down from the witness stand at Keith's killer and he couldn't look me in the eyes, I have put stock in behavioral evidence—how someone behaves after a crime. At a vigil held for his wife just days after she went missing, Peterson arrived late and did not sit with the rest of the family—family friend Sandy Rickard testified that despite repeated pleas from Sharon Rocha, Peterson never responded to her questions about Laci's activities and state of mind the day she vanished. Incredibly, Rickard told the jury that Peterson put Rocha off with excuses about having other things to do. These are perfect examples of behavioral evidence. So is the fact that Peterson grabbed a stack of flyers with his wife's picture on them one afternoon but instead of going out to put them up, went and played golf. I interviewed the manager of the

Red Lion Inn in Modesto at the command center set up by the volunteers searching for Laci, who saw these things happen. I believe him. The jury never heard his testimony, but it is the truth.

In analyzing cases, I take into account something that is not allowed into court when weighing the evidence, and that is statistics. Solving murders isn't divine intervention—it's common sense. I know that most women who are murdered are most likely killed by an acquaintance: a husband, a lover, a boyfriend, the grocery-store clerk, someone they know, someone familiar. When investigating murder cases, police start with the family and move outward in bigger and bigger circles. They start with the home, then go to the office, then to the apartment complex, then to the neighborhood. Stranger-on-stranger murder does not constitute the majority of homicide. That is statistically proven. I know this. The jury can never hear that fact, but it's the truth.

The criminal justice system operates at a relentless pace. I've written about striking one jury while the other jury is out deliberating—there is a constant onslaught of cases. Prosecutors don't have much time to stop and take stock of what's happening. Writing about these issues has reminded me of cases I haven't thought of in a really long time. Every one left its mark, because in nearly every case I dealt with victims of violent crime—victims whom a guilty verdict couldn't heal, nor could it bring back to them the person who was gone forever.

In 2004, I covered the trial of Lynn Turner, an Atlanta woman convicted of murdering her husband, police officer Glenn Turner, by poisoning him with antifreeze. Glenn, then thirty-one, was admitted to the hospital with flulike symptoms in March 1995 but was released. He died the next day. His death was initially attributed to an enlarged heart. Six years later, Turner's boyfriend, firefighter Randy Thompson, thirty-two, with whom she was having an affair at the time of her husband's death, died of the same symptoms. His death was also ruled as heart failure. At the insistence of the victims' mothers, the local medical examiner ran additional tests only to find calicum oxalate crystals—a sign of ethylene glycol known to be the fatal ingredient in antifreeze—in Thompson's kidneys. An examination of Glenn Turner's body revealed the presence of the same crystals.

Due to the similarities in the two deaths, the court ruled that the jurors could hear evidence against Turner in Thompson's death, although she was not charged with the killing at the time. The jury found her guilty of her husband's murder and sentenced her to life in prison. As of this writing, charges are pending against Lynn Turner for Thompson's death.

After the trial, I spoke to the families of both men. Thompson's father said he was relieved the defendant was finally being tried. The family had pleaded with law-enforcement officials to take action long before they did. He ended our conversation by saying, "But he's still gone . . . our son is still gone." The bottom line is, even after a conviction like Turner's, there is nothing joyful in the justice system. That's the reality. There are no happy endings in the courtroom. In this case, the trial revealed that there was a second victim and now there will be a second trial, for the death penalty. Sometimes there is vindication in a courtroom, but never will you find a Hollywood happy ending.

One thing I love about arguing cases on television—and in this book—is that I don't have a judge tossing out truthful evidence deemed inadmissible under the law. I remember one case, in which a millionaire was on trial for the murder of his wife. I never got to tell the jury he refused to pay his wife's funeral bill. He had millions but loathed his wife—the mother of his children—so much that he refused to pay the bill for her funeral. The judge ruled it out as nonprobative, as proving nothing. I disagree. Most families care deeply about the treatment the victim receives and the care their beloved gets at a funeral. I know I did. It is the last thing we can do for the ones we love—bury them. The jury never heard this behavioral evidence. Defense lawyers will argue until they are blue in the face that it means nothing. But it does. And that's the truth.

On air, there is no judge censoring the truth. On *Closing Arguments,* my show at Court TV, I was allowed to speak the truth that defendant Lynn Turner cried in the courtroom in front of the jury but less than ten minutes later she was giggling and laughing out loud, hugging friends, and yakking on her cell phone out in the courthouse parking lot. The jury never knew that, but I did. I can talk about what it means that Scott Peterson turned the baby's nursery into a storage room within weeks of Laci's disappearance, what it means that he sweet-talked his mistress while the police and volunteers worked day and night to find his wife or her body. I can analyze what it means that, when asked if he forced the accuser to have sex, Kobe Bryant paused, for a long time, before he answered no. I can talk about what it means that Robert Blake did not try to save or at least comfort his wife as she lay dying in his car. What I would have given to have the chance, if not to save, but only to comfort Keith as he left this world.

Often people will ask me, "How do you talk about these cases and not get upset?" The reality is, I do. When I do *Larry King Live*, they always have a box of tissues sitting there for me. They know to take the camera off me if I get upset and then come back on when I get myself together again. I very frequently cry during commercial breaks when I hear about a victim—sometimes it happens even if I just look at a photo of the person in life. I cried right through the van Dam trial. I've choked up on air before—and in jury trials I couldn't help it. It's the human element of these cases that pains me. To me, that's what the system is all about—to protect not only the defendant but also the victim. I don't know how you can pretend it's a laboratory experiment, that human emotion, pain, and sorrow are not part of it.

While I know that there are thousands of people watching and listening, when I'm on television and radio, I never think of it. I keep my mind on the victim involved and the truth as I see it. To me, everything is about seeking justice, in whatever forum I find myself. I have a job hosting daily live trial coverage on Court TV and a show weeknights on CNN Headline News doing battle over legal issues. I do not seek or get clients from my appearances. I am not paid for my appearances on *Larry King Live*, *Oprah*, or the morning shows; I work and speak out because I believe in what I'm saying. My opinions are not for sale.

Each night, my conviction to speak out on behalf of regular, hard-working people is renewed by viewers who call in offering encouragement. Even though I never see their faces, their voices are enough to keep me believing and struggling. To those people, I want to say thank you from my heart.

I also get a lot of calls from viewers, asking me why I don't smile more on television. I try to take those comments in stride, but I always wind up thinking, *What's there to smile about?* When I'm on air, analyzing a murder or child-molestation case, it's not just a television appearance. I'm talking about real-life tragedy, involving real people. What am I supposed to smile about?

I've seen firsthand how badly things have spun out of control in the courtroom. I've tried as best I can to share what I have seen with you and offer remedies. It's time we took a hard look at what's wrong with our justice system. It is all we have. There are two things that set us apart from the animal kingdom: our opposable thumbs and the decision we have made as a society to live by the law, to protect those less powerful and less fortunate than others. I believe in our justice system with all my heart. I do not want to see the day it buckles under its own weight, under attack from all sides.

I have great hope that we are and always will be a nation of laws, where every voice, including those that are not blessed with fame or fortune, those victims who are not considered in the Constitution—and even my voice—will be heard. I am optimistic that, as wonderful and powerful as our justice system is and as proud as Lady Justice stands guarding the courts, the best is yet to come. I am willing to fight for that day in court and on air, I am willing to wage battle to freely do what I have done here, with you, in this book: to tell the truth, the whole truth, and nothing but the truth. So help me God.

AND THEN . . .

TIME HAS PASSED, ROARING BY LIKE A locomotive since the original publication of *Objection!* The fixes, predictions, cures, and observations I wrote about have played out, many of them in open court. While disappointments are inevitble, the opportunity for a rough-cut at justice is still a beacon, a light at the end of the tunnel. Since *Objection!* the ride has been bumpy and the road has been hard . . . but Lady Justice needs us all now more than ever.

MICHAEL JACKSON: NOT GUILTY

After covering the Michael Jackson trial day in and day out for months, the long-awaited verdict had finally come. In the course of the trial, as evidence mounted, the outcome seemed clear to me. I believed there was no way the jury could turn away from the evidence presented by the state: not one, not two, but three then-little boys claimed the King of Pop had fondled them, some claiming to have been given alcohol by Jackson beforehand. One "similar transaction" witness, a former youth minister, took the stand and described being fondled by Jackson years before, his face turning crimson during his direct and cross-exam on the stand. He could hardly bring himself to relive the molestation, much less verbalize it in front of strangers. After years in the courtroom, I believed—naively—that the jury would recognize Jackson's course of conduct. I knew it was a tough pill to swallow that a music icon, beloved by millions, could do such a thing, but I chose to believe justice would win out.

   I knew the defense—helmed by the seasoned and disciplined lawyer Thomas Mesereau and his team—had hammered serious cracks into various state witnesses, particularly the child-victim's mom, on cross-exam. But I rationally expected the jury to remember she was tangential to the case. The boy was the alleged victim, not the mom. Another problem for the prosecution as I saw it was that another boy-victim of Jackson's in a multimillion-dollar settlement—twenty million dollars plus—in exchange for silence, was noticeably absent. He made his money years before and never darkened the courthouse steps in the current case.

   As I waited for the verdict, I sat in the Court TV studio in the well-worn anchor chair I have manned for eight years now. By satellite link, I listened with every fiber to my colleague and friend Diane Dimond, who was there at the California courthouse. She had been covering Jackson for years and had been the sole news anchor to break the news of the initial police raid on Neverland, the juggernaut that launched the trial. Jackson had even sued her personally for millions after she followed his case doggedly, never giving up. That suit was long dismissed. Here she sat again, in an eerie case of deja vu. The difference was that this time, District Attorney Tom Sneddon bet the farm and took the case to trial. The Jackson fans who sought to vilify him for doing his job didn't seem to bother Sneddon.

   As I waited, the energy in the darkened studio was crackling. I could see satellite transmissions of hundreds of fans circling the courthouse yelling, chanting, screaming, and singing for the jury to acquit. Diane sat there in a little Court TV tent amidst the mob, covering the goings on in an even voice that never cracked. From my chair on the other side of the country, I did the same.

   The jury entered the courtroom. Since no cameras were allowed, only the sound of the verdict was transmitted out to the tent and directly to my earpiece in New York. Count One: Not Guilty. Okay, I thought. I had expected, even predicted, a split verdict all along. They kept reading. Count Two: Not Guilty. Count Three: Not Guilty. Then I knew, it would be a clean sweep—all Not Guilties.

Jackson would walk.

For some reason, I couldn't seem to process what I was hearing with my own ears, what was going down in a court of law . . . presumably dedicated to reaching a verdict that spoke the truth. An acquittal had been roundly predicted, that no jury would convict even in the face of clear and convincing evidence. I didn't believe it because I didn't want to. I wanted to believe in the system I had represented for so long, had fought for, had cried over, had loved. After all, how many little boys would it take? I remained numb throughout the verdict coverage, calmly announcing the verdict, conducting interviews, broadcasting the news that Jackson would walk free. It was the single highest rated day in Court TV history. I couldn't feel a thing.

I knew that night that Jackson fans around the world would be watching my *Headline News* show, to see how I handled my own ill-fated prediction. I had misplaced my faith in the jury and I was wrong; there were no two ways about it. I pulled out a big sandwich on air at the beginning of the show and "ate crow," admitting I miscalculated and continued the coverage.

My disgust with the jury finally surfaced the evening of June 13, 2005, when I interviewed the Jackson jury foreperson, Paul Rodriguez, for my *Headline News* show. Our exchange went something like this:

GRACE: *Welcome back. We are joined now by the jury foreperson, Paul Rodriguez. Welcome, sir. Thank you for being with us.*

PAUL RODRIGUEZ, JACKSON JURY FOREPERSON: *Thank you.*

GRACE: *Mr. Rodriguez, did you believe the boy who came in, who is now a youth minister, when he stated that Jackson molested him in the past?*

RODRIGUEZ: *Well, we got a little problem with that because he had no idea where some of his money came from, and he didn't want to talk to his mother. And so those kind of things we kind of didn't focus on, but it did keep—we kept that in the back of our minds.*

GRACE: *So would it be safe to say you did not believe him?*

RODRIGUEZ: *Yes, we had a hard time believing him.*

GRACE: *OK. Why do you think Michael Jackson paid out over twenty million to get rid of the 1993 accuser? Was that a stumbling block for the jury?*

RODRIGUEZ: *We took that just for the fact of matter back when. We didn't want to use that for the case now. And we took that for what it was worth, and we thought that what we have to concentrate on is what's happening now. What happened in between the time that this whole thing started in February of 2003 to the end of March, those are the two months that we had to focus on.*

I was incredulous—this guy seemed to explain away all the evidence! As if none of it had even mattered!
Our conversation continued:

GRACE: *We saw Lady Justice play out a jury verdict today in a California courtroom. A thirteen-year-old boy and his family*

thought he had a shot in a case against Michael Jackson. He was
wrong. The jury—clean sweep, all Not Guilty—for Michael
Jackson. Let's go straight back out to the jury foreperson, Paul
Rodriguez. Welcome, sir. You're the foreperson on the jury. One of
the other jurors said right at the get-go they didn't want it to look
like a slam-dunk, so they continued deliberations. Did you guys
take a straw vote at the get-go?

RODRIGUEZ: *No. I didn't agree with that statement. We didn't do
that at all. I didn't like that statement. And I'm not sure who said it,
now that I'm thinking about it, but no, we didn't do that . . .*

GRACE: *How do you explain this guy sleeping with a thirteen-
year-old boy in their underwear?*

RODRIGUEZ: *The thing is, we didn't have the evidence beyond
a reasonable doubt that he did anything with these children. And
when some of these children came in to testify, none of them said
that anything happened. So it was really hard to go in the
direction that he was molesting them.*

GRACE: *Yes. What about the one kid who became a youth
minister, who stated plainly Jackson molested his—fondled his
genitals?*

RODRIGUEZ: *Again, like you said earlier, you know, about his
scenario or his testimony . . . it was hard to buy the whole story,
when he acted like he knew nothing about it. I mean, he acted so
much like the mother of the other accuser, you know, he just
didn't seem that credible. He didn't seem to convince us, like we
wanted to be convinced. And he just—he was leaving too many
little loopholes in his statements.*

Rodriguez had even chosen to disbelieve a youth minister in order to acquit Jackson! I was stunned! This jury was ready to believe that everybody but Jackson was lying—and Jackson never took the stand!

GRACE: *What did you think about the boy's mother?*

RODRIGUEZ: *We thought that she was—from the get-go—that she was not telling the truth, that she was in it for whatever she could get out of it. You know, going back to the JCPenney case and so many other things that came along, she just wasn't a credible witness.*

The mother was the bad guy! Not Jackson! The jury decided to find her guilty, but wait . . . she wasn't on trial!

GRACE: *What did you think about the boy, Paul? What did you think about the boy accuser?*

RODRIGUEZ: *The boy accuser—he was also—sounded a lot like he had been programmed. He sounded a lot like his mother's testimony, and it was really hard to be convinced by him. And that—that's one of the things we were really hung up on. We had to listen to his testimony and discuss it, stop it, discuss it, stop it, you know, just—And going over and over and over it, just to see if we left anything out, if there was something there that we could have used. But again, the evidence was not there beyond a reasonable doubt. It just wasn't there.*

GRACE: *Mr. Rodriguez? Can I ask you a question? What do you think a grown-up man in his forties is doing sleeping with one little boy after the next, all by himself, locked up in his bedroom, every night? That doesn't bother you? It bothers me.*

RODRIGUEZ: *Yes, it does. It bothers us a lot. It bothers us a lot. But again, like I said, we discussed our feelings, our beliefs, and our thoughts, and we cannot base a judgment on anyone that's up there as a defendant. We had to go with what we had as evidence. And if some of the evidence would have been presented or looked into a little more, and given us a little bit more to work with, then this whole thing might have been turned around.*

GRACE: *Mr. Rodriguez, what do you think it would have taken to convince this jury that Jackson had molested this boy?*

RODRIGUEZ: *Like I said, better evidence, and it just wasn't there, or deeper evidence or more evidence. But there was still a lot of things that came out that didn't— They didn't follow up on by giving us more information. You know, they would get our attention, they would go so far with the information, and then they'd say, 'Thank you for your testimony.' And we're thinking, OK, wait a minute. Take this a step further. Give us a little bit more to work with. But they didn't do that.*

GRACE: *You know . . .*

RODRIGUEZ: *So that's what really . . .*

GRACE: *Hey, Paul, I heard one of the lady jurors in your press conference state, "What mother in her right mind would allow this?" So my question is, if nothing wrong happened, then what was this lady juror talking about? Allow what?*

RODRIGUEZ: *I think it was her personal views. And I don't want to speak for her, because I'm really not sure what she was thinking about. I could guess, but I don't want to do that. You know, you*

have to talk to her. That's one thing we did decide on, that we
would not speak for each other. We'd speak [about] what we think
happened and the way we think individually, the direction this
whole thing could have gone or should have gone or didn't go.
But the thing is, again, we had to base our whole decision on the
testimony that was presented to us—all the evidence.

GRACE: *Paul, what did you think about the counts alleging*
that Jackson fed wine to the children?

RODRIGUEZ: *Say that again?*

GRACE: *What was your take on those counts that charged*
Michael Jackson with giving alcohol to a minor?

RODRIGUEZ: *Well, again, it was only hearsay, from the*
information we gathered, that nobody really came across—Ann
Kite, one of the stewardesses—no, not—excuse me, that wasn't
Ann Kite. It was Cynthia Bell, I think, was one of the
stewardesses on one of the flights, and even she said that she
never seen Michael Jackson give any child anything to drink. So
it's hard to base it on anything else other than the hearsay,
maybe from the mother, and the mother didn't seem to be that
credible, like I said.

GRACE: *Yes. Mr. Rodriguez, I understand the theory of*
reasonable doubt. I was a prosecutor many years. But before I let
you go, I've got a question for you. What do you think Jackson,
Michael Jackson, a forty-year-old man, was doing with these
little boys all those nights in bed alone?

RODRIGUEZ: *Well, that's a personal view that I don't want to*
talk about right now.

GRACE: *No, sir!*

RODRIGUEZ: *We all have our thoughts . . .*

GRACE: *You tried him—you tried him for that. He was tried. You were on his jury. That's what he was accused of. What do you think he was doing?*

RODRIGUEZ: *I know. And that's why I say we— We had to just rely on the— I'm not going stick my neck out there on this. We're just— I'm going to base it again on the testimony that was presented to us . . .*

GRACE: *Well, what do you mean, "stick your neck out?"*

RODRIGUEZ: *. . . and there was too much reasonable doubt.*

GRACE: *What do you mean, "stick your neck out?"*

RODRIGUEZ: *Well . . .*

GRACE: *You don't want to say what you thought Jackson was doing with those little boys every night?*

RODRIGUEZ: *Because it's our—it's our own personal beliefs and our own thoughts, and that's not what we have to work with. We had to work with the testimony of the witnesses and the credibility of the witnesses, and that's all we can base it on.*

GRACE: *So what you believe . . . You're telling me what you believe doesn't matter?*

RODRIGUEZ: *Yes. It does matter, but I'm not going to go any further with that.*

GRACE: *Yes, sir. I think you've gone far enough. With me . . .*

RODRIGUEZ: *All right. Thank you.*

I heard it from the horse's mouth. The jury foreperson said he did not want to "stick his neck out." It was easier to turn away and to blame the victim—correction, *victims*—and their families. I can't say I was surprised when the jurors gave a press conference immediately following the verdict. The elderly female juror, Eleanor Cook, attacked the boy's mom immediately, mocking her mannerisms and making clear her contempt for the mom. The others joined in with phrases like "the apple can't fall far from the tree." My stomach turned at what they had done.

And no one was surprised when welfare fraud charges were brought against the boy's mom. She got money from the state she shouldn't have, so the state proceeded full-steam ahead. The irony is overwhelming: She had the guts to take the stand and take the blows on cross-examination. Jackson didn't. Now she will be punished.

It was also no surprise when jurors hit the talk-show circuits, post verdict of course. A day late and a dollar short. The Jackson jurors' greed and thirst for fame is all the more reason that reforms outlined in *Objection!* placing duties, obligations, and censures on greedy jurors is necessary. On August 9, 2005, AP reported two of the jurors who had acquitted Jackson now regretted their decisions but caved in to the pressure to acquit.

Both juror Eleanor Cook and juror Ray Hultman now declare the boy witness was in fact sexually assaulted. Just in time for their book deals! Yes! It's true! They both voted Not Guilty and then pursued book deals to write about how guilty Michael Jackson is! They're the ones who are guilty now—of having neither the guts to vote their hearts and minds nor the conscience to blame themselves for their vote, not some-one else.

As to the Jackson jurors' change of heart, since there is no course of appeal for the state representing the boy victim, Jackson's defense team could afford to be casual about the whole turn of events, offhandedly dismissing the jurors' announcement as "embar-rassing and outrageous." The theory of double jeapardy precludes a second trial after an aquittal, regardless of the jury reversal post-verdict.

The now TV savvy Eleanor Cook went on to say, "I'm speaking out now because I believe it's never too late to tell the truth." Everything I railed about when first writing this book came true during the Michael Jackson trial: the outrageous advantages of celebrity "justice," the des-picable practice of blaming victims as a defense, and the disgusting phenomenon of self-serving jurors blind with greed assaulting Lady Justice.

Now, when conducting press and TV interviews, Eleanor Cook says she's speaking out on her true feelings about Jackson's guilt because it's "never too late." Incredible. Memo to Jackson juror Mrs. Eleanor Cook: Are you listening? It is too late.

AFTERMATH OF THE SCOTT PETERSON TRIAL

Since my last writing, the case of Scott Peterson has become an even greater attack on Laci and her family. The Associated Press reported that Sharon Rocha, Laci's mom, had to petition the courts for Laci's in-surance money because neither Peterson nor his attorney Mark Gera-gos would initially give up Peterson's legal claim to the money until all appeals in his murder conviction were "exhausted." Simply put, we're talking twenty years or so until a decision is reached. An appeal is only "final" when it has completed the entire appeals process. In California, that can take two decades. After much disastrous press and even more public criticism, Peterson backed off.

And as predicted, after losing the Peterson murder trial, pulling a no-show at Peterson's death-penalty sentencing, and being replaced in the Michael Jackson case, defense attorney Mark Geragos is back . . . on the airwaves, that is. Geragos is not only reportedly hawking his own reality show, he is once again a regular legal commentator on CNN's *Larry King Live!* It all goes to prove that cats and defense attorneys do in fact have nine lives!

Last but not least, remember Amber Frey, the star witness in Peterson's murder trial? Today she's getting paid for giving lectures across the country offering advice on how women can bounce back from rough times. She may need the money. In September 2005, The New York *Daily News* reported that the man who had long paid child support for one of Frey's children got a surprise of his own: a DNA test showed he is not the little girl's biological father. Genetic testing indicated that the four-year-old's genetic dad is another man. While Frey sorts out her personal life under the ongoing scrutiny of the press, I'm sure the Peterson defense is kicking themselves for not unearthing this news on their own so they could have spent weeks discussing it with Frey during her cross-exam! See, Amber? There is a silver lining!

HURRICANE KATRINA

One September evening just before air, I learned of the devastating aftermath that Hurricane Katrina had left in her wake after having blown through my beloved home: the Southland. No story, no case, no judge, no courtroom seemed to matter as night after night I saw and reported on the destruction that had been done to Louisiana, Mississippi, and Alabama. The shocking reality that FEMA, our federal government, and the state and local governments of Louisiana had failed its people so completely began to sink in. We knew it was coming. We knew for years the levees could never hold. Why did so many suffer and lose their lives?

Every night we saw images of desperate citizens of New Orleans waiting for food and water while others were dying around them, their bodies literally floating by in streets swollen with water. While we watched helplessly in horror as those images filled our television screens around the clock, it was shocking to realize that no one was coming to help. How could this be?

Local, state, and federal governments were brutally criticized— and rightfully so. Political infighting was exposed at its worst. Instead of protecting its citizens from a long-predicted disaster, elected leaders seemingly joined forces to ignore the obvious while simultaneously pushing through one piece of pork-legislation after the next. Greed and politics trumped saving human lives.

I asked the question repeatedly on my *Headline News* show each night in the aftermath of Katrina. I even interviewed New Orleans *Times-Picayune* reporter John McQuaid who had predicted a Katrina-like disaster and had written about it endlessly, begging officials for help. Here is one of the transcripts, this one dated September 6, 2005.

GRACE: *I'm going to go straight to John McQuaid with the* Times-Picayune.

John, when I hear Christiane describing what they will find— when the water subsides, the nightmare that is under that water . . . You have been predicting this for years. You have called on the government to help you. Explain.

JOHN MCQUAID, *TIMES-PICAYUNE* REPORTER: *In 2002 my colleague Mark Schleifstein and I worked on a series of stories that looked at the catastrophic risk facing New Orleans. And we talked to a lot of emergency managers and the Red Cross, and they outlined this scenario almost exactly.*

*And we wrote about it in a series that said, basically, hurricane
risks in south Louisiana and New Orleans are worsening. And the
government isn't really doing anything about it.*

*And we described pretty much the exact scenario, in the story
called "The Big One," that has unfolded over the past week.
And believe me, it's not something you want to be right about.*

GRACE: *John, what efforts? I mean, you've written about it,
you've written about it, you've written about it. Why do you
believe, John, that no one in Washington would listen?*

MCQUAID: *Well, I don't really know. I mean, this type of risk is
considered by emergency managers to be relatively remote.
I mean, the Corps of Engineers rated these levees at being a one-
in-three hundred chance each year of having this type of
catastrophe occur.*

*And that seems pretty low. But, in retrospect, obviously, with an
extreme risk that people knew could happen, then something
should have been done about it.*

*But there were all sorts of other concerns. There was terrorism,
of course, a focus on terrorism in the federal government.
Even locally, there was a focus on more mundane flood-control
issues.*

GRACE: *Yes, and they had to build that big bridge in Alaska
for, what, $200 million? Had to have that.*

The interview went on and on, detailing warning heaped upon
warning McQuaid had given publicly.

John McQuaid was not a lone voice in the wilderness by any means. Many spoke out; none were heard.

There was a strong emphasis placed on the issue of citizens looting. It didn't seem to matter that most of these people were shown carrying food, diapers, and other supplies out of abandoned buildings. While I sat in a darkened television studio, I wondered, how did it reach that point? Our government surely has the money to pay back grocery store owners, gas stations, and many others for losses not covered by their insurance carriers. Police and National Guard were within their rights to break store locks and feed the needy. Why were ordinary people doing the same thing immediately characterized as criminals? And no, I'm not defending the thugs who ran by TV cameras stealing VCRs and electronics or the criminals who cleaned out the gun department of Wal-Mart . . . book 'em!

But it was the children and the elderly who suffered the most in those early days after Katrina because of governmental bungling. Of course, all looting was not for noble purposes. That was clear. But the point remains the same: Justice did not play out, and our government failed the citizens who need it the most. I knew that when I saw images of "authorities" turning guns on citizens who were taking food from grocery stores or, in another instance, turning evacuees away from various locations at gunpoint.

Now the injustice continues to play out in the handling of insurance coverage or lack thereof. Claims of incredible personal losses are being turned down by long-standing and "reputable" insurance carriers who argue exclusions for "water and flood damage" govern Hurricane Katrina losses as opposed to full coverage for "hurricane" damage. These exclusions truly leave victims with nothing, although many of the existing policies claim to offer "full and comprehensive" coverage. Now affected Katrina victims are left wondering why they paid, year after year, on insurance premiums that are apparently worthless. The stench of unfair trade practices on the part of the insurance carriers is unbearable.

As the weeks following the storm played out, I interviewed anyone

and everyone I could find in hopes of helping to make a difference. I
am still haunted by the horrific conditions at the Superdome, the New
Orleans Convention Center, and across the Gulf. While my CNN
Headline News show did manage to reunite many families torn apart
by Katrina, I was left with the knowledge that it is nearly impossible to
bring about governmental change. Politics played such a role in the
debacle in Louisiana, from local government right up to state and federal government. As of this writing, the courthouse in New Orleans remains closed. Files and evidence have literally floated away. Families
remain separated, lost from each other. Registered sex offenders have
scattered to the four corners of the earth. It seems daunting, overwhelming. There is only one word for those of us who care: persevere.

Not only perservere, but fight. Already civil attorneys are fighting
giant insurance companies on behalf of policyholders. Class-action
groups have already formed to create strength in numbers. According
to CNN, Richard Scruggs, who did legal battle to help win $250 bil-
lionfrom the tobacco industry, is taking on big insurance companies
over Katrina flood coverage.

In his court filings in Pascagoula, Mississippi, Scruggs argues that
by excluding water damage in hurricane policies, insurers "preyed upon
trusting American families and taxpayers," and calls for reform. On
September 25, 2005, I brought Scruggs's legal battle to the airwaves.

> GRACE: *Believe it or not, big insurance companies are now
> refusing to pay victims' claims after Rita and Katrina. It's hard
> to believe—oh, yes, I pay premiums just like you all the time.
> I'm going to go straight out to Richard Scruggs, trial attorney.
> He has filed a lawsuit on behalf of many Katrina victims. And
> this guy, don't let him be modest, didn't you handle some of the
> tobacco litigation?*

> RICHARD SCRUGGS, FILED LAWSUIT ON BEHALF OF
> KATRINA VICTIMS: *Nancy, I had a hand in it, of course, and*

I was one of the core group that took on that challenge, which was monumental in a different way from this one. It is unfortunate quite frankly that lawyers, it looks like, are going to be required to force these companies to do the right thing and to stop them from evading the same contractual liability they had to the victims of 9/11. They're trying to do the same thing to the victims of hurricanes Katrina and Rita.

GRACE: *Regarding the tobacco lawsuits, as a nonsmoker, I want to thank you for that.*

SCRUGGS: *You're welcome.*

GRACE: *Now, what got into you? Why did you feel that you had to take on the insurance companies after Rita and Katrina?*

SCRUGGS: *Well, you know, this is not something I sought out. This was sort of a draft, but it's become an issue of passion for me. My—The boys and girls—now men and women—that I grew up with are family. The photograph right here is my brother-in-law, Trent Lott, of all people. The rubble of his home. And he is being jacked around by the insurance companies just like everyone else. The same guys that tried to evade the contractual obligations to the victims of 9/11 are doing the same thing now here.*

GRACE: *To Ali Velshi, CNN anchor and reporter, Ali, what's the loophole, what's the technicality the insurance companies are using, and who are the insurance companies?*

ALI VELSHI, CNN CORRESPONDENT: *Well, we are talking about some of the biggest insurance companies going, Allstate and State Farm are the two big names that—*

GRACE: *Oh, whoa, whoa, whoa, whoa! Allstate is mine. And State Farm is my family's. We're up the creek without a paddle.*

VELSHI: *I'm talking to a bunch of people who are lawyers and, as a financial journalist, I would never tell people not to read through their homeowner documents. But, you know, I've got to tell you, I may not well have looked through mine. Here's the issue. See that water coming through the window?*

GRACE: *Yes.*

VELSHI: *Water comes in through the bottom, it's a flood. Water comes in through the roof during a hurricane, it's hurricane damage. It's unclear whether water coming in through the window is one or the other, but that's the issue. Federal flood insurance is—*

GRACE: *Wait, wait, wait, wait, wait, wait, wait, whoa, whoa. I have got two legal degrees and you got that one by me. What?*

VELSHI: *Yes. And if you had your house destroyed, you are really not interested in listening to this argument, but the fact is the insurance companies are saying that if it is a flood, if it is water that comes in—not from damage, not from wind—it's not the hurricane, it's the flood that damaged your house. If it's a flood that damaged your house, they don't pay. "You should have other flood insurance," is what the insurance companies are saying.*

And that's what Dickie Scruggs is going up against. He's sitting here saying, wait a second, house is destroyed. That's a clause that may not be familiar. Now, Dickie, I don't want to speak for you, but

is that true? GRACE: *Yes, you would never do that, Ali.*
[To Richard Scruggs,] Let me get this straight. So the insurance
companies, Allstate, State Farm, and who's the other one, Richard?

SCRUGGS: *It's Nationwide, and the gentleman is just*
misinformed. All of the coastal homeowners from Florida
around to Texas have been forced to pay an additional premium
for what's called a "hurricane endorsement" or "hurricane
deductible endorsement." And I have got one right here off of an
Allstate policy that's in current force on the Gulf Coast. It's
typical of all three companies. It is a hurricane endorsement that
is unique to coastal residents. And if you can see the definition
of hurricane, it refers you to the National Weather Service.

Now, here is the National Weather Service's definition of
hurricane. And you will see that in the first example there is storm
surge in addition to wind.

GRACE: *OK. So it has got to be.*

SCRUGGS: *Yes, it has got.*

GRACE: *Then I guess, Ali, it has got to be a storm surge. But I*
guess the gist of what I'm getting from you, Ali, is that it has got
to be—they're saying the water caused by the hurricane is a
flood, not a hurricane?

VELSHI: *Yes. And when you're—and I really do defer to Mr.*
Scruggs, because I certainly—I agree that these are complicated.
And if you are going home to a house that has been destroyed,
the last thing you need is the technicality of, "Was this a flood?
Was this a surge that had come in?"

*The idea that the insurance companies are trying to put forward
is that damage caused to your home by rising water or by a flood
is something that they say that the homeowners should have had
flood insurance through FEMA if you live on a flood plane.
That's what they're trying to say.*

GRACE: *OK.*

VELSHI: *Mississippi Attorney General Jim Hood disagrees and
says this is a clause. He's trying to get that excluded. He's suing to
get that clause excluded so that people can claim the damage that's
done. Now here's what the insurance commissioner in Mississippi is
saying. He wants federal money to hire engineers to go and look at
every house and determine whether it was a hurricane wind that
caused [the damage] or rising waters from a flood.*

GRACE: *Holy moley. Hey, Elizabeth, put up the Allstate
response. Let's be fair to them. Since most homeowners',
condominium, mobile home, or renters' insurance policies don't
cover a flood, find out if you're eligible for a flood insurance
policy. And also, Elizabeth, when you can get to it, get me the
State Farm response.*

*With me, also, Joseph Annotti. He is the—Oh, there you go. State
Farm offers flood insurance through the National Flood
Insurance Program, although the government actually provides
the coverage. To Mr. Annotti, he's the senior vice president of
Property Casualties Insurers Association of America.*

Mr. Annotti, response?

JOSEPH ANNOTTI, SVP PROPERTY CASUALTY
INSURERS ASSN. OF AMERICA: *Well, Nancy, flood*

*insurance has been available from the federal government since
before Hurricane Camille hit the Gulf Coast in 1969. That's
almost forty years. And private insurance has—Insurers have
excluded flood damage in very clear language for decades before
that happened.*

*If you read [the] policy, it is crystal clear. I have next to me
case law after case law after case law where this policy's been
tried and tested. You know, I think Mr. Scruggs is trying to
appeal to people's emotions in an effort to twist arms and force
companies to pay for claims for which [a] premium was never
collected.*

GRACE: *Wait a minute. OK . . .*

ANNOTTI: *And for risk that was never insured.*

GRACE: *I understand what you're saying, but I need to clarify
something in my own mind.*

ANNOTTI: *OK.*

GRACE: *Is there hurricane coverage for these people?*

ANNOTTI: *There is wind damage coverage and there is flood
damage coverage. Wind damage coverage is covered under your
homeowners' policy. Insurers are out there paying claims every
single day since the day after the storm hit.*

GRACE: *OK. Right, right, right, right, right. Thank you, but I
don't need a history lesson. Go ahead.*

ANNOTTI: *Flood damage coverage.*

GRACE: *Yes. That's what I want to hear about. Flood damage coverage.*

ANNOTTI: *Flood damage coverage is available through the National Flood Insurance Program, has been for almost forty years. If your home is damaged by a flood, you turn to that policy to get coverage. If you don't have a flood insurance policy in place, then what you need to do is apply for a grant or a loan to FEMA.*

GRACE: *OK. Got you, got you, I got it. I would like to just go directly to the questions at hand. And my question is, Hurricane Rita and Hurricane Katrina, wouldn't you classify them as wind under the wind damage?*

ANNOTTI: *Much of the damage was in fact caused by wind. And that damage is going to be paid for under the homeowners and business insurance policy contract. It is being paid for every day.*

GRACE: *OK. Mr.—Let me go back to our attorney, Richard Scruggs. Response?*

SCRUGGS: *Well, the response of course is that the homeowners' policy contains the endorsement that you see in front of you, wherein the homeowner pays an additional substantial premium for a hurricane endorsement on his policy. And "hurricane" is defined the way the National Weather Service defines it, as you can see from this particular—from this particular.*

GRACE: *We can't see that piece of paper. So just tell us.*

SCRUGGS: *Sorry.*

GRACE: *That's OK. Just tell me the bottom line on this. Your argument is going to be what?*

SCRUGGS: *Well, the bottom line is we want these companies to honor their clear contractual undertakings to the homeowners on the coast. Mr. Annotti's trying to cherry pick a few provisions from the standard homeowners' policy without referring to the hurricane endorsement.*

GRACE: *Final thought, Ali?*

VELSHI: *The insurance companies aren't scared of too much in life. Richard Scruggs might be the one thing that they are scared of. He's not afraid to take on a lot of things. There might be a compromise here; there might be a middle ground. There's a congressman who's trying to get a bill passed to say we want to be able to let these people apply for that flood insurance retroactively and let them get paid out for their flood damage.*

GRACE: *You know, Ali, I know what you're telling me makes good business sense, but middle ground? After I saw that video, after what Anderson told me . . .*

VELSHI: *The middle ground might let them get the money. The bottom line, it's only middle ground, but it will let them get their money. It is—Insurance companies, as you know, are not very willing to sit and make compromises because that may lead to something else.*

In their response, the named insurance companies claim their policies specifically exclude flooding caused by storm surge, regardless of what policyholders believed. I will be watching and waiting to see how this chapter of the aftermath of Hurricane Katrina unfolds. While the carriers predict this and similar lawsuits will go nowhere fast, I predict Lady Justice may have a very different opinion!

GOOD NIGHT, COCHRAN

I close with my thoughts on an event that will forever remain etched in the memory of my legal career: the moment I learned that Johnnie Cochran had passed away. I knew Johnnie had been very ill for a long time, although I rarely commented on his condition, even when asked directly.

Johnnie became a household name when he defended O. J. Simpson, but in the years leading up to his death he avoided the limelight. Not long before Johnnie passed away, he told me he was "feeling pretty good," never once complaining. Cochran tried more cases than most of the "talking heads" put together, and while I rarely agreed with him, I did learn from him. When I was first paired on air with Cochran on our Court TV show, I was the sidekick to his celebrity. But you know what? He never let on.

Sitting at Cochran's memorial service in New York, I looked around the church and saw so many people there genuinely mourning him. As I walked out into the warm air coming up off the pavement, I remembered our nightly signoff: "Good night, Gracie," he said every evening. And I would respond: "Night, Cochran." So now, a final "Good night, Cochran."

As I end this chapter, my deepest thank-you is to you, for inviting me and all of my legal stories and analysis into your home. I hope we meet again, be it on the airwaves, in the written word, on the streets of New York City, or back home in the Southland. Thank you for sharing so much time with me. And until then, Good night, friend.

ACKNOWLEDGMENTS

FROM MY HEART, I THANK MY DEAR FRIEND AND coauthor, Diane, who believes in me and this story. Our long days and nights of work together bring a smile to my heart . . . no words serve to thank you, dear friend. We have shared so much more than our book . . . and it all started with a cup of coffee.

To Bob Miller, Will Schwalbe, Ellen Archer, Katie Wainwright, and Zareen Jaffrey, who made *Objection!* possible, thank you for giving me this forum, friends. My special thank-you to our editor, Gretchen Young, who believed in our message long before we ever met. You walked into the room and suddenly everything was possible. I don't know any other words than "thank you."

To Court TV and Henry Schleiff, thank you for the years of trials, the opportunities you've given me. To Larry and the wonderful staff at *Larry King Live*, Wendy and Dean, you allowed the victims' voices to be heard. Thank you to Mr. Slaton, who gave me a courtroom to find my voice.

And above all, to my dearest family and my beloved, you are my joy and my rock. You accept my flaws and find joy in my triumphs— what good are they without you? Thank you for weathering at my side all the years of courtroom battle, the highs and the lows. And Father God, thank you for your strength, and for all my many blessings.

—Nancy

I had the good fortune to receive an incredible amount of support and wise counsel from many sources during the writing of this book. All of it is deeply appreciated.

Thank you, Nancy, for trusting me with your story and for your friendship. Your passion for your work is incredible and inspiring. It's been quite a journey.

I am so grateful to have had the opportunity to work once again with the great creative, committed, and enthusiastic team at Hyperion. A special thanks to our editor, Gretchen Young. You're the best! Your guidance, good humor, and endless patience made all the difference.

A huge thank-you to Michael Anderson, who, in addition to being my assistant for ten(!) years, served as the tireless researcher for this book. Your dedication to this project meant the world to me.

Thank you to my many friends who cheered me on during the writing of this book, especially Liz McNeil, Natasha Stoynoff, Elinor Morris, and Elissa Zelman.

I have been blessed with an incredibly loving and supportive family who never seem to tire of listening to my tales of the highs and lows of a writer's life, and I love them for it. To my parents, who passed on their great love of books to me, I miss you both. There is not a day that goes by that I do not think of you. I take comfort in knowing you are still looking out for me from above, and for that I will always be grateful.

Finally, I want to thank my husband, Jim Donovan. Nothing I ever do would mean anything without the love you show me every single day.

Throughout this process you have always been there with your uncommon common sense to listen, make me laugh, and remind me about what's really important. I love you.

—Diane

SELECTED BIBLIOGRAPHY

CHAPTER ONE
Bugliosi, Vincent. *Outrage: The Five Reasons Why O. J. Simpson Got Away with Murder* (Island Books, 1996)

Stapley, Garth, "In the Courtroom: For the Defense—Geragos Says He's Driven by Duty, Steep Challenge" (*Sacramento Bee,* April 26, 2003)

CHAPTER THREE
Selcraig, Bruce. "Buying News" (*Columbia Journalism Review,* July/August 1994)

CHAPTER FOUR
Bell, Rachel. "Serial Killers/Most Notorious: John Wayne Gacy" (Court TV's Crime Library)

CHAPTER SIX
Riedl, Brian, M. "Ten Guidelines for Reducing Wasteful Government Spending" (The Heritage Foundation, February 12, 2003)

CHAPTER SEVEN
Gado, Mark. "A Killing in Central Park: The Preppy Murder Case" (Court TV's Crime Library)

Meili, Trisha. *I Am the Central Park Jogger: A Story of Hope and Possibility* (Scribner, 2003)

Robinson, Bryan. "Celebrity and the Accused: How the Different Fortunes of R. Kelly and Michael Jackson Illustrate Sex-Crime Victim Bias" (ABCNEWS.com, May 20, 2004)

CHAPTER NINE

O'Sullivan, John. "Deadly Stakes: The Debate Over Capital Punishment" (*National Review*, August 30, 2002)

Sanction, Thomas. "A Matter of Life or Death: McVeigh Case Shows How Differently Europe/America View Capital Punishment" (*TimeEurope*, May 21, 2001)

CHAPTER TEN

Hallam, Judge Oscar. "The Lindbergh Kidnapping Hoax: Some Object Lessons on Publicity in Criminal Trials" (*Minnesota Law Review*, March 1940)

Ridenour, Amy. "The Supreme Court Is Wrong to Ban Camera Coverage" (*National Policy Analysis: A Publication of the National Center for Public Policy Research*, November 2000)

INDEX

Nancy Grace is one of the hottest names in cable television. She is the host of *Closing Arguments* on Court TV and *Nancy Grace* on CNN's Headline News. One of the most sought-after legal commentators in the country, she appears regularly on *Larry King Live* to offer expert analysis on important cases and trials. Prior to her career in television, she worked in the Atlanta Fulton County District Attorney's office, where she served for a decade as special prosecutor compiling a perfect record of nearly one hundred felony convictions at trial.

Diane Clehane is a *New York Times* bestselling writer and journalist whose work appears regularly in *People, The New York Post, Variety,* and *TV Guide.* She lives in Westchester County, New York, with her husband and is currently at work on her first novel.

A portion of the authors' proceeds will go to the National Center for Missing and Exploited Children, a private, nonprofit organization that provides services nationwide for families and professionals in the prevention of abducted, endangered, and exploited children.